Frank Duerden was born in Nelson, Lancashire, in 1932 and, although now living in Essex, still regards himself as a Northerner. He started walking and rock climbing on the wild moorlands of the Pennines whilst still at school. In thirty years of active rambling he has walked in most parts of the British Isles and along many of the long distance footpaths. He has completed many of the classic routes such as the Three Peaks Walk of Yorkshire and the Lyke Wake Walk, and is interested in walking events, usually entering about ten or so each year. He is a member of the Ramblers' Association, Youth Hostels Association and Long Distance Walkers Association. He is married with three daughters and is currently a senior lecturer in polymer technology at the Polytechnic of North London.

Frank Duerden

The Complete Rambler

MAYFLOWER
GRANADA PUBLISHING
London Toronto Sydney New York

Published by Granada Publishing Limited
in Mayflower Books 1980

ISBN 0 583 13135 2

First published in Great Britain by Kaye & Ward Ltd 1978
under the title *Rambling Complete*
Copyright © Kaye & Ward Ltd 1978

Granada Publishing Limited
Frogmore, St Albans, Herts AL2 2NF
and
3 Upper James Street, London W1R 4BP
866 United Nations Plaza, New York, NY 10017, USA
117 York Street, Sydney, NSW 2000, Australia
100 Skyway Avenue, Rexdale, Ontario, M9W 3A6, Canada
PO Box 84165, Greenside, 2034 Johannesburg, South Africa
CML Centre, Queen & Wyndham, Auckland 1, New Zealand

Set, printed and bound in Great Britain by
Cox & Wyman Ltd, Reading
Set in Monotype Times

Granada ®
Granada Publishing ®

Contents

Acknowledgments

It would have been extremely difficult, if not impossible, to have written this book without the information, help and advice so freely given by so many people. I would like to acknowledge to the full my debt to them all and to express my gratitude for their help.

Mr Alan Mattingly of the Ramblers' Association very kindly wrote a Foreword to the book and I also received help both from him and from his staff during the course of preparation. I wrote to about 150 companies, organizations and organizers of challenge walks requesting details of their products or work. In all cases they replied and in most cases they later checked my copy for accuracy.

In particular, I would mention those who kindly read the chapters in draft form and made many useful comments: Tom Lyons and John Lintott (Chapter 2), Mr J. E. Traynor of Berghaus (Chapter 3), Mr Tony Wale of Silva Compasses (London) Ltd (Chapter 4), Ann Sayer and John Carey (Chapter 5); Mr J. Newcombe, Chief Training Officer, of St John Ambulance and Mr Cyril Cheney (Chapter 6), Mr Bernie Sluman of the Countryside Commission and the officials of the National Parks (Chapter 7); Mr Geoffrey Berry, Keith Chesterton, Mr P. H. E. Carter, Mr Ernest Kay, Mr Frank Noble and Tony Youngs (parts of Chapter 8), Chris Steer (Chapter 9), Miss N. Eggenberger of Edward Stanford Ltd and Mr Graham Heath of the International Youth Hostel Federation (parts of Chapter 10), John Feist and Mike Powell-Davies (Chapter 12); Frank Thomas, Mr Paul Clayden of the Commons, Open Spaces and Footpaths Preservation Society and Mr Don Gresswell (Chapter 14). Mr Robert Lawrie also kindly gave me his time.

In common with other authors I consulted widely both books and rambling journals in order to gather information.

In particular, I must mention the excellent publications of St John Ambulance and the Commons, Open Spaces and Footpaths Preservation Society, without which Chapters 6 and 14 could not have been written.

Mrs E. Pocock typed the manuscript in a most thorough and efficient manner; not an easy task with my method of writing. My three daughters also gave great help: Christina prepared most of the diagrams, Beverley helped on my rambles and did much of the proof-reading and Sharon typed many letters.

Finally, on a more personal note, I must express my gratitude to my parents to whom I owe a great deal; to my wife, Audrey, without whom little would be accomplished or be worthwhile; and to my many friends in the rambling world who have helped me over many difficult miles. These words are an inadequate expression of my true feelings.

FRANK DUERDEN

Foreword

There are 55 million people living in Britain, and every one of them is a rambler. Young and old, fit and disabled, artisan and academic – they all enjoy a walk in our glorious countryside at one time or another. For some, a short stroll around a local nature trail is the limit of their outdoor experience; others may remain dissatisfied until they have climbed all the peaks in Britain over 3,000 feet (or, as we should now say, 914 metres). The experience is vastly different, but the motivation is the same – a simple desire to get away from the artificial constraints of twentieth-century life and relax (not necessarily without the expenditure of a good deal of energy) in the great outdoors.

The opportunities for exploring the mountains, hills, valleys, fields and woodlands of Britain are infinite. Not only do we have a most wonderfully varied countryside (to take but two examples, contrast the sweeping views across the South Downs with the intricate patchwork of fields and woodlands a few miles to the north; or the grandeur of the Lake District with the sylvan hillsides of nearby Arnside); we also have a unique heritage of footpaths, commons and open spaces which offer a right of access to those of us among the 99·5 per cent of the population having no claim to ownership of land in rural areas. But, like freedom (with which it is closely allied), the price of public access to the countryside is eternal vigilance. For example, if it were not for the dedicated efforts of footpath societies and branches of the Ramblers' Association up and down the country, the great majority of our public rights of way would have been 'rationalized' out of existence long ago. If it were not for the concerted lobbying and militant action taken by the mass trespassers of Kinder Scout in the 1930s and 1940s, we would still have no right of access to those gritstone moors of Derbyshire. And if it were not for the vision and persistence of the founders of the National Trust, there would be many precious stretches of coastline and mountain, today preserved for the refreshment of the public, which would otherwise be fenced off or concreted over.

And it is interesting to record that, although popular concern for the environment is generally regarded as a post-war social phenomenon, the countryside campaigns to which I have been alluding do in fact go back much further in time than this. James Bryce introduced his 'Access to Mountains Bill' in Parliament as long ago as 1884. The first *national* amenity organization – the Commons, Open Spaces and Footpaths Preservation Society – was founded in 1865 as a result of successful efforts to save Epping Forest. The first recorded footpath society was set up in York in 1824, and, believe it or not, the earliest known legal action on behalf of a public right of way was initiated in 1669 when a landowner was prosecuted for ploughing up a public right of way.

But, enough said. I would not wish to offend the hospitality of the author and publisher of this fine volume by using the space they have given me for an undiluted advertisement for the Ramblers' Association. But readers will doubtless discover that the more they walk in the countryside, the more they come to realize that the exercise of rights entails the acknowledgment of responsibilities – not just the common sense responsibilities laid down in the Country Code, but also the responsibility of contributing in some way to the essential work of protecting an endangered heritage. The opportunities for making such a contribution are considerable – as a glance at the list of voluntary countryside organizations in Chapter 11 will show. All you really need is the willingness and ability to help.

One last point before concluding with a word about Frank Duerden's book itself. Don't be put off by caricatures. Outdoor enthusiasts are fair game for writers and playwrights, and some highly amusing portrayals come to mind – the jolly, shorts-and-camp-fire members of the 'National Union of Hikers' in Compton Mackenzie's 'Monarch of the Glen'; or Keith and Candice-Marie, the hilarious pair of social misfits tramping the Dorset Coast Path with military timing in the TV play 'Nuts in May'. But don't be dissuaded by such satirical episodes from donning a pair of walking boots and setting off with a rucksack on your back. Apart from being essential equipment on most occasions, these traditional trademarks of the rambler are being purchased and used by an increasingly large and varied section of the population. Schools encourage their kids to take it up; retired folk find that rambling offers an inexpensive but healthy and delightful pastime; and professional people in mid-career discover that a week-end's walk eases the tension and sets them up for another week at the factory or office. And somehow, rambling enhances your sense of humour; once you get started, you find that the last thing worth worrying about is being laughed at by other people.

I sincerely hope that this book will introduce many more people to rambling. It provides a comprehensive basic reference text. But, much more than that, Frank Duerden has skilfully managed to combine succinctness with an expression of natural enthusiasm. His attention to detail is impeccable, but he has throughout written with an inspiration born of his own rich experience in exploring the countryside on foot. And the delightful thing is that his experiences can be shared by everyone.

October 1977   ALAN MATTINGLY

CHAPTER 1

Introduction

Over the past 25 years or so there has been an enormous increase in the popularity of most outdoor leisure pursuits. Canoeing, fishing, golf, horse-riding and mountaineering all come readily to mind as examples of activities which now attract far more attention and have far more active participants than formerly.

The reasons for this growth probably include the increased amount of leisure time that people now enjoy, the greater affluence generally which allows more to be spent on equipment and the improved facilities available in most areas. In addition, a greater proportion of people are involved in sedentary types of work and are likely to find attractive recreational activities which involve some physical effort. But, perhaps most of all, people have discovered that these activities are a valuable and enjoyable antidote to the increased uncertainty and tension that unfortunately are so often features of modern life.

Rambling is another outdoor pursuit which has grown in a remarkable way over the same period. Thirty years ago, when I began, it had nothing like the same popularity that it has today. For those who doubt this statement let me point out the following facts which should be considered:

(1) Membership of the Ramblers' Association, which is the main organization for the rambler, more than trebled between 1952 and 1975, although it has fallen slightly since.

(2) The growth of the Youth Hostels Association, both in members and in the use of hostels, has been very remarkable. Between 1966 and 1978 the yearly total for hostel 'overnights' set a new record each year! (Figure 1). Probably about three-quarters of YHA members are walkers.

(3) Challenge Walking, a semi-competitive activity related to orienteering and race walking, has always had some

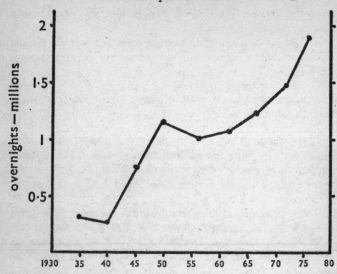

Figure 1. Graph of YHA overnights

enthusiasts but has grown out of all recognition since the late 1950s. There are now at least 60 organized events each year and the number is growing. The Lyke Wake Walk, a challenge walk which can be done at any time and involves walking about 40 miles (64 km) within 24 hours, is now completed by about 8,000 walkers each year.

(4) The first long-distance route, the Pennine Way, was opened in 1965. To date, eleven have been created by the Countryside Commission and about double that number have been devised by other organizations or individuals.

(5) The first National Park was established in 1950 and the first Area of Outstanding Natural Beauty designated in 1956. There are now ten and 33 respectively occupying a total of about 18·5 per cent of England and Wales.

(6) A high proportion (about 40 per cent) of the 'useful' organizations given in Chapter 11, i.e. walking and rambling associations, amenity societies, etc. have been established

since the Second World War and memberships have risen considerably.

(7) The publication of footpath guides has become almost a major industry, about one new or revised edition appearing each week on average.

(8) So much effort has been put into the design of clothing and equipment that the walker is now faced with an almost bewildering variety.

These developments were described in the numerous catalogues, guide-books and magazines, and in the journals of walking clubs and amenity societies, that were published over the period. 'The Complete Rambler' is an attempt to bring all this information together into one volume which will be a reference book to the facilities available to walkers and a guide to walking as an absorbing outdoor pursuit.

It has been suggested to me that walking is so natural an activity for most people that there should be no need for a book on the subject. I cannot agree. Of course it is true that you can ramble in the countryside without any special equipment and without any knowledge of map reading and thoroughly enjoy yourself. But that is only one part of the story. Another part includes the fit, knowledgeable and experienced hill-walker, well-equipped and able to find his way safely and surely across wild mountain country under winter conditions, selecting his own route and dealing efficiently with each obstacle that he meets. He is playing a very different game indeed. I am not in any way implying that one is inferior to the other as a pleasant activity, but it is obvious that the latter demands a level of preparation and competence of quite a different order. To bridge the gap does demand a book.

'The Complete Rambler' has been written for all who walk in the countryside, whether they are beginners or experienced 'hard men'. The beginner wants to know which equipment to buy, how to read maps and plan a route, estimate time and distance and cope with difficult ground. The more experienced walker requires a reference book which will bridge the gaps in his knowledge and to which he can refer over and over again for details of guide-books, long distance footpaths, challenge walks, useful organizations, etc. I have tried to cater for both of these requirements.

Although we live in a comparatively small group of islands we can enjoy an astonishingly wide variety of countryside. Just consider the variety that is represented, for example, by the fields and orchards of Kent, the bare chalk ridge of the South Downs, the flat black fen country of Norfolk or Lincolnshire, the wide moorlands of the Peak District, the limestone country of the Yorkshire Dales, with its pavements, caves and pot-holes, and the rugged mountains of the Lake District, North Wales or Scotland. Add to these a coast line of high cliffs, sandy shores, pebble beaches and dunes; a varied agriculture; a people rich in local dialect and accent; a turbulent history which has left us a fine legacy of earthworks, castles, country houses and fortified towns and you can then understand the interest and variety which await you. You can enjoy them by using a complex network of over 100,000 miles (160,900 km) of public footpaths and bridleways which have grown up over the years. Local paths used by villagers for easy access to mill, manor or church, old Roman roads, coastguard paths, drove roads over moor and fell, and even some rights of way created specially for the walker. You can find these by using a series of detailed Ordnance Survey maps which are unsurpassed for quality by any in the world.

I have been a rambler for over 30 years and each year has given me tremendous enjoyment and rich memories. Watching a red sunrise over miles of frozen moor on a cold winter morning in Derbyshire. The sun reflecting from the snowy crest of a ridge in the Pennines. Wild geese rising from the bare Essex marshes. The aurora borealis displaying across a northern sky. The sound of a nightjar across a shoulder of moorland as I walked home in the gathering dusk. The view from the South Downs towards the Weald. The feeling of spring deep in a forest. And a hundred others. If you start rambling you also will gather such memories. I guarantee it.

I cannot pretend that all your days will be as enjoyable.

There will be days of heavy rain when you are cold and wet through and long for a bath, dry clothes and a hot meal. There will be weary miles towards home at the end of a day. There will be blisters and stiff muscles and bruises. But you will find that the good memories greatly outnumber the bad ones and that it is the good ones which are the most vivid and lasting. In 30 years I have never regretted a single walk. I have only regretted the times when I couldn't or didn't go out walking.

You may think that you are much too old for rambling or suffer from some physical disability that will prevent you altogether. If you do think this, then turn to pages 31 to 33, read them carefully and then decide if you still feel the same. Walking will do more for the physical and mental well-being of the vast majority of people than any amount of time in front of a television set.

I hope that you will try rambling. I know that you will enjoy it, no matter whether you are content to walk a few miles only on a warm summer afternoon along the local footpaths and lanes or whether you aspire to long, hard backpacking expeditions in the mountains or the toughest of challenge walks. There is a place for everyone in the walking world. If this book fails to persuade you to try rambling then it is a pity and I am sorry, because I know what you will be missing. If it does persuade you then just one last thing. Do it now! Today, if possible! Don't say 'Yes, I must do that sometime.' Because 'sometime' has a habit of never arriving and that would be even more of a pity.

CHAPTER 2

Making a Start

Of all spare-time activities, rambling must be one of the easiest to start. You do not really have to buy any special equipment, you will not have to learn and then practise any difficult techniques, it can be done almost anywhere and at any time. You can simply go into the countryside and start to walk. Many people start this way and some grow into great enthusiasts. At the same time, unfortunately, very often the first experience is also the last. If the route is not planned properly in advance then you may finish with blisters and feeling very tired after a long trudge home. If the weather turns bad then you may become cold and wet through simply because your raincoat, quite adequate for the town, could not cope with the bad weather that you met. Footpaths that appeared inviting on the map may prove to be non-existent, and a walk across a ploughed field on a wet winter's day is not the best way to start. Every year people are killed whilst taking a short walk in the British mountains.

If only a little thought and time is given to preparation before you start then the first ramble can be the thoroughly enjoyable experience that it should be, instead of a miserable time to be got over as quickly as possible and most certainly never to be repeated.

Selecting a route

Work out the route beforehand in the comfort of your home when you have plenty of time to think about it, and not when you are ready to start.

The easiest way is to buy a guide-book describing the walks in your area, and there are literally hundreds of these books which cover most parts of the British Isles (Chapter 7). The majority of these are competently written and are fairly easy to follow. You will do the best walks this way, as the author has probably made a selection of many known to him and modified these so that they visit the most interesting and beautiful places. In addition you are not likely to meet any local opposition as the paths will be regularly walked. Take an Ordnance Survey 1 : 50 000 map with you however so that you can find your way back if you do lose the route; in any case, this will give you some valuable practice at map reading. I would strongly recommend that you start this way as your walks will then probably be very successful and you will be fired with enthusiasm for more.

An alternative is to work out your own route on a 1 : 50 000 or 1 : 25 000 map. This can be great fun, but at the same time involves more risk of disappointment. Some footpaths may be in a bad condition and force you to negotiate ploughed fields or very muddy and rutted lanes. Stiles, signposts and even small bridges may be missing and give you difficulties in finding the route. You may meet recalcitrant farmers, boisterous dogs and ominous-looking bulls. But, mile for mile, this will give you a great deal more fun than following in someone else's footsteps. Here are a few hints if you follow this method:

(1) Select the area within which you would like to walk. Can you get there relatively easily by car or public transport? If the latter then you will probably be restricted in your choice of starting point. If so, then mark the points on the map.

(2) Are there interesting places that you would particularly like to visit? Then mark these on your map as well. Use a soft pencil for marking maps so that the marks can be rubbed out afterwards. An excellent way of marking maps is to use small, round, red, self-adhesive labels (about $\frac{3}{16}$ inch diameter). These will stick to the map but can be removed easily afterwards without damage and are very prominent.

(3) Decide the approximate distance that you intend to walk. Do not be over-ambitious at the beginning; five miles is enough for anyone who has not walked seriously for a long time. Then gradually increase your distance without over-tiring yourself. The distance will depend upon the

weather, the time of year and the composition of the party. Always plan for the weakest member of the party.

(4) Look for any prominent footpaths near to the starting point and the points of interest. A good method is to cut a piece of string against the map scale so that it is the same length on the map as the distance that you intend to walk. Anchor one end of this on your starting point and the other end on your finishing point and try to 'work' it over the paths on the map. This will help a great deal to give you a route of the desired length.

(5) When you have selected your route, measure the actual distance (Chapter 3) and estimate the time required.

(6) Settle on the method of travel to the starting point and for your return journey and for your meeting time and place. Make sure that the other members of your party are informed.

Estimating time

You should always estimate the time that a ramble will take you. The method for doing this was first described by W. W. Naismith of the Scottish Mountaineering Club in 1892 and is therefore now known as Naismith's Rule:

> For ordinary walking allow one hour for every three miles and add one hour for every 2,000 feet of ascent; for backpacking with a heavy load allow one hour for every two and a half miles and add one hour for every 1,500 feet of ascent.

Thus, suppose your route is twelve miles long and that you have estimated that you will be climbing a total of 3,000 feet:

Then time required $= \dfrac{12}{3} + 1\frac{1}{2} = 5\frac{1}{2}$ hours

or $\quad \dfrac{12}{2\frac{1}{2}} + 2 =$ approx. 7 hours (backpacking).

This method was easy to apply with the one-inch Ordnance Survey maps, as all heights were marked in feet, but a modified method is necessary with the new 1 : 50 000 maps which have replaced them. In the 1st series of 1 : 50 000 maps the spot heights and contour values are given to the nearest metre, but the interval between contour lines (vertical interval) is still 50 feet. In the 2nd series the vertical interval is now ten metres. In those cases therefore you must adopt one of several methods. (You will find this easier after Chapter 3.):

(1) 1st Series. Estimate your walking distance in miles as before. Determine the total ascent in feet by counting the number of contour intervals and multiplying by 50. Then proceed as before.

(2) 2nd Series.

(*a*) Estimate the total ascent in metres and convert to feet, i.e. multiply by 3·3. Then proceed as before.

(*b*) Estimate your walking distance in kilometres and your total ascent in metres. Allow one hour for every five kilometres and one hour for each 600 metres ascent (ordinary walking), or one hour for every four kilometres and one hour for each 450 metres ascent (backpacking).

Naismith's Rule does not, however, make any allowance for (1) rest periods, (2) the degree of fitness of the party, and (3) the weather and roughness of the ground. It must therefore be considered as only an approximate guide to walking time, and probably underestimates the time needed by the average walker.

A rough method of calculating total time, which *includes* reasonable stops for rest and food, uses the following figures:

Party which includes young children	$1\frac{1}{2}$ mph
Party of moderate walkers who walk perhaps once or twice per month over lowland areas	2
Small party of fit walkers walking regularly over lowland areas	3

Divide the total distance by the appropriate speed, add an allowance for ascent as above, and the final figure is the *total* time required.

Starting out

Make sure that you have all the equipment that you are likely to need before you leave home. Take plenty of food with you and always carry a drink of some kind. A typical list of equipment for an ordinary country walk lasting a morning and afternoon would be:

Rucksack
Waterproofs (certainly a top garment, preferably
    over-trousers as well)
Food (more than you think you will need)
Drink (preferably hot in winter)
Guide-book and/or map
Compass (not essential, except in wild country, but
    often helpful)
Torch (particularly in winter)
A few first-aid plasters (for cuts, blisters, etc.)
Small pocket knife (for cleaning your boots before
    entering a pub or boarding a bus)
Handkerchiefs (two)
Extra sweater

These can all be packed into your rucksack or into your pockets. These are in addition, of course, to your walking footwear and clothing.

From the beginning aim to achieve a steady pace with easy regular strides. Many walkers prefer to start rather slowly and then speed up a bit after a mile or two. But always aim at a steady walking rhythm. This will be much less tiring than a fast and irregular pace broken by frequent or long stops.

Ensure that you maintain a good balance at all times. The weight of the body should be moved slightly forward, i.e. a slight forward stoop, with a short, smooth swing of the arms. The sure sign of a good walker is the manner in which he makes it all look very easy, as if he could go on all day without tiring. By all means have a good look at the scenery, but keep a watch on the ground a few feet ahead, particularly on rough ground, so that you can see the ruts or the tree roots that will trip you up.

When walking uphill you will probably find it easier to lean slightly into the slope. Always place the feet fully on to the ground, resisting the temptation to walk only on the toes as this will be very tiring. With every footstep look for small roughnesses, such as tufts of grass or small protruding rocks, so that you can place your feet horizontally upon them. If this is not possible then it will usually help to splay your feet out somewhat. But each foot should be placed carefully and precisely upon the ground. Rhythm is vital and never go too fast. If you can chat to your companion or whistle without getting out of breath when walking uphill then your speed is probably about right. In very steep parts a zig-zag route will be better than one going straight up. When walking downhill over grass or bare ground the weight should be moved forwards. Put the weight on to the heels and again use small irregularities to keep your feet horizontal. If the ground is soft you can dig your heels in somewhat. In really steep places it may be better to move down in zig-zags. Keep the knees slightly bent and loose so that you absorb any sudden shocks and are not constantly jarring the body.

Stop about every hour or so for a short rest and a small snack. But five to ten minutes is quite long enough, provided that you relax so as to obtain maximum benefit. A good plan is to eat little but often. By all means have rather more at lunch or teatime, but don't eat a large meal or you will be fit for nothing afterwards, never mind an afternoon of walking. But do have a good breakfast about an hour before you start out. When you do stop for a lengthy period put on the spare sweater right away if the weather is chilly. Otherwise you will start to get cold during your stop. Take the sweater off again when you start. Only wear what is necessary to keep you warm. If you get too hot then again you will tire more easily.

Walking along roads always requires care, particularly with a large party and at night. Keep in single file and walk along the side facing the oncoming traffic. At night, wear light-coloured clothing or squares of white cloth pinned to the chest and back. If you have a torch shine it ahead, but not into the driver's eyes, so that he can see you. Keep a watch on cars approaching you to ensure that you have been seen in sufficient time for avoiding action. It is also sound policy to glance back at all cars approaching from behind, as there is the real risk of being run down by a car overtaking another just before reaching you.

You may find that your boots slacken off as you walk. When you stop check on this and re-tighten the laces if necessary. White Petroleum jelly smeared over your feet before putting on your socks will help to prevent the formation of blisters.

Leading a party

1. Make sure that the walk is advertised in good time beforehand stating date, time of starting, meeting place, approximate distance and any particular difficulties on the route. Include also a brief but attractive description of the route so that people will be interested in coming along. Also mention if it will be possible to cut the route short at some point by taking public transport. Many people may not wish to do the full distance but would come along for, say, the morning part.

2. Work out the route beforehand and if possible walk over the full distance. There is nothing worse than leading a demoralized party around the countryside whilst trying to discover where you are.

3. Do not be put off by bad weather (but see Chapter 5). If you advertise a walk then turn up and do it unless the weather is really exceptional. In practice anyhow it will be almost impossible to let everyone know of a cancellation on the day.

4. Allow a few minutes after the advertised time for late arrivals before moving off.

5. Ask another member to stay at the rear of the party to ensure that no one is left behind during the walk.

6. The leader chooses the route, sets the pace and decides when and where to stop for rest or food.

The pace must be suitable for the slowest member of the party even if some others find this too slow.

7. Do not let the party get too strung out. Stop occasionally to let the party reform. Always stop at a serious obstacle to reform the party and help people across it.

8. Never let people get ahead of you and keep the party together at all times. If you do lose someone then stop the party and organize a search.

9. Ask your party to walk in a single file across a field which has been ploughed over or put down to crops, thus leaving a well-marked but narrow path. This is also a good idea for popular moorland tracks which otherwise tend to grow wider with continued use.

There should be no need to enforce these few simple rules with rigid discipline. A ramble is a pleasant, informal affair but the rougher and wilder the country the more important they become.

Forming a rambling club

There are many ramblers who walk regularly on their own or in the company of a few friends and who never join a rambling club. However, I suggest that you do join a club as there are a number of positive advantages to membership. You will meet people with similar interests and be able to discuss equipment, new routes, walking areas or the best accommodation; they will also put you in touch with others who have special interests such as footpath clearance or backpacking. The club will hold regular meetings and these will introduce you to many excellent walks that you have never tried before. There will be week-ends and even holiday weeks away from your normal walking area; for example, a southern club may visit Scotland, North Wales or the Lake District. You will be able to share cars to take you to walks, each person contributing to the costs. Your walking horizons will broaden and your interests widen.

Your local library will probably be able to give you some information about local clubs. You can also write to the Ramblers' Association who will be able to put you in touch with a group or an affiliated club. The district newspaper will probably include information on walks held by local clubs. Generally, walking clubs welcome guests and you will be able to go out once or twice with them, although naturally they will expect you to become a member if you wish to continue. If all these fail then you can form your own club.

You will need first of all to discover if there is sufficient support. Put an advertisement in the local paper advertising an inaugural meeting or walk and see what support you receive. You may be able to get the local paper to include a small article free of charge for the same purpose. If you do take the initiative in this way then you must be prepared to carry out most of the work yourself during the first year or so, but aim from the beginning at building up a small group of activists. For long-term viability you ought to have a minimum of about 25 members with perhaps half-a-dozen who are prepared to help you to run the club.

With a small group the duties of secretary, treasurer and chairman can be combined and a committee of four or five others is sufficient. Later on, when the group is much larger, it will be better to divide these duties up amongst several people. Two other useful officials are a publicity officer and a footpaths secretary; the latter keeping a check on local footpaths, probably in collaboration with the local group of the Ramblers' Association.

During the first year one walk per month is probably sufficient. You can increase the number if there is a demand from members and provided that you can get enough leaders. You will probably find that the latter is the main problem. But, apart from that, you can increase the frequency of walks considerably. One large club now organizes three walks in each week of the year: Saturday, Sunday and one mid-week. Another club runs three walks on each week-end to cater for walkers of different ability. It is a good idea to send a questionnaire to each member at the end of the first year in an attempt to discover what they think of the club's activities and what they would like for the future.

Regular group walks will form the basis of your activities

but there are many other possibilities for your programme and it is a good idea to introduce as much variety as possible. Some ideas that are worth considering are:

(*a*) Mid-week walks for retired members. These can be very popular as the pace can be reduced if necessary for more elderly walkers.

(*b*) Walks in the long, light evenings of summer; about two or three hours around some local beauty spot.

(*c*) A regular 'Rambling Week' in which there is a walk each day with perhaps two or three walks of different length on the final Sunday.

(*d*) A group walk over a long distance footpath. There are several that can be done over an Easter or Spring Bank Holiday 'long week-end'.

(*e*) A walking holiday in an area which offers different scenery, with the advantage of cheap group travel.

(*f*) Organize a small local challenge walk (Chapter 9). Do not be too ambitious for a start, a route of ten miles with unmanned checkpoints is quite sufficient. Advertise the event widely, make it an open event and you will be surprised at the number of non-members who come along and who will later join your club.

(*g*) Arrange a footpath survey and clearance. Even if you do not wish to become very involved in this type of work the local Ramblers' Association group will welcome help once or twice each year.

(*h*) Get in touch with other clubs in adjacent areas and arrange exchange visits. In this way you will draw upon their local knowledge and they, in turn, upon yours.

(*i*) Evening meetings with films or holiday slides. Several films can be hired or members can bring along holiday slides and provide a short commentary.

(*j*) Always have an annual dinner or party. It will probably prove to be the most popular event of the year.

You should always be on the watch for more unusual group rambles with which you can vary your programme. A few suggestions are:

(1) Are there any local streams which can be followed to their mouth or source? In many cases footpaths exist along or near to the banks.

(2) Follow old Roman roads. Some of these are marked on Ordnance Survey maps and exist now as straight green roads which provide excellent walking. One guide is 'Roman Roads in Britain'. Ivan D. Margary, John Baker.

(3) Old drove roads. There are many of these crossing high ground which were originally used for driving sheep to the markets.

(4) Abandoned railway lines. Some of these may be followed as rights of way and are clearly marked on Ordnance Survey maps.

(5) Canals or rivers. Usually a towpath can be followed and can give surprisingly quiet walking even into the heart of large cities. In the case of some canals a permit may be required. Some stretches are a little spoilt for walkers, however, by the presence of anglers who congregate in surprisingly large numbers.

(6) Coast paths. Paths exist around most of our coasts and can give very quiet walking with lovely views over cliff, beach or salt-marsh. Generally they are better in the winter months when there are few holiday-makers about.

(7) Are there any well-known local antiquities which could be joined by a single route? The Crosses Walk over the North York Moors started in this way.

(8) Are there any large stretches of woodland, for example, which could be walked from one end to the other or whose boundary could be followed? Epping Forest, which penetrates deep into suburban London, can be followed almost throughout its length of about 15 miles without walking along a single road at any point.

A useful little book (unfortunately now out of print) which gives numerous suggestions in some of these categories is:

'Hike Projects and Challenges'. Keith Pennyfather, The Scout Association.

Keeping a record

Always keep a record of all the walks that you complete. It settles endless arguments afterwards, is a source of countless ideas for 'repeat walks' and is a never-ending source of pleasant memories. It will also show how your walking ability is improving year by year. A cheap, hard-backed note-book is quite sufficient for a record of the date and times, miles covered, companions and enough directions to enable you to retrace the route afterwards. A note on the weather and the main incidents of the walk will complete the record. It is amazing how quickly memory can fade unless jogged in this manner.

Rambling for young people

You might as well start them off early. For this purpose there are some excellent carriers ('Papoose' models from Karrimor) which weigh about $2\frac{1}{4}$ lb (1 kg) and are suitable for children from six months to walking age. The carriers, which fit on to the back like a rucksack, have an adjustable metal frame with hip belt and a seat of polyurethane-coated nylon. It is doubtful if this early start will fill the child with a love of the Great Outdoors, but it will certainly help Mother and Father to get into it!

Once the child starts to walk strongly then it will be possible to go for short local walks. But: firstly, don't over-do it. A long walk in which the end is 'just a bit further' but never seems to arrive, will not encourage him on the next occasion. Secondly, make sure that he is properly equipped. Several firms (e.g. Berghaus) produce, for example, light-weight waterproofs and boots specially for children and, later on, there are packframes which can be adjusted to allow for growth. Thirdly, interest them in the countryside so that each walk is an adventure. There are lots of nature trails about, usually fairly short, which are ideal. But, let's face it, most children under ten will not be so enthusiastic about walking, so progress slowly.

For older children there are many opportunities. Here are some ideas:

(1) Joining a local YHA Group. These are made up largely of young people who will be organizing group walks, night hikes, week-end hostelling and similar activities. (See Chapter 11).

(2) Adventure holidays. There are a number of these specifically for young people. Walks along long distance footpaths, for example, or a 'package' holiday with activities in several pursuits such as canoeing, sailing, hill walking and pony trekking.

Youth Hostels Associations. (See Chapter 11).
P.G.L. Young Adventure Ltd, Adventure House, Station Street, Ross-on-Wye, Herefordshire, HR9 7AH.

(3) The Duke of Edinburgh's Award Scheme. The Scheme has three awards – bronze, silver and gold – and is open to all young people from their 14th to 25th birthdays. Appropriate subjects are expeditions, mountain rescue, mountaineering, orienteering, rock climbing, as well as rambling.

The Duke of Edinburgh's Award, 5 Prince of Wales Terrace, London, W8 5PG. 01 937 5205.

(4) Challenge Walks. Most of these are too tough for young people and there is usually a minimum age limit of 14–18, but some are suitable; for example, the Rodings Rally in Essex. (See Chapter 9).

(5) The Scout and Girl Guides Associations have always encouraged walking, camping and related activities. Age limits: 8–20 years, (Boys), and 7–18 years (Girls).

The Scout Association, Baden Powell House, Queens Gate, Kensington, London, SW7 5JS. 01 584 7030.
The Girl Guides Association, 17–19 Buckingham Palace Road, London, SW1W 0PT. 01 834 6242.

Rambling for the elderly

Rambling is by no means an activity purely for young

people. In fact, one of the best things about rambling is that it can be continued long after the point where a retirement pension is being collected. There are many walkers in their late fifties or sixties who think nothing of completing 40 or 50 miles, and some in their seventies and eighties who are still fit and active.

If you have been a regular walker for most of your life then by all means keep it up so long as you are physically able to do so. If you are taking the pursuit up in middle age, perhaps after a long period without strenuous physical activity, then you should be more cautious. If, in addition, you are overweight or smoke heavily then even greater caution is needed. Unfortunately, mountain rescue teams are frequently called out for walkers and climbers who have suffered heart attacks whilst in the hills.

It is advisable to consult a doctor who will be able to give you a physical examination before you commence any serious walking. This, at least, will put your mind at rest before you do start exerting yourself. If you are a smoker then try to cut it out altogether, and if overweight start a diet under the guidance of your doctor. Your return to serious physical activity should be very gradual, by no means attempt to rush it. It may be hard, but it will be well worth the effort. You will be astonished at the improvement in your general well-being.

A very popular book on physical fitness is: 'The New Aerobics'. Kenneth H. Cooper, Bantam.

Rambling for the disabled

Rambling can give a great deal of pleasure to disabled people. Some clubs have been formed especially for them. Examples are the Deaf Mountaineering Club who have a full programme of visits to mountain areas, the Rambling Club for the Blind which has been active in the Manchester area for over 40 years and the Disabled Campers Club. Membership of ordinary walking clubs, however, should be encouraged, as this is of great value in helping disabled people to integrate into the community.

Disabled people should be encouraged to join and should be accepted as ordinary members of a club; at the same time their handicaps must be appreciated and, if necessary, allowance must be made for them. This does not mean that you act in a patronizing manner, they will most certainly not thank you for that. But it does mean that you do not ignore their handicaps and that your plans will take them into account.

It is a little difficult to generalize about the help needed by disabled people as this will depend considerably upon the type and severity of handicap suffered. Some spastics, for example, can enter fully into club activities whilst blind people will need sighted walkers to guide them. It is best to treat each disabled person as a special case, the help required being determined by the handicap. Generally, however, disabled people will have to walk more slowly than other walkers, will tire more quickly and will find stiles, gates, ditches and rough ground more difficult to negotiate. Balance will often be poor and a walking stick will be found useful. It will be necessary for a party to go at a slower pace and to stop more frequently.

Read: 'Outdoor Pursuits for Disabled People'. Norman Croucher, Disabled Living Foundation, 346 Kensington High Street, London, W14 8NS.

To more fully appreciate what can be achieved by a disabled person read: 'High Hopes'. This is the story of Norman Croucher who had both legs amputated, but went on to climb the Matterhorn, Mont Blanc and other high mountains. Hodder and Stoughton.

Rambling for the mentally handicapped

Rambling is popularly considered solely as a recreational activity, but it can also be used as a valuable therapeutic exercise for certain groups.

The Firwood Ramblers is a rambling club which was formed in 1970 for the mentally handicapped and/or disturbed patients resident in the Firwood Ward of the Brockhall Hospital at Blackburn, Lancashire. The members all have some degree of mental handicap, and often suffer from some physical disability. Nevertheless, in the period since 1970 the activities of the group have been expanded so that rambling is now a valuable part of a wider rehabilitation and socialization programme.

The club holds regular weekly rambles in the nearby Pennines and Forest of Bowland. Regular five-day visits are paid to sites in the Yorkshire Dales, Lake District and North York Moors. Several longer expeditions have been organized along the Coast to Coast Walk and the Pennine Way. Competent leadership combined with a very disciplined approach has resulted in complete freedom from accidents during the seven years of the club's existence.

The Country Code

Every year damage is caused by visitors to the countryside. Much of this may be due to the holiday-maker or to the motorist having a day out with his family, but some is certainly caused by ramblers.

In an attempt to reduce this damage and to create good-will between town and country people the Countryside Commission has prepared a short list of simple rules to guide the visitor, which is known as the Country Code:

> Guard against all risk of fire
> Fasten all gates
> Keep dogs under proper control
> Keep to the paths across farm land
> Avoid damaging fences, hedges and walls
> Leave no litter
> Safeguard water supplies
> Protect wild life, wild plants and trees
> Go carefully on country roads
> Respect the life of the countryside

Other interests

The enjoyment that you gain from rambling will be increased even more if it is accompanied by a knowledge of the countryside, its wild life and the lives of its inhabitants. Most walkers find that their interests tend to broaden as the years go by. Some of the subjects that you may enjoy are:

(1) Ornithology. Bird watching is a fascinating hobby. There are over two hundred birds which are reasonably common in the British Isles, with about the same number which may be classed as rare. No equipment whatsoever, except a good guide to the various species, is really necessary, but a pair of 8 × 30 or 8 × 40 binoculars will help enormously and add to your enjoyment.

Read: 'Beginner's Guide to Bird Watching'. Reg Harrison, Pelham.

(2) Botany. The number of different types of plants growing in the British countryside is really amazing. Good pocket books are:

'Collins Pocket Guide to Wild Flowers'. David McClintock and R. S. R. Fitter, Collins.
'The Observer's Book of Trees'. W. J. Stokoe, Warne.
'Collecting and Studying Mushrooms, Toadstools and Fungi'. Alan Major, Bartholomew.

(3) Archaeology. The British Isles are immensely rich in archaeological remains of many types: earthworks, stone circles, old mines, Roman roads, ancient crosses, forts, hill figures and others. These can be found and explored or examined without any equipment except a good guide book. One such book is:

'Collins Field Guide to Archaeology'. Eric S. Wood, Collins.

(4) Architecture. No walker can fail to notice the wealth and variety of country and town houses, churches, cottages, old market halls, farm buildings and castles which are to be found throughout this land. Many are open to the public (Chapter 11).

(5) Geology. A good introductory text-book is 'The Amateur Geologist'. Peter Cattermole, Lutterworth.

Also, 'The Hamlyn Guide to Minerals, Rocks and Fossils'. W. R. Hamilton, A. R. Woolley and A. C. Bishop, Hamlyn.

(6) Meteorology. Apart from its interest, it also has a practical value in helping the walker to predict weather changes.

'Instant Weather Forecasting'. A. Watts, P. Davies.

(7) Farming methods. Walkers often tend to forget that the countryside is the workplace of a large proportion of our population. Their lives should be respected, their work also makes an interesting story.

Magazines and journals

(a) Journals

Several organizations publish official journals which are of particular interest to the walker. The main national ones are:

1. *Backchat*. Bi-monthly. Backpackers Club.

2. *Hostelling News*. Quarterly. Youth Hostels Association (England and Wales).

3. *Rucksack*. Three per year. The Ramblers' Association. The R.A. also publishes two other periodicals which can be obtained for an additional subscription:

Footpath Worker. Reports of decisions on public path orders, court cases, etc.
Press Bulletin. Digest of press extracts on footpaths, National Parks and similar matters.

4. *Strider*. Three per year. Long Distance Walkers Association.

Copies are sent free of charge to members. Information on the organizations is given in Chapter 11.

(b) Magazines

1. *The Great Outdoors*. Monthly. Specializes in articles

on walking, lightweight camping and backpacking with reviews of new equipment and suppliers, guides, books, etc. Holmes McDougall Ltd, 12 York St, Glasgow, G2 8LG.

2. *Climber and Rambler*. Monthly. This is actually the journal of the British Mountaineering Council. Good articles on routes, equipment, books, etc., but tends to concentrate on hill walking and, in any case, devotes a lot of space to climbing news. Holmes McDougall.

(c) Annuals

1. *The Mountain Year* was first published end 1976 and is intended as an annual publication. Includes lists of centres for hill-walking courses, professional mountain guides, films and lecturers. Holmes McDougall.

2. *The Backpacker's Guide*. Kate Spencer Agency Ltd, Warwick Avenue, Whickham, Newcastle upon Tyne. Full of information on backpacking.

CHAPTER 3

Clothing and Equipment

Some outdoor pursuits require a considerable outlay before a start can be made; hang-gliding and yachting are good examples. The very opposite is true for rambling. You can start without any special equipment whatsoever. A pair of old, but sound and comfortable shoes, an old pair of trousers, shirt and pullover are fine for short walks in the summer. For walking in lowland areas in winter however they would be inadequate. For moorland and mountain walking at any time they would be both inadequate and dangerous. When you become enthusiastic you will want to buy special clothing and equipment in order to extend your walking possibilities.

Fortunately, most walking equipment is only moderately expensive. You should be able to buy good quality clothing, boots, rucksack, etc., for about £125. These will last a minimum of about five years (some items will last far longer). Maintenance costs are very low. So we are talking of an expenditure of about £25 per year at current prices.

Usually, but not always, quality goes with price for walking equipment. It is a better policy to buy more expensive but good-quality equipment slowly item by item over a long period than to buy a complete set of cheap but poor quality goods all at once. You will find that the poorer-quality equipment is a constant source of irritation and will probably let you down when you most need it. The cheap anorak will usually tear in the middle of the heaviest downpour and the rucksack strap will most likely break under the heaviest load. Good quality equipment is well worth waiting for.

CLOTHING

Apart from skirts and underclothing, clothes for men and

women are substantially the same; the main differences being in weight and style.

Generally speaking cotton and wool, which are natural materials, are superior to synthetic materials such as nylon or rayon. Nylon shirts, for example, tend to become moist and uncomfortable in summer and have little insulation value in winter.

Light cotton shirts are ideal for summer use, whilst woollen shirts, usually with a tartan pattern, are very popular for winter wear. For very cold conditions extra underwear can be worn. Damart Thermolactyl underwear is particularly good for colder conditions.

Shorts, jeans or light cotton trousers are all good for summer walks in lowland areas. None of these are entirely suitable for use in mountain areas in summer or winter. Shorts give little insulation and no protection to the knees and legs for rock scrambling; jeans are cheap and hard-wearing but give little insulation when wet; light and thin cotton trousers are cheap but are neither hard-wearing nor give much wet insulation. Shorts can, of course, be worn in such areas provided that trousers are carried which can be slipped on over the top if the weather deteriorates.

Woollen trousers are far better. They are warm when dry or wet and are hard-wearing.

Walking or climbing breeches (Plus Two's) are best of all. They are available in thick wool or cotton. These finish just below the knee where they are fastened with a buckle or Velcro strip. For extra strength and life they have a double layer in the seat, crotch and knees.

Long sleeved woollen pullovers provide extra warmth. It is usually better to carry two light, thin garments than a thick one of similar weight as these will be warmer when worn together. You can also wear one only for in-between warmth. Javlin Jackets are popular which have a wind-proof and durable outer surface with a soft-pile inner lining.

Windproof and rainproof outerwear

Ideally two types of garment are necessary:

(a) *A wind- and shower-proof anorak or jacket*

In cold weather it is important to protect the body against the cooling effect of wind. Wind will increase the rate at which heat is lost from the body, producing the same feeling of cold as would be experienced on a still day at much lower temperatures. This effect can be very marked: for example, a wind of about 20 m.p.h. will produce at 0°C a similar effect to a drop in air temperature of about 15°C.

Anoraks made from closely woven cotton are popular. These are of thigh length, have draw cords at the waist and neck, elasticated inner cuffs and hood. Two front pockets and a large map pocket across the chest are very useful. Although used primarily as windproofs they will be sufficient for short light showers. They do tend to become too warm on occasions and for this reason some walkers prefer a walking jacket which can be opened partly or completely down the front for greater comfort.

(b) *Rainproofs*

The body is constantly giving out water vapour, particularly if hard walking is being undertaken. A garment which is waterproof will not allow this water vapour to escape so that heavy condensation will occur on the inner surface. Although waterproofs can be designed to provide some ventilation, it is very difficult to remain dry if they are being worn. Rainproofs should be put on only when it is absolutely necessary and should be removed as soon as the rain abates to allow inner garments to dry.

Walking capes (ponchos) are not very popular nowadays but give less condensation than waterproof anoraks. They are made from proofed nylon and fasten up the front and sides with press-studs or zips. They are designed to give a very loose fit and can be put on over large rucksacks.

Normally, however, they do not provide sufficient protection for mountain walking, particularly where heavy winds are encountered.

Rainproof anoraks or jackets, made from single-layer proofed nylon, are better under these conditions. They can be rolled up and are very light (9–15 oz or 255–425 gm). These should be provided with hood and elasticated inner cuffs. Matching trousers (6–10 oz or 170–283 gm) can also be worn but tend to increase condensation considerably.

These lightweight types have limited life and more durable models are made from heavy duty nylon coated with polyurethane or neoprene. Weight is higher (1 lb 2 oz–1 lb 10 oz or 510–737 gm) but they are to be preferred for long life and for use in mountainous country. Cagoules are rainproof anoraks which extend down to the knees providing greater protection in severe conditions.

For cold conditions nylon jackets filled with down or polyester fibres (duvets) can be worn.

An important development in recent years has been the use of GORE-TEX fabrics for waterproof clothing. These were developed by an American company, W. L. Gore and Associates, and are now being manufactured in the United Kingdom by a subsidiary. The main component of these fabrics is a thin film of PTFE (polytetrafluoroethylene) expanded to a microporous state. The PTFE film is too weak to be used alone however and laminates have therefore been used in which the film is bonded to a woven fabric. The early two-layer fabrics tended to discolour in areas of greatest pressure and they have now been replaced by three-layer laminates which have an inside layer of a knitted fabric. This inner layer has the added advantage of giving a more comfortable feel. It is claimed that outer garments made from GORE-TEX are rainproof but give greatly reduced condensation compared to coated fabrics. The theory of this action is that water vapour will diffuse outwards provided that there is a higher water vapour concentration on the inside compared to the outside, i.e. the situation with a rambler walking 'hard' and perspiring heavily on a cold and wet day; but that raindrops cannot diffuse inwards.

At the present time jackets, overtrousers and gaiters are being made from this material by several United Kingdom manufacturers. They tend to be more expensive than similar garments made from coated fabrics.

Head coverings

These are much more important than many walkers imagine. In hot sunny weather light cotton 'jungle' hats give useful protection. In winter a considerable amount of heat can be lost from the head and a woollen hat should be worn. A woollen balaclava is excellent as it can be worn rolled up or pulled down for additional warmth.

Gloves

Gloves should be carried on any walk in winter time. Woollen mitts, i.e. with one compartment for the fingers and another for the thumb, are probably warmest. In rain or snow conditions these can be covered with lightweight waterproof mitts made from nylon.

FOOTWEAR

This is probably the most important part of the walker's equipment. If your boots are not right then you will probably suffer from blisters and sores, feel miserable and may be put off walking for good.

The best advice that can be given is that you should go to a reputable supplier and let him help with the selection of a suitable pair. You can obtain boots by mail order and most leading retailers supply a large number in this manner, but it is better to visit their premises. If you do obtain boots by mail order then the retailer may supply a special order form which will tell you which foot measurements to take. It is important to complete this carefully to ensure a good fit. But with care you should be able to obtain a satisfactory pair of boots by this method.

About 25 years ago walking boots were fitted with metal nails, such as clinkers or hobs, which were inserted into the face and edge of a leather sole. These have now been superseded almost entirely by one-piece moulded sole and heel units made from hard black rubber which have a pattern similar to that of a tyre tread and are attached to the leather middle sole. The sole is fairly thick to give long life and to eliminate discomfort from stones, etc., on the ground. Rubber soles are more comfortable than nails and give an excellent grip on dry rock, grass or soft snow. They do not give a good grip, however, on wet rock, particularly if mud or lichen is present, on wet grass or on ice. In these cases care is necessary. Unfortunately, this change from leather soles with metal nails to rubber soles has probably resulted in some reduction in the average life of boots.

The sole is not flat but is bow-shaped so that only the middle part rests on the ground, unlike climbing boots where a flatter sole is usually provided. This shape gives greater comfort and is less tiring. A shank, made from wood or plastic, is added to the instep region for reinforcement but the sole should still have some flexibility.

The boots are fastened by laces which are taken through rings and hooks on the outside of the boot; the rings are on the lower part of the boot and the hooks on the upper.

The upper should preferably be one piece with a seam at the rear and have a two-layer construction. Padding is often provided around the top and sides of the ankle region for extra comfort, but this increases the time required to dry the boots after a wetting. It is important to prevent water entering the boots in the lace region and this may be done in several ways. In one method the gap is closed by a soft flexible leather flap (the bellows), whilst in another method the upper folds over in the same manner as a coat. The tongue is usually padded to protect the upper of the foot from chafing.

A special type of boot is produced by Norman Walsh. These have a 'V Ripple' sole which gives excellent grip, soft leather uppers for comfort and are very light. They are much in favour for Challenge Walking particularly over long distances. (See Chapter 9).

You should select your boots very carefully. Take your time over this; normally it will take at least an hour to make a selection.

(a) Make it clear what kind of walking you intend to do.

(b) Put on two pairs of thick woollen stockings or whatever you have found most comfortable. Always try on both boots of a pair as your feet will probably not be exactly the same shape or size.

(c) Lace the boots as tightly as possible. Start from the bottom through the bottom hooks with equal lengths of lace on the two sides and lace up in a criss-cross manner. At the top start to lace down in a similar manner, finally tying your bow on the second hook down. Tying at the top may cause a sore spot to develop where your foot flexes against the knot.

(d) Stand up and check that there is adequate space around the toes. This is important as otherwise your toes will be damaged, particularly when descending hill sides.

(e) Walk around the shop. You may find that your heels tend to move up and down slightly within the boot at this stage, but this should stop after you have worn the boots a few times and they conform more to the shape of your feet.

(f) Holding the top of a cupboard or strong shelf step back on to your toes so that the soles are roughly vertical. Kick the ground gently. You should not be able to feel the end of the boot with your toes.

When you arrive home wear the boots indoors for a while to ensure that they are comfortable. If you have not worn them outside then the retailer will probably be prepared to change them for you. Break the boots in gently. Walkers recommend all sorts of methods for doing this, but the best method is simply to walk as much as possible starting with short distances and gradually working up. You should not get any blisters or experience any real discomfort if you select your boots carefully in the first place and then break them in slowly.

It is important to look after your boots properly. Clean them immediately after you return from a walk as this will be much harder later. Mud in particular becomes difficult to remove if it has dried. Remove the laces and carefully scrape off as much mud as possible with a blunt knife or a strong wood edge. Do not try to clean into the welt with a knife point or edge as this may cut the leather or stitching. Then clean the boots thoroughly in cold water using a fairly hard brush. When all the dirt has been removed, rinse the inside and outside of the boot with cold, clean running water. Allow the boots to dry naturally in a well-ventilated room. Never place the boots in front of a fire to dry. It is a good idea to stuff newspaper into the boots for the drying period. Finally, apply a dressing of wax polish to the leather, preferably rubbing it in with the fingers. Occasionally a dressing of dubbin should be given to keep the leather supple.

You can expect a life of about four to five years of regular use from a pair of boots, although this will depend upon, the person as well as the type of walking.

Gaiters

These give excellent protection in snow or very muddy conditions and are becoming very popular. Ankle gaiters fit over the upper of the boot and are held in place by a cord which runs under the instep. Knee-length gaiters are similar and are tied under the knee. They prevent snow, mud and stones from getting into the boots and the knee-length type keep stockings and trousers reasonably clean. They are made from either cotton duck or heavyweight nylon.

Stockings

Most walkers wear two pairs of long thick woollen stockings, and some even include a pair of soft ankle socks underneath for further comfort. Make sure that they are the right size and put them on smoothly. Darned stockings are all right for the shorter walks but may produce sores over greater distances.

RUCKSACKS (Rucsacs)

Your choice of rucksack will depend primarily upon the load that you wish to carry and you will probably find that you will need two types: a small one for day use and a larger one for backpacking or walking holidays.

Basically there are three main types:

(a) Frameless day sacks

These are intended, as the name implies, for day or week-end use where loads are likely to be light. They have one large compartment with perhaps one or two outside pockets and two adjustable shoulder straps. Some models have a padded back which helps to reduce possible discomfort. About twenty years ago all rucksacks were made from thick brown cotton canvas and this is still used today. These tend however to become heavier when wet and must be thoroughly dried afterwards to prevent deterioration due to mildew attack. Nevertheless, cotton sacks are hard wearing and should give from ten to 15 years of regular use.

Most walkers today prefer nylon sacks. These are proofed, usually with polyurethane, to make them rainproof. They are available in various attractive colours and are lighter than canvas sacks. A typical sack would weigh about 8–12 oz or 227–340 gm. In order to reduce condensation where the sack rests on the back, many nylon models incorporate a canvas panel between the shoulder straps.

(b) Pack frames and sacks

A pack frame is constructed from light aluminium alloy tubing; the sections being joined together by screwed joints or by welding. It consists of two vertical tubes, capped with rubber or plastic mouldings, and three or four horizontal tubes. The vertical components are usually given a slight curve in the form of a shallow 'S' so that they conform roughly to the shape of the back. Some frames have a small platform at the base. Adjustable-length frames are available for young people who are still growing. Two or three broad strips of fabric (Back bands) are held horizontally under tension around the frame. Two adjustable fabric shoulder straps and a waist belt are attached to the frame. Special shoulder pads can be slipped over the straps and padded waist belts are sometimes provided.

The sack is made from proofed nylon or cotton canvas and can be attached to the frame by straps at the top and bottom. The neck of the sack can be closed by a drawcord and a large flap which extends well down over the sides and front of the sack. Side pockets are sometimes provided. Most leading manufacturers have designed their products so that any sack can be fitted to any frame and it is best to choose these separately. (This may not apply to frames and sacks from different manufacturers however).

It is important to choose a frame of the correct length. A recommended method for doing this is to measure the length of the walker's back from a point midway between the shoulder blades (approximately level with the shoulders) to the hip bones. This should be the same as the length of the frame from the point of attachment of the straps to the bottom edge of the lower band. When the loaded frame is worn the bottom band will rest on the hips and the curve of the frame will follow the contours of the back.

The sack size should be determined by the load that you are likely to carry. Outside pockets are very useful for holding spare maps, food and drink as they can easily be reached when required.

Hip belts are available on most models and can help to distribute a considerable part of the load of the sack on to the hips, the wide padded versions being most efficient.

The weight of a frame and sack will be about $3\frac{1}{2}$–5 lb or 1·6–2·3 kg. The pack frame and sack is far superior to the ordinary frameless sack for the carrying of heavy loads. Condensation is also less of a problem as there is space between the back and the sack for air to circulate.

(c) Anatomic (ergonomic) sacks

The main feature of these sacks is the shape of the backwall which is contoured in three dimensions to fit the wearer's back. Top tensioning straps can be tightened to draw the sack close to and slightly over the shoulders. A light aluminium alloy frame may be incorporated into the fabric wall; this helps to distribute the load and to maintain the shape of the backwall. The backwall is padded for comfort and made of cotton to reduce perspiration problems which would be experienced with a close-fitting nylon wall. A further distribution of the weight is achieved by a broad hip harness.

Rucksacks of this type are an alternative to the pack frame and sack for the carrying of heavy loads.

Packing a rucksack

In heavy rain a rucksack may not give full protection to the contents. In practice considerable seepage can occur, particularly with older models. It is a good idea therefore to use a large thick polyethylene bag inside the sack as an inner lining.

With a small day sack you will be carrying comparatively little so that packing will not be particularly important. The rainproof clothing can be folded neatly before being placed into the rucksack. Food can be carried in polyethylene containers. A polyethylene bottle with drink and any light foods such as nuts or chocolate can be put into the outside pockets where they can be reached easily.

Rather more care is needed on a backpacking holiday. There are two factors to bear in mind: first, it is important to get the heaviest objects towards the top of the sack and close to the back, and second the contents must be packed so that they are readily accessible when required. The lightest items can be put towards the bottom.

Figure 2 shows a rucksack packed in a typical manner for a backpacking expedition.

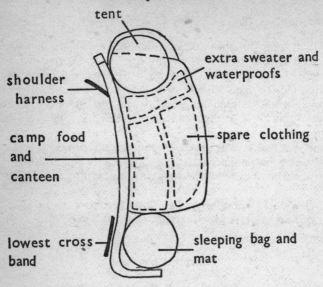

tent

extra sweater and waterproofs

shoulder harness

camp food and canteen

spare clothing

lowest cross band

sleeping bag and mat

side pockets: 1. cooking stove and fuel
2. food for journey and drink

Figure 2.   Packing a rucksack

MISCELLANEOUS

Compass

See Chapter 4.

Map-cases

These are transparent, about one foot or 30 cm square, with a zip or Velcro fastening and provided with carrying rings and cord. They are very valuable in wet weather to keep maps clean and dry.

Torch

A useful accessory when a walk continues into the darkness. A small plastic torch is probably sufficient, but some walkers equip themselves with elaborate head-strap torches with leads to batteries held in a pocket.

Walking sticks

There was a time when the walking stick was considered an essential item of equipment for any rambler, but those days are long gone and nowadays the vast majority of walkers regard a stick as an unnecessary encumbrance. But, nevertheless, many elderly or handicapped walkers will probably find a stick invaluable as a 'third leg' to help them along. It is also useful to slash down tall nettles, push away nasty briars and to ward off offensive dogs and inquisitive cattle.

Whistle (metal or plastic)

Unnecessary for lowland rambling, but usually recommended for all moorland and mountain walking in case help is needed.

EQUIPMENT MANUFACTURERS AND SUPPLIERS

The firms listed below are some of the leading manufacturers and suppliers of walking clothing and equipment. In most cases they will supply directly but in addition their products can often be obtained at numerous shops throughout the country.

1. Banton & Co. Ltd, Meadow Lane, Nottingham, NG2 3HP.
   Nottingham 868011. (Point five cold weather clothing).

2. Blacks of Greenock, P.O. Box 6, Port Glasgow, Scotland, PA14 5XN.
3. Berghaus, 34 Dean St, Newcastle upon Tyne.
   Newcastle 23561.   (Waterproof clothing, rucksacks).
4. Bradsport, 82 Edge Top Rd, Thornhill, Dewsbury, West Yorkshire, WF12 0BH.
   Dewsbury 467510.   (Waterproof clothing).
5. Damart Thermowear (Bradford) Ltd, Bingley, West Yorkshire, BD16 3BR.
   Bingley 7071.   (Thermolactyl underwear).
6. Edward R. Buck & Sons Ltd, Bukta House, Brinksway, Stockport, Cheshire, SK4 1ED.
   061 480 9721.   (Bukta Rucksacks).
7. Hebden Cord Co. Ltd, 17–23 Oldgate, Hebden Bridge, West Yorkshire, HX7 6EW.
   Hebden Bridge 3152.   (Breeches).
8. G. T. Hawkins, Overstone Rd, Northampton.   (Boots).
9. Henri-Lloyd Ltd, Smithfold Lane, Worsley, Manchester, M28 6AR.
   061 790 2277.   (Waterproof clothing).
10. James Boylan and Sons Ltd, Mullan Mills, Emyvale, Co. Monaghan, Eire.
    Emyvale 5.   (Boots).
11. Javlin International Ltd, Javlin House, Edgedale Rd, Sheffield, South Yorkshire, S7 2BQ.
    Sheffield 57413.   (Warm wear jackets).
12. Karrimor International Ltd, Avenue Parade, Accrington, Lancashire, BB5 6PR.
    Accrington 385911.   (Rucksacks).
13. Lytham Leisure Products, Preston Rd, Lytham, Lancashire.
    Lytham 738311.   (Waterproof clothing).
14. Mountain Equipment Ltd, George St, Glossop, SK13 8AY.
    Glossop 3770.   (Cold weather clothing).
15. Norman Walsh, 20 St Helens Rd, Bolton, Lancashire. (Lightweight boots).
16. Perard (Yorkshire) Ltd, Bradford Rd, Birstall, Batley, West Yorkshire.

Batley 478481. (G & H Products waterproof clothing).

17. Robert Lawrie Ltd, 54 Seymour St, Marble Arch, London, W1H 5WE.
    01 723 5252. (Clothing, boots).

18. Vango (Scotland) Ltd, 47 Colvend St, Glasgow, G40 4DH.
    041 556 7621. (Rucksacks).

CHAPTER 4

Maps and Map Reading

MAPS

The Ordnance Survey

The idea of a national survey was debated by Parliament during the middle years of the eighteenth century but no subsequent action was taken. In 1783 however a joint Anglo-French project was begun to determine the difference in latitude and longitude between the observatories at Greenwich and Paris. This involved triangulation work between the two observatories and necessitated the purchase of new and accurate instruments. On completion of this project the instruments were bought by the Duke of Richmond who held the post of Master General of His Majesty's Ordnance, a department responsible for military stores and equipment. In 1791 he initiated the Trigonometrical Survey, later to become the Ordnance Survey, part of whose immediate aim was a one-inch to one mile map covering the entire country.

The 1st Edition (Old Series) of the 1″ Ordnance Survey map covered England and Wales in 110 sheets and was published between 1801 and 1873. The 1″ map series was published in a total of seven editions; the first two by 1890, the next three 1890 to 1935, the sixth or 'New Popular' edition after the Second World War, and the final and 7th edition which was withdrawn by 1976. The one inch to one mile maps were replaced by the 1 : 50 000 scale series.

There is a separate Ordnance Survey for Northern Ireland.

Ordnance Survey maps

A wide variety of maps are published, of which the main types are:

1. Motoring Maps.
   (a) Route Planning Map of Great Britain 1 : 625 000

(*b*) The Routemaster 1 : 250 000 (9 sheets).

2. Tourist and Special Maps. Most of these use a scale of one inch to one mile and cover the more popular holiday areas, giving a considerable amount of information on facilities of interest to the holiday-maker. Separate sheets are published for Ben Nevis and Glencoe, the Cairngorms, Dartmoor, Exmoor, New Forest, Lake District, Loch Lomond and the Trossachs, North York Moors, Peak District, Snowdonia (half-inch to one mile) and Wales and the Marches.

3. 1 : 25 000 Outdoor Leisure Maps. A series of maps which deal with areas of particular interest to walkers and others interested in outdoor pursuits. These give more detail than the previous series. Sheets have been issued under the following titles: The Dark Peak (i.e. the northern half of the Peak District National Park), The Three Peaks (Part of the Yorkshire Dales National Park), The English Lakes (i.e. Lake District National Park), Wye Valley and Forest of Dean, Malham and Upper Wharfedale (Part of the Yorkshire Dales National Park), Brecon Beacons, Snowdonia, The High Tops and the Cairngorms, The Cuillin and Torridon Hills, Brighton and Sussex Vale, South Pennines, The New Forest, The Purbecks and South Devon.

4. 1 : 50 000 Series. The 1st Series maps were published between 1974 and 1976; these are now being replaced by the 2nd Series maps. The entire area of England, Scotland and Wales including off-shore islands, but not Northern Ireland, are covered by 204 sheets.

5. 1 : 25 000 Series. The 1st Series maps were published between 1945 and 1956 and cover England, Scotland and Wales except for the Scottish Highlands and some islands. Since 1965 some of these maps have been replaced by 2nd Series maps which are based upon a new survey.

6. Archaeological and Historical Maps. Some of these are of interest to the walker, e.g. Hadrian's Wall (two inches to one mile).

7. Large scale maps, e.g. 1 : 1250 (about 50 inches to one

mile). These are of little interest to the rambler and are intended mainly for local planning purposes.

8. Geological and Soil Survey maps.

For further information consult the catalogue obtainable from Ordnance Survey, Romsey Road, Maybush, Southampton, SO9 4DH. Southampton 775555.

For maps of Northern Ireland write to The Chief Survey Officer, Ministry of Finance, Ordnance Survey, Ladas Drive, Belfast, BT6 9FJ. 0232 54580.

Scale

The scale of a map is the relationship between the distance apart of two points on a map and the distance apart of the actual points which they represent on the ground.

This may be expressed in three ways:

(*a*) Words. The expression 'one inch to one mile' means that one inch on a map represents one mile on the ground.

(*b*) Figures. The expression 'one inch to one mile' may be represented as:

$$\frac{1}{63,360} \text{ or } 1 : 63\ 360.$$

These are all the same because there are 63,360 inches in one mile. The current Ordnance Survey maps which are most useful to walkers are the 1 : 25 000 and 1 : 50 000 series. These are based upon the metric system, one centimetre on a map being equivalent to $\frac{1}{4}$ or $\frac{1}{2}$ kilometre respectively.

(*c*) Scale line. This is simply a straight line divided up into suitable units. (Figure 3). The scale line shown is that included on all sheets of the 1 : 50 000 map series.

It is essential to know the scale of a map so that you can determine the distance between two points, e.g. between two villages. Apart from this the scale of a map is important because:

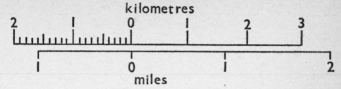

Figure 3. Scale line

(*a*) it will determine the size of the actual area covered by a map, and

(*b*) it will determine the amount of detail shown on the map.

Maps such as the O.S. 1 : 1250 series (about 50 inches to one mile), are known as large-scale maps; whilst those such as the O.S. 1 : 625 000 series (about ten miles to one inch) are known as small-scale maps.

Thus: a large-scale map covers only a small area of ground but gives a lot of detail.

A small-scale map covers a larger area of ground but gives less detail.

Selection of suitable scale

The Ordnance Survey published a wide variety of maps for the United Kingdom and it is important to select the best map for a particular purpose.

For travelling by car from town to town where only main or trunk roads are to be used the O.S. 1 : 625 000 map will be suitable. For travelling by car where more information regarding minor roads is required the 1 : 250 000 series could be used. These would also be very suitable for a holiday tour by bicycle.

Walkers will find that the 1 : 50 000 and 1 : 25 000 series maps are the most suitable. The 1 : 50 000 maps will be sufficient for most purposes and will be the ones that are most frequently used. They indicate public rights of way and give sufficient details of landscape features such as woods, streams and contours for routes to be followed without difficulty. In addition public houses, post offices, churches, castles, etc., are all marked. This map will probably prove insufficient however for some areas with numerous small fields, particularly where all traces of footpaths have been removed by ploughing or the blocking of stiles. For this kind of country the 1 : 25 000 maps will be superior. Larger scale maps such as the O.S. 1 : 10 000 are unnecessarily detailed for walkers.

Subsequently sections will therefore be confined to the 1 : 25 000 and 1 : 50 000 series maps.

The 1 : 50 000 scale maps

The index of sheets is given in Figure 4.

Conventional signs

The position of a large number of features, such as churches, post offices, woods, sandy beaches, cliffs and so on, have to be included on a map. Words alone would not be a satisfactory method of representing such objects; it would be difficult to determine their exact position and the map would become very congested. Words are therefore used in very few cases to mark the position of a feature. In most cases symbols are employed. These symbols are called 'conventional signs'. This is a shorthand which enables the mapmaker to put a great deal of information into a very small space. Colour is also employed to distinguish between different features, for example, different grades of roads; this also helps the map-user to distinguish some features more clearly. Six colours are used on the current maps. In the 1 : 50 000 map series most of the signs bear some resemblance to the actual objects themselves so that they can be remembered more easily.

Some typical conventional signs from the 1 : 50 000 map are shown in Figure 5.

You will notice that the conventional signs may be divided into two groups:

(1) The signs which represent features of the landscape

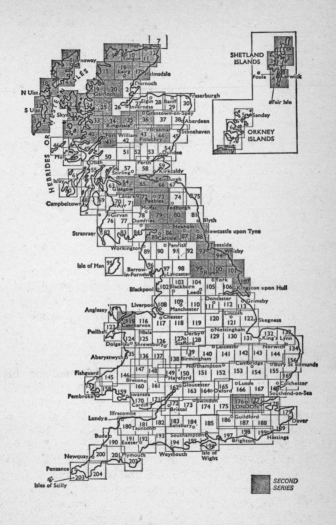

Figure 4. Index for 1 : 50 000 sheets. (From Ordnance Survey)

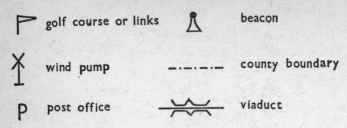

Figure 5.   Some examples of conventional signs

which can be seen, e.g. roads, cliffs, woods, windmills, etc.

(2) The signs which represent features which cannot actually be observed, such as county and parish boundaries, sites of battles, contour lines.

Contours

It is very important to be able to assess the nature and particularly the relief of the ground over which you are planning to walk. Obviously your walking pace is going to be greatly affected by the steepness of slopes along your route; and also because it will be difficult to follow a route through mountainous country without a knowledge of the position and direction of valleys, ridges, etc.

Contour lines are used on the 1 : 50 000 map for this purpose. A contour line on a map is a line drawn through all points which are the same height above mean sea-level.

The contour lines are brown and adjacent lines are separated by the same vertical difference; on the 1st Series maps this is 50 feet whilst on the 2nd Series maps this is ten metres. This difference is called the vertical interval. Every fifth line, e.g., after 50 metres, is thicker. At intervals the contour lines are broken and the height above mean sea-level is given as a number (Figure 13). The actual height at particular points is also noted, e.g. the summit of a mountain.

The closer the contour lines are to each other the steeper is the ground. If the ground is so steep that a cliff is formed then the lines are terminated and a cliff is indicated.

The 1 : 25 000 scale maps

These maps give considerably more detail than the 1 : 50 000 maps. In particular, field boundaries are shown; this makes them much more useful in areas where all signs of a footpath have been removed. The area covered by a sheet is much smaller however. A 1 : 50 000 sheet covers an area of 40 × 40 kilometres, whilst a 1 : 25 000 sheet covers an area of only 10 × 10 kilometres (1st Series) or 20 × 10 kilometres (most 2nd Series). You will therefore require sixteen or eight 1 : 25 000 sheets respectively to cover the same area as one 1 : 50 000 sheet. Price is a further consideration. On current prices the 2nd Series 1 : 25 000 sheets will be seven times more expensive than the equivalent 1 : 50 000 sheets.

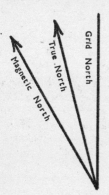

Figure 6. Directions North

THE COMPASS

Direction North

This term has three meanings (Figure 6):

(*a*) True or Geographical North. The Earth turns daily on an axis which passes through the Earth's surface at the Geographical North and South Poles. A line which runs along the Earth's surface from pole to pole in a south to north direction is called a line of longitude (also a meridian). These indicate the direction of the True North.

(*b*) Magnetic North. This is the direction taken by a compass needle. This direction is not usually the same as the line of longitude through that point. This arises because the Magnetic North Pole of the Earth does not coincide with the Geographical North Pole. The angle between these two directions will vary from place to place and from year to year. This angle is called the Magnetic Variation or Magnetic Declination.

(*c*) Grid North. This is the direction of the 'vertical' grid lines marked on the 1 : 50 000 maps; north being at the top of the map. Only one grid line can coincide exactly with a line of longitude and the discrepancy between Grid North and True North becomes greater as you move away from the true origin of the grid (see later). This discrepancy therefore varies from one place to another but remains constant from one year to the next.

When using a compass it is more useful to relate Magnetic North to Grid North rather than to True North. This information is provided on the 1 : 50 000 sheets. For example, Sheet No. 126 (Shrewsbury) states that Magnetic North was about 8° West of Grid North in 1974, decreasing by about $\frac{1}{2}$° in eight years. Thus, it will be $7\frac{1}{2}$° in 1982, 7° in 1990 and so on. This angle is called the Grid-Magnetic Variation. In 1974 for the UK mainland it varied between 7° and 10° West.

Bearings

A bearing is simply the direction between two objects given as an angle measured clockwise from Direction North. Thus, in Figure 7 Point B is east of Point A, and the bearing of B from A is 120°. Figure 8 shows how these bearing angles relate to the points of the compass. As there are three Norths there must also be three bearings. In practice, we will use two: Grid Bearings which are taken from the map and are therefore also called Map Bearings, and Magnetic Bearings which are measured outdoors with a compass and are therefore also called Compass or Field Bearings. Obviously one can be calculated from the other by use of the Grid-Magnetic Variation.

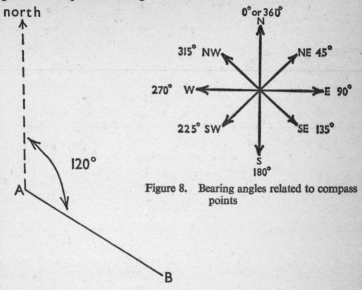

Figure 7. Example of a bearing

Figure 8. Bearing angles related to compass points

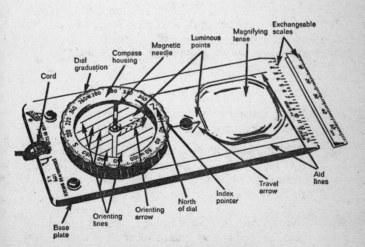

Figure 9. The Silva compass.

The Silva Compass

The Silva compass is extremely popular with walkers, as it is with orienteers and climbers. A typical model is shown in. Figure 9, although there are a number of other types available. The directions given in the following sections are based upon the Silva compass, although they may also be applicable to other makes with a similar construction.

When you are using a compass ensure that it is well clear of any iron or steel objects such as a knife, lighter, pen, etc., as these will cause considerable deflection of the magnetic needle. In some areas the needle will also be affected by local rocks.

MAP READING

Estimating distance

It is easy to measure the shortest distance between two points on a map. The Silva compass has a scale on the side of the base plate which can be used for this purpose. A scale is also provided on O.S. maps. It is far more common however to have to estimate the length of a walking route which twists and turns and is anything but a straight line.

There are three ways by which this can be done:

(1) *With a pencil and sheet of paper* (Figure 10)

As an example, suppose that you want to measure the length of the footpath from the church to the cross-roads.

Step 1   Lay the paper flat on the map so that the corner lies on the church and the paper edge lies along the footpath to the first bend. Mark the point of the bend on the paper.

Step 2   Now rotate the paper around the mark until it is alongside the next length of footpath. Mark the second bend.

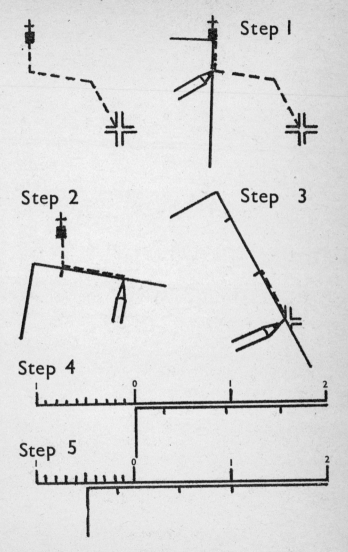

Figure 10. Estimating distance with paper and pencil

Step 3 Repeat for the third length of footpath.

Step 4 Lay the paper alongside the map scale with the corner on zero. You will see that in this case the distance is not a whole number of miles.

Step 5 Move the paper to the left until the final pencil mark coincides with a whole number of miles. The sum of the distances on the left-hand scale and on the right-hand scale gives the total distance. In the example this is 1·5 miles.

(2) *With a length of string*

Use a length of string in a similar way to the paper edge in method (1).

Tie a knot in one end of the string, and place the knot on to the church symbol holding it with your left index finger. Move your right index finger along the string pulling it taut so that it lies along the first section of the footpath. Move the left finger along and repeat drawing the string taut along the second part of the footpath. Repeat to the end of the footpath. Then lay the string along the scale and measure the length.

(3) *Using a Map Measurer*

This is a handy little instrument, easy to use and fairly cheap (Figure 11). The instrument is held in the hand and the measuring wheel is run along the footpath line on the map. At the end of the footpath line the dial gives a reading of the total distance traversed in miles and kilometres.

These methods all tend to underestimate the distance as they 'cut corners' and 'straighten out' lines.

Judging the ground

Gradients

Gradients are usually expressed in the form of a ratio be-

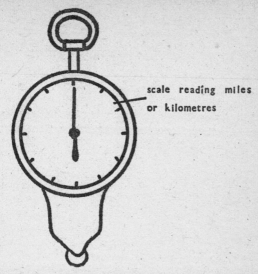

scale reading miles
or kilometres

Figure 11.   A map measurer

tween the rise in the height of the land and the horizontal distance on the map. Thus in Figure 12 (*a*) the inclined line is at a gradient of 1 in 10. Figure 12 (*b*) shows various gradients to give you an idea of what they look like.

A road of gradient 1 in 10 will be hard for the average cyclist, probably causing him to dismount, whilst 1 in $2\frac{1}{2}$ is the gradient of the steepest road found in this country.

The gradient of a slope can be calculated from an examination of the contours on a map. In Figure 13 point A is on the 250 metres contour and points B and C are both on the 310 metres contour. The distance from A to B and A to C can be measured using the scale.

Distance from A to B = 1,400 metres.
Distance from A to C = 2,400 metres.

Gradient from A to B = 1 in 24.
Gradient from A to C = 1 in 40.

The total height to be climbed is the same in both cases,

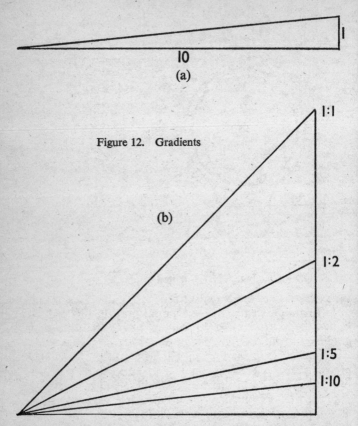

Figure 12. Gradients

of course, but the footpath from A to B would be shorter but steeper than that from A to C. This is the reason why paths in mountainous areas often go in 'zig-zags' rather than directly up a slope.

It should be noted that Figure 13 only shows the relative gradients of the two slopes; it will only show the actual gradients if the horizontal and vertical scales are the same.

The spacing of the contour lines will give you an idea of the steepness of a slope. Contour lines which are close to-

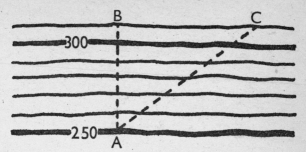

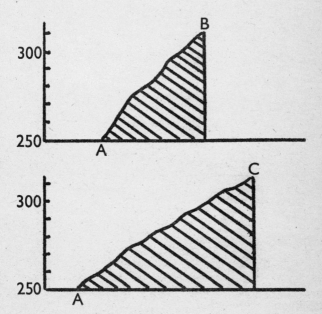

Figure 13.   Estimating gradients

gether represent a steep slope and those which are further
apart represent a more gradual slope.

Figure 14. Distinguishing between

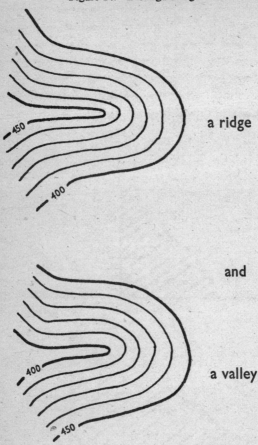

a ridge

and

a valley

Profiles

You can deduce the profile of a slope by an examination of the contour pattern. There are three types of simple slope: straight, convex and concave. In the straight slope the distance between successive contour lines remains constant, i.e.

the gradient is constant. In the convex slope the interval between contours gradually increases up the slope, i.e. the gradient gets less. In the concave slope the interval gradually decreases up the slope as the gradient increases.

It is very important to distinguish between a ridge and a valley (Figure 14) although there are usually other features which help you to do this.

National Grid references

A grid reference is used to pin-point a position. There will be many occasions for this; for example, to let members of a rambling party know where to meet. This can be done, of course, by referring to a cross-roads, or a church in the area, but it is usually better to add a grid reference to reduce the possibility of a mistake.

With any rectangular area, such as a map, the position of any point can be accurately defined by giving its distance from the left-hand edge and its distance from the bottom edge. This is the basis of the grid system. The grid of a map is therefore established by two lines at right angles, one north-south and the other east-west which intersect, not necessarily at the south-west corner of the map, but somewhere to the south-west. These two lines are called the axes of the grid and their point of intersection is called the origin; the distance east and north of the origin are called the easting and northing respectively. The lines drawn parallel to the axes are called grid lines.

Unfortunately the discrepancy between the grid line and the meridian increases as you move away from the axis. This makes it desirable to put the origin into the centre of the grid area so as to reduce this variation to a minimum. But this would necessitate a method of differentiating between the four quarters (using, for example, negative numbers or letters). To avoid this the true origin is still placed in the centre of the area, but a 'false origin' is chosen so that the entire area to be covered lies to the north-east of it. The 'false origin' of the British grid (called the National Grid)

lies to the south-west of the Scilly Isles. All grid references
are given with reference to the 'false origin'.

In the National Grid the entire area of the British Isles,
excluding Ireland, is covered by 100 km squares (Figure 15).
These squares were originally designated by a number, but
nowadays letters are used. Each 100 km square is then divided
into smaller squares of 1 km side. These lines are marked on
the 1 : 50 000 maps.

Giving a grid reference

Figure 16 shows a section of a 1 : 50 000 map with a church
indicated. Let us assume that this shows an area from 100
km square SP. It is necessary to give a grid reference for the
church.

Step 1   Note the number of the 'vertical' grid line to the
         left, i.e. west of the church.
Step 2   Imagine that the interval between this grid line and
         the next is divided into tenths. Estimate the number
         of tenths that the church lies east from this
         line.
Step 3   Note the number of the 'horizontal' grid line below
         the church, i.e. south.
Step 4   Estimate the number of tenths north of this line.

The full grid reference is SP-213575.

If there is no doubt as to the 100 km square intended, then
a six figure grid reference only need be given, i.e. 213575.

Remember that the easting is placed before the northing.
If you have difficulty in remembering this then you may find
that the sentence 'In at the door and up the stairs' helps you.
Or, alternatively, you could remember that in the alphabet
the 'E' (in 'Easting') comes before the 'N' (in 'Northing').

The number of tenths between adjacent grid lines may be
estimated by eye, but it can be measured accurately using a
Romer. Some types of compasses contain Romer scales. A
Romer is simply two scales at right angles, each of which is
marked off in tenths and equal in length to the distance
between two adjacent grid lines.

Diagram showing 100 kilometre squares and the letters that designate
them

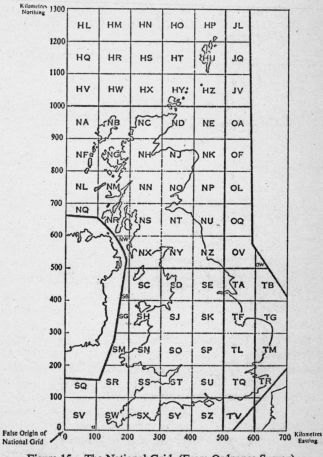

Figure 15. The National Grid. (From Ordnance Survey)

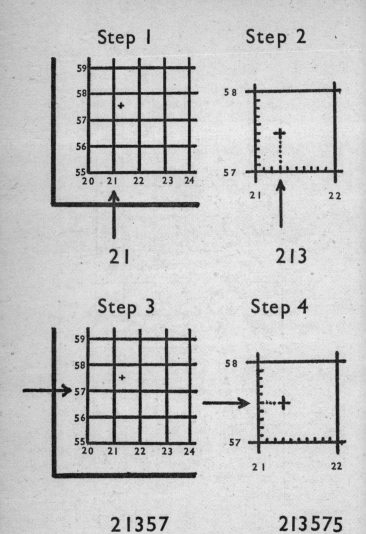

Figure 16.   Finding a grid reference

Setting the map

This simply means that the map is held so that all points on the map are in the same direction to each other as the actual features are on the ground. Thus, if you look along the straight line joining your position on the map with any other point on the map then you will also be looking towards that point on the ground. Whenever you are following a route or using the map outdoors you should always start by setting the map.

There are basically two methods:

(1) *By eye*

Using the map identify at least two prominent features in your vicinity. Rotate the map until the points on the map are in the same direction as these features. This is very easy provided that you can see and identify prominent local landmarks. It cannot be used, for example, on a flat moorland covered in thick mist.

(2) *Using Direction North*

(*a*) *With a compass.* This can be done roughly by ignoring Grid-Magnetic Variation. Place the compass on to the map so that the grid lines are parallel to the orienting lines and the orienting arrow points to the top. Then rotate the map until the magnetic needle points to the N on the dial. The top of the map now points to the Magnetic North.

For accurate setting the Grid-Magnetic Variation must be taken into consideration. The method is the same as before, except that the map should be rotated until the magnetic needle points to 352°, i.e. assuming that Magnetic North is 8° west of Grid North.

(*b*) *Without a compass*

(i) By the sun. The sun is due east at 6 a.m., due west at 6 p.m. and moves east to west during the day. At mid-day

it is due south. This will give you an approximate guide
to direction. A better method uses an ordinary watch.
Hold the watch horizontally so that the hour-hand points
towards the sun. The line bisecting the angle between
the hour-hand and 12 o'clock in a clockwise direction
points to the south. Remember that if British Summer
Time is operating then one hour should be deducted
from the hour-hand time. Therefore, in the example
shown in Figure 17, the 4 should be pointed towards the
sun and not the 5.

(ii) By the stars. During the night the stars appear to revolve
in the form of a huge wheel around a fixed point. This
point is in the direction of the Geographical North Pole.
There is no reasonably bright star at this point but the
Pole Star (Polaris) is very near. This star may be found
easily starting from the prominent and well-known
constellation, the Plough (Great Bear or Ursa Major).
Polaris is in the constellation of the Little Bear (Ursa
Minor), which is similar in shape to that of the Plough
(Figure 18).

Following a route by compass bearing

This method is used when your position is known and you
wish to travel directly across open country to another point
some distance away.

Step 1   Measure the grid bearing.
         Place the compass on the map so that the long edge
         of the transparent base plate joins your location to
         the objective. Rotate the compass housing until the
         orienting lines are parallel to the grid lines and
         the orienting arrow points to the top of the map.
         The index pointer on the compass gives the grid
         bearing.
Step 2   Convert grid bearing to magnetic bearing. Rotate
         the compass housing to increase the angle by the
         amount of the Grid-Magnetic Variation, i.e. at
         present increase the angle by 8° or other local value.

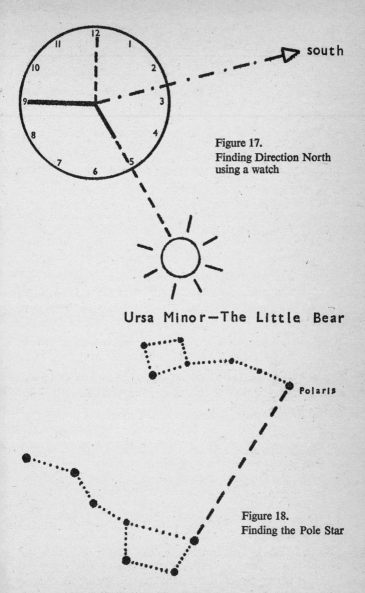

south

Figure 17.
Finding Direction North
using a watch

Ursa Minor—The Little Bear

Polaris

Figure 18.
Finding the Pole Star

Ursa Major—The Great Bear

Step 3   Rotate the entire compass until the magnetic needle coincides with the N on the scale. The travel arrow then indicates the direction of travel.

Step 2 can be omitted, but this will introduce an error of about 8° in the direction of travel. This will produce a deviation of over one-eighth mile after one mile of walking.

When following a bearing it is best to proceed via a chain of objects on the required line of travel. Stop, identify some prominent object or feature in the required direction and then walk towards it, repeating the procedure when you reach it. At night a star can be used provided that the direction is regularly checked to allow for stellar rotation. On very rough but featureless moorland in misty conditions one member of a party can be directed ahead for a reasonable distance and used as a marker, the procedure then being repeated.

Determining your position

Two methods are available:

(1) Lining-in

Set the map.

Look into the distance and pick out some prominent object, e.g. a church, and some other object, e.g. the edge of a wood, in line with it. Identify these on the map and draw a line through them. Now pick out two more objects in a similar manner in a direction approximately at a right angle to the first pair. Repeat the above procedure. The point where the two lines cross is your position.

(2) Taking cross bearings with a compass (Resection)

This technique may be used when you can identify two local features or landmarks on your map.
Step 1   Take a field bearing. Hold the compass horizontally and point the travel arrow in the direction of the

first feature. Rotate the compass housing until the magnetic needle points to N.

Step 2   Convert magnetic bearing to a grid bearing by rotating the compass housing so as to reduce the angle by the amount of the Grid-Magnetic Variation.

Step 3   Lay the map on a flat horizontal surface and without altering the setting place the compass on to the map so that the edge of the base plate goes through the symbol of the object chosen. Then rotate the entire compass until the orienting lines are parallel with the grid lines on the map and the orienting arrow points to the top of the map. Draw a thin pencil line through the symbol along the base plate edge.

Repeat Steps 1–3 with the second feature. The two lines will intersect at your position.

The methods can also be used to identify some prominent landmark on the map.

NOTE

In later chapters all map numbers refer, unless otherwise stated, to the 1 : 50 000 series. For easy location of Youth Hostels, etc. position is indicated in each case by a 1 : 50 000 map sheet number and Grid Reference; for example, (100–613839) indicates Grid Reference 613839 which can be found on O.S. 1 : 50 000 map no. 100.

CHAPTER 5

Mountain and Moorland Walking

Most experienced walkers would probably agree that mountain and moorland areas offer some of the finest walking available. This is shown for example, by the popularity of the National Parks which, with one exception, are all substantially areas of wild country. One reason for this must be the magnificent scenery that is to be found in mountain areas, much of it available only to the walker who can penetrate into the more remote regions away from roads. Generally, also, there are fewer restrictions to walking although, despite what many may think, mountains are owned by someone and are not common property. Perhaps most important of all, however, is the challenge that mountains and moorlands offer to the walker. Walking over rough ground and the ascent, and descent, of steep slopes make a heavy demand upon strength and stamina. The loneliness and remoteness of these areas force the walker to depend upon his own resources and ability and upon those of his companions. Route finding may be difficult due to the absence of landmarks or to mist on high ground, and yet nowhere is it more important. The weather can change rapidly and can be a vital factor in the difficulty of a route and the time necessary to complete it. Mountains and moorlands offer adventure and this appeals to walkers of all age groups.

The term 'fell-walking' is very commonly used in the north of England; a fell being a mountain or shoulder of moorland.

SOME MOUNTAIN FEATURES

(a) Cirque (Cwm in Wales, corrie or coire in Scotland, combe or cove in the Lake District and Pennines)

This is a U-shaped valley cut into the side of a mountain by a glacier. It has a characteristic long-section (Figure 19)

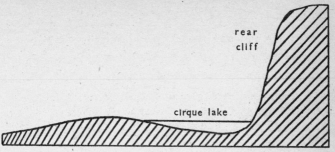

Figure 19. Long-section of a cirque

with a steep, often precipitous, back wall. A good example is Cwm Idwal in North Wales where the rear wall consists of the great cliffs of the Devil's Kitchen and Glyder Fawr.

These were sometimes cut high up into the side of main valleys by subsidiary and less eroding glaciers so that they are left hanging above the main valley. In this case the lip of the cirque lies some distance up the wall of the main valley and a climb is necessary to reach it. These are called hanging cirques. Great Langdale in Cumbria is an example of a main glacial valley; Langdale Combe and the valley containing Stickle Tarn, which both open into it, are examples of hanging cirques.

(b) Lakes (Llyn in Wales, Loch or Lochan in Scotland, Tarn or Mere or Water in the Lake District)

These are a common feature of glaciated mountain districts. The hollow in the bed of the cirque caused by the glacial action is sometimes further enhanced by material called moraine deposited on to the lip of the cirque by the glacier. In most cases this hollow has been filled by water forming a cirque lake. Lakes can also occur in the main valleys. There are about 450 lakes in the Lake District alone.

(c) Ridge and Arête

A ridge is an arm of a mountain formed between two cirques. In extreme cases the two cirques became so close together as the glaciers eroded their head walls that they are separated only by a thin rock edge. This rock edge is called an arête (Crib or Cribin in Wales, Fiacaill in Scotland, Edge in the Lake District). Good examples are Striding Edge in the Lake District and the ridges of the Snowdon Horseshoe in North Wales.

Where the ridges descended into the valleys they were often cut away by the glaciers in these valleys. In these cases the ridges end in a cliff and are said to be truncated. Spurs projecting out from a main ridge or arête are usually truncated in the same manner.

(d) Pass or Col (*Bwlch in Wales, Bealach or Lairig in Scotland, Saddle or Hause in the Lake District*)

The name given to a saddle between two mountains which is often a convenient route for crossing from one valley to another.

(e) Cliff or Crag (*Craig or Clogwyn in Wales, Craig or Creag in Scotland*)

A common feature of glaciated mountain areas they are often split by ravines or clefts which are called gullies. A buttress is a massive face of rock standing out from the main cliff or mountain side which is often flanked by gullies.

(f) Scree

Mountain crags are continuously being broken up by the action of frost. Water enters into cracks and crevices in the rock where it freezes; this is accompanied by an increase in volume which produces a considerable force on the sides of the crevice. As a result the rock is shattered and ultimately small pieces fall away and accumulate on the slopes below. This is called scree, an old Norse word which means rubble which will slide when trodden upon.

(g) *Cairn* (*Carn in Wales*)

A pile of stones used to indicate the summit of a mountain or to mark parts of a path. Some mountain tops, however, have many cairns which seem to indicate nothing in particular.

(h) *Streams* (*Afon or Nant in Wales, Allt or Burn in Scotland, Beck or Gill in Lake District and Pennines*)

These are characterized in mountain areas by a high gradient and a narrow, V-shaped valley with steep sides. They often flow over small cliffs and into ravines. In U-shaped valleys they have low gradient and may meander.

SUMMER WALKING

Equipment

It is essential to be properly clothed and to carry adequate equipment before venturing on to the hills. There will of course be long days of hot weather when shorts and a light shirt are most suitable, but warmer clothing should always be carried. A cold wind on the tops, a clammy mist or a rapid change in the weather can produce sudden chilling with the possibility of exposure (hypothermia). There have been many cases of this in the British hills in mid-summer. The small extra weight carried is a small price to pay for the extra security gained.

The following is a sensible list for average British summer conditions:

Waterproof anorak (or cagoule) and overtrousers
Windproof anorak or jacket
Sweater
Walking breeches or woollen trousers
Two pairs of long woollen stockings
Gaiters (not essential but useful for boggy moorland)
Walking boots

Woollen hat
Rucksack
1 : 50 000 map with waterproof map-case
Compass
Torch with spare batteries and bulb
Whistle
Pocket knife
Small first-aid kit
Food (more than you think you are likely to need)
Emergency rations
Drink (preferably hot tea, coffee or soup in a vacuum flask)
Two handkerchiefs
Survival bag
Watch
Money

Suitable emergency foods are chocolate, barley sugar, Kendal Mint Cake, dried fruit and glucose tablets. These should be kept for emergencies and not used for occasional snacks.

About 50 feet of No. 2 or 3 nylon rope should ideally be carried in very rough areas, e.g. for scrambling, where there are inexperienced members in the party. But it is important that the leader knows how to use the rope correctly.

Safety

The information given in Chapter 2 on the selection of route, estimation of time, walking technique and the responsibilities of a leader are even more important in hill-walking. But some further points need to be made.

The majority of walkers should not go into the hills on their own, a party of two or preferably three giving a much greater margin of safety. It would be wrong however to condemn solo walking in the hills for everyone. Solo walking can give a great deal of pleasure and is done every day by scores of walkers without any mishap, but the increased risk must be clearly recognized. It should be attempted only by fit and experienced fell-walkers who are properly equipped.

Check your equipment carefully before you leave home. It is no use discovering that you have left your spare sweater behind when you are feeling the cold, or that your emergency rations are missing when you are benighted.

Leave a note of your route with a responsible person before you go. If you are missing after an agreed time then search parties can be organized and they will then know where to look for you. Make sure that you notify the person concerned when you return; there have been many instances of searches being organized for 'lost' walkers who were eventually found many miles away in a comfortable hotel or hostel.

A party should stay together at all times, particularly if the hills are misty or the weather is bad. The leader of a large party has a particular responsibility in this respect. On no account should any member of a party be left behind in the hills, unless help is being sought after an accident. A reliable member should bring up the rear of the party to prevent anyone being left behind. Eight novices would be a maximum number for two experienced walkers.

It is vital to keep warm at all times. You may begin to feel cold due to the following:

(*a*) Change in the weather. Weather forecasts are unreliable for local mountain areas and, in any case, the weather can change very quickly.

(*b*) Rise in height. The temperature will usually fall as you climb, generally at an average rate of 0·6°C per 100 metres (i.e. about 3°F for every 1,000 feet); this is known as the Lapse Rate.

(*c*) Wind. This can be much more important than generally realized, and for this reason a windproof top garment should always be carried.

(*d*) Rain.

Overheating should always be avoided. It can easily occur on the ascent of very steep slopes, particularly if sweaters have already been put on. It is better to wear less clothing and put on the extra sweater when higher and into wind, or when a stop is made. Waterproofs also should not be put on until rain is met as these cause heavy condensation and overheating.

Accurate map reading and compass work are much more important than in lowland areas. Learn and practise the use of these before you start. You must take particular care during the later stages of a walk when the party may be tired and rushing to get home. Accidents occur frequently during this period.

Obstacles and techniques

Generally the most popular routes on mountains avoid difficulties and take the easiest line. Some difficulties may however be encountered in any walk in the hills. There is also a great deal of enjoyment in deliberately tackling difficulties, provided always that they lie within one's capabilities.

1 Bogs

These are a feature of most moorland areas. Some are certainly dangerous and walkers have died in them, but this is very rare. Nevertheless it can be a very alarming experience to sink up to the knees or waist. A very flat area covered with bright green moss should always be viewed with suspicion. So also should areas of bare peat after prolonged and heavy rain, particularly if very flat or in a hollow where water can collect. Proceed with care testing each footstep carefully before trusting your weight to it. Usually it is safe to put your feet on to small tufts, or even a few blades of grass, as this indicates firm ground. Do not attempt to rush across a bog except over very small areas with the certainty of firm ground beyond, otherwise you may find yourself marooned out of reach. Proceed slowly and carefully and be prepared to make endless detours to keep on reasonably firm ground.

2 Boulder slopes

Some hill sides and tops are covered with large boulders

which can give slow and laborious passage. Proceed slowly and rhythmically placing your boots flat on to convenient rock faces or across the sharp edge of boulders, using hand holds for balance where necessary. Try to avoid taking a long stride to reach a hold, usually you will find an intermediate one which will help you to keep your balance and rhythm. If you dislodge a boulder shout immediately to warn anyone below you. Do not climb immediately above another walker but, preferably, off to one side.

3 Clints and grikes

Limestone districts, notably in the Yorkshire Dales National Park, contain large platforms, often acres in extent, of flat, horizontal rock. By the action of weathering these platforms have become deeply grooved and furrowed; the grooves, often several feet deep, are known as grikes and the areas between known as clints. The clints are bare rock free from any vegetation whilst the grikes often harbour many unusual plants growing out of reach of grazing sheep.

Clints are relatively easy to walk over in dry weather but need care as a false step can lead to a damaged ankle in a grike. In wet weather the limestone can be slippy and dangerous. Walking across clints at night can be particularly hazardous.

4 Groughs (*Pronounced 'gruffs'*)

These are channels cut into the soft top surface of peat moors by running water. The source area of many streams often consists of a number of groughs running in roughly the same direction. Some are narrow and only a few feet in depth and can be easily jumped. Others however are far too wide for this and can be 12–15 feet deep. The walls are usually steep and consist of black, bare peat; the bottom varying from sandy beds over which it is a delight to walk to slime in which the boots sink. With the larger specimens it is often best to walk a few yards along the grough to find a spot where the side has collapsed forming a grassy stairway down to the bottom. As an alternative if the side is not too steep is is possible to climb down and then up the opposite side using the boot edges in the soft peat. Groughs need care, not because they are particularly dangerous, but because they can result in a wild, undignified slide to the bottom with the walker becoming covered in a foul slime.

5 Mist

Mist is essentially cloud at ground level. It will be frequently encountered in British mountains, usually above 1,500 feet (457 m). It tends to destroy some of the enjoyment as the view is lost and it makes route finding much more difficult. It can also be very alarming to beginners.

Before you climb into mist or before it becomes denser always stop and check your position carefully. For route finding in dense mist it is essential to use a compass and to keep a close check on the route being followed, so that you do not reach a situation where you simply do not know where you are. In the event of being uncertain it is best to retrace your steps back to the last known point before proceeding afresh. If the mist clears temporarily then stop and recheck your position before it thickens again.

The most dangerous situations occur in the descent of steep slopes in mist where a cliff may be encountered. It is essential in these cases to move with great caution and be prepared to stop if the ground becomes excessively steep. In this event it is best to contour the hillside until an easier way down can be found.

6 Pot-holes, mine shafts and tunnels

Pot-holes are vertical shafts, often of considerable depth, found in limestone country which have been formed naturally by the action of water. In most cases they are unfenced. The edge of a pot-hole should be approached with care, particularly if the rock is wet. Caves also abound in such areas but should not be explored without proper equipment as they may contain difficult or complex sections or even open shafts.

Some mountain areas have been extensively mined and open disused mineshafts and tunnels are found. The areas of Tan Hill Inn and Cross Fell on the Pennine Way and many parts of Derbyshire are examples. It is best to keep well clear of shafts. Tunnels should not be explored as the years of neglect have rendered many particularly dangerous.

7 Ridges

Generally these offer the best routes to the top of mountains. They tend to be dry and they are a very definite mountain feature which can be easily recognized on maps. Some ridges can however be rocky as mentioned earlier. The lower part of a ridge into a valley often ends in a cliff and a detour is then necessary.

8 Rock faces

Generally the walker should avoid climbing any rock faces; rock climbing should be attempted only after instruction and with proper equipment. Each year many walkers become 'crag-fast', i.e. they are unable to move up or down, and have to be rescued.

There are however a number of shattered mountain ridges that can be tackled with safety by anyone with a clear head for heights and who proceeds with care. This type of activity, on the borderline between walking and climbing, is called 'scrambling' and can be great fun. Good examples of scrambling ridges are the North Ridge of Tryfan and Bristly Ridge on Glyder Fach, both in North Wales.

As far as possible keep the body vertical and avoid the tendency to lean inwards towards the rock. Try to maintain three points of contact at all times. Keep a clear head, plan your moves carefully in advance, and then climb slowly and calmly up the rock. Don't grab at holds or rush at the rock. Don't use your knees on a hold as it can sometimes be difficult to move away again, and you may finish up with both feet stuck out behind and unable to move! Try to use your arms to provide balance and your legs to push you up. Remember that your legs are a lot stronger than your arms.

Descent is usually easier facing outwards when you can lower yourself from hold to hold with a good view of the rock and holds below. On steep rock however it will be easier and safer to face inwards to the rock where you can use more positive hand-holds. Even on shattered scrambling ridges there will be some areas of rock which will require a higher technical standard of climbing and it is essential therefore that you choose your route carefully so that you can advance, and if necessary, descend safely. There will also be exposed sections where a slip could result in a long fall with serious results.

9 Scree

Scree slopes are very laborious to ascend. Climb slowly, placing your feet flat on to the ground or on larger pieces of rock so that your boots are nearly horizontal. Do not ascend directly in front of other walkers as you may dislodge rocks on to them. Spread out into an arrowhead formation. It is possible to descend scree slopes very rapidly if the scree is sufficiently small and runs easily. Keep your weight back and your legs straight and dig your heels into the scree whilst taking long, low paces downhill. You can work up quite a pace by this method which is called 'scree-running', but be careful not to build up such a speed that you lose control. Also ensure that you can see the whole slope and that no small cliffs lie on the route of descent. Unfortunately many scree slopes in popular areas are becoming worn out with overuse.

10 Streams

These can provide one of the best guides to position in mountain and moorland areas. In addition, on moorland, they will sometimes give excellent walking conditions along the banks and enable fast progress to be made. Generally,

however, in mountain areas streams should not be followed
closely as they rarely offer the best route. They will usually
give rough walking, occasionally go over cliffs or into ravines
and can also give boggy and slimy sections. Provided that
the stream can be kept in sight it is usually better to walk
some distance away and higher up along the shoulders of
the stream valley.

Streams in mountain areas can rise very rapidly after a
period of heavy rain. For this reason tents should always be
pitched well above the normal stream level. Never attempt
to cross streams which are badly swollen by rain, in these
cases make a diversion to a suitable bridge. The crossing of
a river at any time requires considerable care and should be
carried out only with the aid of a safety rope held from the
bank.

11 Thunderstorms

These can be alarming in the mountains when the lightning
and thunder are very noisy and appear to be close. Some
people have also been killed by lightning in the British
mountains. In such conditions drop well down from high
ridges and summits, avoiding any prominent objects and lie
down flat or close to the ground until the storm passes.

12 Vegetation

Grass slopes These usually give the easiest walking provided
that the grass is fairly short. They can be very slippery however when wet or covered in snow, particularly if smooth
leather or rubber-soled footwear is being worn. Even dry
grass can be difficult with this type of footwear.

Bracken In the absence of paths this will give hot and
laborious walking. Bracken growing on rock-strewn slopes
is ankle-twisting country and walking will be even more
difficult.

Heather Walking through deep heather can be tiring as it

impedes movement of the feet. It is probably best to lift the
feet clear at each step, but this is almost as bad. Rock-strewn
slopes covered with heather are both difficult and treacherous.

WINTER WALKING

Walking the hills in wintertime can be a great delight but
also holds dangers. All the hazards of summer are present,
but in winter you may also meet snow and ice which require
special techniques. The days will be shorter and temperatures lower, and conditions can become much worse. The
points made earlier apply but are even more important.

Equipment

All the equipment given earlier should be carried, plus an
extra sweater and increased food. In addition, if snow or ice
is likely on the route, then the following equipment is also
necessary:

> Ice-axe
> Instep crampons
> Gloves (woollen with waterproof cover)
> Snow goggles

An ice-axe consists of a straight shaft, made from metal or
wood, fitted with a steel spike at one end and a steel head at
the other. The head has a pick and a broad adze. The entire
axe is about 60–85 cm long. Lightweight types are available
for walking.

An instep crampon consists of a metal plate with small
spikes which fits flat into the instep of the boot and is held
in place by straps over the boot upper. For more serious
work full crampons are used. These are very helpful on hard
snow particularly if boots with hard rubber soles are being
worn.

This extra equipment may seem extravagant under most
conditions but remember that areas of snow and ice may
not be visible from the valleys and that conditions can

change very quickly. It is far better to carry this equipment half-a-dozen times unnecessarily than be without it on the one occasion when it is needed.

Specific winter features

1 Snow and ice

Snow and ice can vary considerably and care is required to recognize the various types. Their nature can change fairly quickly with changes in the weather and from one part of a mountain to another.

(*a*) Freshly fallen snow (powder snow). New snow is made up of ice crystals which have collected together in a loose, fluffy mass which is three to four times larger in volume than the water from which it was formed. This should be treated particularly carefully as it takes time to compact and to adhere to the ground underneath and may avalanche if lying on a steep slope. Deep snow will slow up the walking pace considerably.

(*b*) Old snow (névé, firn). This is older, harder and slightly darker snow which has become compacted until the individual crystals have joined together to form a sponge-like material. It now occupies about twice the volume of the water formed when it melts. It adheres more strongly to the ground underneath and is excellent for making steps or walking with crampons.

(*c*) Ice. Snow will gradually become more compacted and harden to form ice. It will still contain some bubbles of air and be white in colour.

(*d*) Verglas. A coating of ice on rocks caused by rain or melted snow freezing on the surface.

As a general rule, walkers should avoid ice and any long slopes which are more than about 35° from the horizontal.

2 Cornices

A cornice is an overhanging lip of snow formed by the wind over a steep slope at the edge of a plateau or ridge. It presents two possible hazards: firstly, collapse down a slope on to the walker, and secondly, collapse under the weight of the walker precipitating him down the slope. A cornice will break off much further back from the lip and further down a slope than might be expected. Generally a cornice will break off at the same angle as the slope underneath. In mist or a heavy snowfall it can be difficult to detect the edge of a cornice and great care is needed. The term 'white-out' is used for conditions when local features cannot be distinguished in a uniform whiteness.

3 Avalanches

Although these are usually associated with higher mountain ranges, nevertheless they do occur on British mountains resulting in loss of life. Fresh snow on steep slopes of ice or grass is particularly liable to avalanche.

Techniques

1 Ordinary walking

The most likely accident on snow slopes is slipping. It is important to keep the body upright. Leaning into the slope, whether on ascent or descent, will increase the risk particularly if rubber-soled boots are being worn.

Walking in thick freshly-fallen snow can be tiring as the boots will sink in at each step. Gentle slopes of old snow are best tackled in a zig-zag manner using the edges of the boot to avoid slipping. Steeper slopes will require either the use of crampons or steps kicked into the snow. Kick the boot into the snow keeping the sole horizontal. On steep slopes it is easier and safer to walk in zig-zags rather than straight up. On descent face outwards and dig the heels into the snow.

2 Use of crampons

Instep crampons are probably sufficient for ordinary hill-walkers although full crampons are better. When not in use they can be carried on the outside of the rucksack. When used ensure that these are fitted correctly to the boot and that all straps are straight and firm. Place the boots down flat to the ground with a slight stamping action so that all the points penetrate together even on slopes. The boot is then lifted until the spikes are clear and then placed firmly into the next position. Keep your feet apart to avoid catching on the crampon points. Snow may tend to accumulate between the crampon points and should be removed by a small knock from the ice-axe on the side of the boot.

3 Use of ice-axe

When not in use the axe can be carried spike uppermost either in the rucksack or on the outside. Special carrying straps are provided on some types of rucksack. The head of the axe should be protected with a cover and plugs are available to put on to the spike.

Gentle slopes can be tackled either directly or in zig-zags. When ascending or descending slopes directly the axe can be held by the head in a similar manner to a walking stick, pushing the spike into the snow. In ascending in zig-zags the axe should be held in the same manner by the up-slope hand; or alternatively, the axe can be held diagonally across the body with the up-slope hand on the axe-head (pick downwards) and the other hand on the shaft lower down the trunk.

In the event of a slip the axe can be used as a brake to arrest motion. The easiest fall to arrest occurs whilst ascending slopes when the body will probably fall facing the ground with the axe held by the head. Both hands should grip the axe-head with the shaft held under the arm, and the pick is then pressed into the snow until the fall is arrested. Crampons and the axe-spike should be lifted well clear of the ground. If a fall occurs whilst descending the walker will probably fall on to his back. In this case he should roll over as quickly as possible and apply the technique above. A rough 'head-over-heels' fall is most difficult to arrest and every effort should be made to assume the face-down position.

4 Glissading

It is possible to descend snow slopes rapidly by this technique but it is easy to lose control. It must only be carried out on slopes which have been carefully surveyed, particularly to ensure that there are no small cliffs on the slope, that there is a gentle run-out at the bottom and that the snow is firm throughout. It is in essence a controlled slide which can be carried out either in the standing or sitting positions.

It is very important that the techniques described are practised in a safe spot, preferably under expert guidance, before they need to be used. It should also be realized that hill-walking in winter merges into snow and ice climbing, in the same way that scrambling merges into rock climbing. In the last analysis the decision to turn back must be left to the individual.

The above is an outline of the techniques required for hill-walking in winter. A full description is beyond the scope of this book. An excellent and more detailed account can be found in 'Mountaineering. From Hill Walking to Alpine Climbing'. Alan Blackshaw, Penguin Handbooks.

THE MOUNTAIN CODE

The Mountain Code was suggested by the British Mountaineering Council and drawn up with help from a number of other organizations. It was revised recently by the BMC Safety and Technical Committee.

Copies may be obtained from the British Mountaineering Council, Crawford House, Precinct Centre, Booth Street East, Manchester, M13 9RZ. 061 273 5835.

CHAPTER 6

First Aid and Safety

FIRST AID

First aid is the skilled treatment of injuries or illness, using materials and facilities available at the time, which is given until a casualty can be placed into the care of a doctor. Medical aid indicates treatment given by a doctor.

Injury or illness can occur during the course of a walk just as they can occur in the home or at work. In rambling however there are two additional factors which should be borne in mind. Firstly, conditions may be more severe, as for example on a mountainside in mid-winter, and secondly the remoteness of places in which accidents can occur. These suggest that in some cases considerable time may elapse before medical aid can be obtained and hence the greater importance given to first aid.

Ideally, every person should be trained in first aid. At the present time this is obviously far from the case nor indeed are the training resources available to bring this about. Nevertheless, courses are held regularly throughout the country by the voluntary aid societies and it is recommended that a walker should take any opportunity to join. In some areas special short courses for walkers and climbers are offered.

In the event of an accident any doctor or Certificated First Aider present will automatically take charge. In most cases, however, a trained person will not be present and the first aid will have to be given by an untrained person. This chapter is intended therefore to cover this eventuality by giving a brief and simple description of likely injuries and illnesses and directions for their treatment.

For a much more detailed guide read:

'First Aid Manual'. The authorized manual of The St John

Ambulance Association and Brigade, St Andrew's Ambulance Association and The British Red Cross Society.

A more specialized book, but still written for a lay person, is 'First Aid for Hill Walkers and Climbers'. J. Renouf and S. Hulse, Penguin.

General rules

(1) Stay calm. Act quickly but quietly and methodically.
(2) If nobody is already competently in charge, then take charge yourself.
(3) Calm those around you, particularly the patient.
(4) Ensure that the party is safe and that there is no immediate danger of further injury. If not, then take appropriate action.
(5) Examine the patient.
    (*a*) If you do not already know, find out from the patient or from others the circumstances of the injury or illness.
    (*b*) If the patient is conscious ask him how he is feeling.
    (*c*) Examine the patient.
        (i)   Is he fully conscious or not?
        (ii) Are there signs of internal or external bleeding?
        (iii) Are there any obviously deformed limbs?
(6) Treat the injuries in the following order of priority:
    (i)   If the patient has stopped breathing give emergency resuscitation.
    (ii) Control heavy bleeding.
    (iii) Treat fractures, strains, sprains, etc.
    (iv) Treat minor bleeding.
(7) Ensure that the patient is in a comfortable position. Reassure him at intervals. Handle as gently as possible. Move as little as possible unless the injuries are obviously of a minor nature. Ensure that the patient is warm. Shock will probably be a factor in all but minor injuries.
(8) Decide if help is needed from the local Ambulance Service or Mountain Rescue. If so, then ensure that someone goes for help as soon as possible.

In all first aid an element of common-sense is necessary

and the foregoing notes are only intended as a guide.

Emergency resuscitation (artificial respiration) must be applied as quickly as possible when it is observed that breathing is beginning to fail or has ceased altogether. Any delay may have serious consequences.

(1) Place the patient on to his back with his face sideways and remove anything which is obviously causing obstruction, such as vomit or false teeth.

(2) Turn the face upwards with some support for the back of the neck, press the head back and the chin up so that the air has a free passage. If breathing commences then place the patient on to his side as vomiting will probably occur.

(3) If breathing does not commence then respiratory resusciation must be given. Close the patient's nose by pinching the nostrils together, take a deep breath and blow into the patient's mouth until his chest rises; remove your mouth and wait for the chest to fall before repeating. Continue until natural breathing resumes. Then place the patient on to his side as above.

Specific injuries and illnesses

Blisters

Blisters caused by burns or scalds should not be pricked. Blisters on the feet should however be treated differently.

Prevention:

(*a*) Ensure that your boots are large enough to take at least two pairs of thick woollen stockings.

(*b*) Rub the feet liberally with White Petroleum jelly before putting on stockings and boots.

(*c*) Ensure that stockings are clean, free from darns and are put on smoothly.

(*d*) If any foot discomfort is felt whilst walking then stop, remove the boot and investigate. Put a small strip of adhesive tape over the affected area which will probably be red and tender.

Treatment:

(*a*) Wipe all dirt from the area of the blister.

(*b*) Sterilize a needle with antiseptic liquid or by holding in a match flame and allowing to cool.

(*c*) Pierce the blister on one side and repeat on the other side.

(*d*) Gently press out all liquid using clean cotton wool. Dry.

(*e*) Apply a clean, dry dressing to the area.

The pain from blisters may be greatly reduced by immersing the feet in cold water for ten minutes or so. It is much better to prick blisters in this way than to let them burst during a walk. Burst blisters are painful, the immediate area of the stocking becomes wet and there is risk of infection.

Burns and Scalds

Burns may occur during the use of open fires or stoves and scalds during cooking. Correct and careful procedure to prevent accidents should be followed at all times. If a person's clothing does catch fire however then immediately quench the flames with cold water. If none is available, then smother the flames by wrapping a rug or garment over the area of the flame so as to exclude air. (Garments or rugs made from nylon or rayon or similar materials should not be used as these are highly inflammable.) A victim on his own should roll on the floor or smother the fire with any available material as above.

Treatment:

(*a*) Gently place the affected part into cool water for at least ten minutes. This will restrict damage and reduce pain.

(*b*) Remove any articles such as rings which are on or near the affected area as swelling may occur.

(*c*) Remove any clothing from a scald or burn unless it is adhering to the affected area.

(*d*) Cover the area with a dry sterile dressing or clean sheet, etc. In addition, with bad burns lay the person down, immobilize any badly affected limb and treat for shock. Seek medical aid.

Ointments, etc., should not be applied nor should blisters be pricked.

Cramp

This is defined as a sudden, involuntary and painful contraction of a muscle or group of muscles. It may be caused by chilling during exercise (swimming outdoors is a well-known example) or by excessive loss of salt and body fluids from heavy sweating, diarrhoea or constant vomiting.

Treatment:

Straighten the affected limb thereby stretching the contracted muscle. In the case of salt and fluid deficiency give frequent drinks of cold water containing half a teaspoonful of salt to each pint of water.

Dog bite

The damage may be a combination of lacerated, contused and punctured wounds. See under Wounds.

Drowning

Give emergency resuscitation as quickly as possible in an attempt to restore breathing and seek medical aid.

Foreign matter in the eye

Small particles of dirt in the eye can be painful and can give difficulty in seeing. Do not rub the eye or attempt to remove any particles which are on the pupil or embedded in the eye (or sticking to the eye). In these cases the eye should be closed and covered with a pad of cotton wool until medical aid can be obtained.

Treatment:

The patient should face the light so that particles can be more easily seen.

(*a*) Pull down the lower lid of the eye. Remove any particle visible with the corner of a clean handkerchief moistened with water.

(*b*) Whilst the patient looks down pull the upper eyelid over the lower.

(*c*) The patient should blink under water.

If the patient wears contact lenses then these should be removed before treatment.

Fractures

A fracture is a cracked or broken bone. In some cases the broken bone may protrude through the skin.

Symptoms:

(*a*) Pain which increases with movement and when the injured area is gently pressed.

(*b*) Swelling.

(*c*) Inability to move the injured part.

(*d*) Deformity.

(*e*) Unnatural movement of the member.

(*f*) Grating of bone. (But do *not* try to produce this.)

Treatment:

Do not try to move the patient or to straighten out any bent or deformed limbs. Obtain medical help whilst keeping the patient warm, dry and as calm as possible.

If absolutely necessary then the injured limb must be arranged so that there is no movement of damaged bone, e.g. if the patient is in very great pain.

(*a*) Support the injured part.

(*b*) The injured part can be tied with bandages against the patient's body or by using a splint for support. All bandages should be sufficiently tight to prevent movement but not to restrict circulation. Check for over-tightness at intervals as swelling may occur. Tie knots in the bandage away from the injured part. Place soft padding between skin surfaces to prevent chafing and consequent discomfort. A splint must be rigid and sufficiently long to cover the fracture. If a proper splint is not available use a walking stick, piece of fencing, a straight tree branch, ice-axe or even a firmly folded magazine.

Heat exhaustion

Caused by exposure to excessive heat, as for example by hard exercise on a very hot day when excessive sweating causes unusual fluid and salt loss from the body.

Symptoms:

(*a*) Muscular cramp.
(*b*) Exhaustion and possibly restlessness.
(*c*) The face becomes pale and cold with a clammy sweat.
(*d*) Rapid pulse and breathing.
(*e*) Headaches, dizziness, nausea and vomiting, diarrhoea. Abdominal cramp.
(*f*) Fainting.

Treatment:

(*a*) Lay the patient down in a cool place, loosen tight clothing at neck and waist, raise legs and turn head to one side.
(*b*) Give the patient a drink of cold water. Where excessive sweating, cramp, diarrhoea or vomiting has occurred, half a teaspoonful of salt should be added to each pint.
(*c*) Seek medical aid if symptoms are severe.
'Accolade' is a preparation which many walkers have found useful in hot weather.

Lightning

The clothing may be set alight causing burns; these may also occur due directly to the lightning, particularly where metal objects have been worn. The patient may become unconscious or be killed. If necessary, give emergency resuscitation in an attempt to restore breathing. Treat burns. Seek medical aid.

Mountain hypothermia (Exposure)

Normally the inner part of the body (trunk and brain) is maintained at a temperature of 98·4°F (37°C) by a regulating bodily process; the outer layer of the body being slightly cooler. In certain circumstances however this temperature-regulating process can fail and the temperature of the core will fall. This leads to definite changes in the behaviour of the individual and in more extreme cases to unconsciousness and death.

It is important to know how to prevent the onset of this condition, how to recognize the symptoms when they do occur and what action to take when such symptoms are established. When cold, wet and windy conditions prevail on a mountain, a walker must maintain a close watch for the appearance of symptoms both on himself and on his companions.

Prevention:

(*a*) Avoid excessive chilling of the surface of the body by wearing insulating materials, e.g. woollen shirts and pullovers. These should be covered with windproof and showerproof garments (or waterproof in very wet weather).

(*b*) Avoid becoming exhausted by excessively hard walking or climbing. Rest and take energy-giving foods at regular intervals.

Symptoms:

Some or all of the following may be noticed although not necessarily in the order given:

(*a*) Cold, tiredness and cramp. Violent shivering. Stumbling.

(*b*) Physical and mental lethargy. Failure to understand simple questions and instructions.

(*c*) Failure or abnormality of vision.

(*d*) Slurring of speech.

(*e*) Irritability. Often unexpected violent or irrational behaviour.

(*f*) An extreme pallor.

(*g*) Collapse and coma.

Treatment:

(*a*) Stop immediately. Do not attempt to 'walk it off'.

(*b*) Place the patient into a sleeping bag in a horizontal position. If unconscious place in recovery position. Put a companion in with him if there is room or beside him if there is not. Provide cover for the head, i.e. a woollen cap or balaclava.

(*c*) Erect a tent over the patient or carry him into the tent if this is not practicable. Use a survival bag if a tent is not available.

(*d*) If the patient is conscious then supply warm food or sugar in an easily digestible form, e.g. condensed milk.

(*e*) Comfort the victim to reduce his fears and anxieties.

(*f*) If respiration fails then apply emergency resuscitation until normal breathing is restored.

(*g*) In severe cases send for help from Mountain Rescue.

ON NO ACCOUNT attempt to warm the patient rapidly by (1) increasing the walking pace, (2) lighting a fire or applying hot-water bottles, (3) rubbing, or (4) giving alcoholic drinks. These may produce a rapid increase in blood circulation and a further fall in core temperature leading to collapse and death.

Poisoning

May be caused by eating some types of berries or plants, or from infected foods. Symptoms are nausea, vomiting, pain and diarrhoea. Seek medical aid.

Shock

This condition may occur in a person who has been involved directly or indirectly in an accident. Symptoms are extreme paleness associated with a cold skin, heavy sweating, nausea and vomiting, thirst, dizziness and fainting. There may also be obvious signs of anxiety. Breathing may be rapid but shallow and the pulse rapid and weak.

Lay the patient down providing insulation from the ground and a light, and if necessary waterproof, covering to keep him warm and dry. Loosen any tight clothing. Raise legs unless fractures are suspected. Do not use heat or give a drink but the lips may be moistened. Reassure to reduce anxiety. Deal with any injuries or illness which may have caused the state of shock.

Snakebite

Many people become very frightened after snakebite and develop symptoms of shock, even though deaths from this cause are very rare (ten in England and Wales this century). Lay the patient down and reassure him, particularly if he is agitated. Wash the affected part with soapy water, cover with a clean dressing and immobilize the bitten part. Obtain medical aid as soon as possible. Give emergency resuscitation if breathing begins to fail.

Stings from bees or wasps

If the sting is still in the flesh then remove it using tweezers or a needle which has been sterilized with an antiseptic solution or a flame. Apply surgical spirit or an antihistamine cream if available.

Strains and sprains

A strain is associated with a muscle, whilst a sprain occurs at a joint. Both are characterized by pain, which will increase when the patient tries to use the muscle or joint, and by swelling.

Treatment:

If a strain is severe then place the patient into a comfortable position supporting the injured part whilst medical aid is obtained.

In the case of a sprain the patient should also be placed into the most comfortable position whilst the joint is either treated with a cold compress (towel soaked in cold water) or covered with cotton wool and wrapped with a firm bandage.

The most likely parts for a sprain are the ankles. In this case do not remove the boot but loosen the laces if swelling causes discomfort. The boot acts as a good support for the joint.

If in doubt treat as a fracture.

Sunburn

This normally occurs in hot sunny weather in summer, but reflection on snow may result in the same condition. Exposure of the skin to hot sun at the beginning of summer should be gradual. Symptoms of sunburn are redness and soreness of the skin, swelling and even blistering. If sunburn does occur then avoid further exposure until the symptoms disappear and use one of the proprietary soothing creams available. A doctor should be consulted for severe cases.

Wounds (*including cuts*)

These may be of five kinds:

(*a*) Incised. A clean cut caused by a sharp instrument such as a knife. Heavy bleeding usually occurs in this case.

(*b*) Lacerated. A torn wound caused by barbed wire, thick brambles or animal claws. Less bleeding than with (*a*) and probably more dirt.

(*c*) Contused. Bruising of an area caused by a blow or a fall.

(*d*) Punctured. Caused by penetration of a sharp pointed instrument such as a knife.

(*e*) Gunshot. A small entry hole but possibly with deep penetration, internal injuries and a larger exit opening.

Treatment:

Ascertain any areas of external bleeding, removing clothing if necessary.

(1) Slight external bleeding will usually stop very shortly but if necessary the following can be tried.

   (a) Lay the patient down and reassure him.
   (b) If dirt is present wash the wound with running water.
   (c) Dry with clean cotton wool, place a dressing over the
       wound and apply light pressure by hand, or by ban-
       dage or adhesive plaster.
   (d) Raise the injured part and support.

(2) Heavy external bleeding must be stopped immediately.
   (a) Lay the patient down and reassure him. Lower the
       head if possible.
   (b) Apply pressure to the bleeding area, preferably over a
       dressing. If possible press the edges of the wound
       together.
   (c) Raise the injured area and support (but not if a frac-
       ture is suspected).
   (d) When bleeding has ceased or decreased clean the
       wound gently and carefully with cotton wool from the
       centre to the outside.
   (e) Apply a dressing to the wound and bandage firmly or
       hold with adhesive plaster.
   (f) Immobilize the injured part. The arm, for example,
       can be put into a sling.
   (g) Obtain medical aid.

Internal bleeding may occur due to injuries and may be
difficult to detect. If blood flows from the ears, nose, mouth
or is noticed in vomit, urine or excreta then this indicates
internal bleeding.
   (a) Place the patient immediately at rest with legs raised.
       Reassure.
   (b) Loosen all tight clothing about his neck and trunk.
   (c) Keep him warm by providing insulation to ground
       and air.
   (d) Obtain medical aid.
Do not provide drink or food and keep careful note of
any symptoms and also of pulse and breathing rate.
   Bruises may be relieved by a cold compress (towel soaked
in cold water) or ice bag (polythene bag two-thirds full of
crushed ice).

SAFETY

Animals

Bulls

The presence of a bull in a field which has to be crossed can be very alarming to many walkers. It can also be dangerous. On average three farm workers are killed and 50 injured each year by bulls in England and Wales, death occurring by crushing and/or goring. In general all bulls should be regarded as potentially dangerous and, if possible, a field containing a bull should be avoided. If this is not possible, then keep to the perimeter of the field walking quietly and quickly to the other side.

Dogs

Generally most farmyards will contain at least one dog. They can be noisy and intimidating rather than dangerous. Usually the best policy is to ignore them or to talk quietly to them. Do not run, stop or show signs of fear.

Horses

Generally these are harmless and will give no trouble although they may be curious and trot over, particularly if you are eating food. Again the best policy is to ignore them and act in a calm manner.

Snakes

The adder is the only poisonous snake to be found in the British Isles and this will not usually attempt to bite unless deliberately disturbed, stepped on or accidentally cornered. It may be recognized by the dark zig-zag markings along the back. Do not meddle with snakes or kill them. They are normally harmless creatures, happy to get on with their own lives if allowed.

Bivouacs

A bivouac is an overnight stop in the open when proper camping equipment is not available. This can be done from choice and, provided that the weather is fine, can be a delightful experience. In many cases however a bivouac has to be taken because a party cannot continue or reach its destination before nightfall. This may happen because planning was faulty or navigation poor so that the journey took longer than anticipated, an injury to a member of the party or because of a severe deterioration in the weather.

If possible the decision to establish a bivouac should be taken early, before the onset of night or before conditions become too severe, and certainly before any member of the party becomes exhausted. Possible methods are:

(1) It is vital to stay warm during the night. Choose a sheltered place out of the wind, such as the lee of a wall or rock. Provide insulation from the ground using grass, heather, bracken or your rucksack. Put on all spare clothes, ensuring particularly that the clothes next to the skin are dry. Put on waterproofs to keep out the rain or cover yourself with a survival bag. A survival bag is made from thick polyethylene and is large enough to cover the entire body (but the face must not be covered to allow breathing). Eat nourishing food as necessary.

(2) In snow conditions a semicircular wall of snow may be built against a rock outcrop or stone wall to provide additional shelter. As an alternative a snow hole may be dug with an ice-axe. Dig two narrow but deep holes about six feet apart into a deep drift of hard snow and then join them together to form a cave. Block up one entrance with snow and provide an air hole. The other entrance can be blocked temporarily with rucksacks.

Carry out precautions as given under the previous paragraph. In very cold weather make sure that your clothing is not unduly tight and slacken your boots to ensure that the blood circulation is not restricted. Members of the party should huddle together.

Mountain rescue

(1) In the case of slight or moderate illness or injury apply first aid and take all reasonable steps to get the patient down off the mountain and to home or a centre where further treatment can be given.

(2) If however the injuries are more serious or may be aggravated to a serious extent by further walking then the Mountain Rescue Service should be called after appropriate first aid treatment has been applied.

(*a*) Ensure that the patient is safe, only moving him if it is essential for his continued safety. Shelter him by erecting a tent or building a wind-break around him. Provide insulation under him to keep him warm. Use a survival bag if one is available.

(*b*) In a party of two persons the patient will have to be left on his own. Provide him with torch and whistle so that he can attract attention if in a fit state to do so.

In larger parties someone should stay with the patient whilst one, or preferably two, persons go for help.

(*c*) Make a written note of the position of the injured walker, e.g. a grid reference, bearings on to local prominent features or a marked map. Add a note of the time and nature of the accident and the extent of injuries suffered. The messenger should take the note with him and not trust to his memory.

(*d*) The messenger should make his way quickly but carefully to a telephone or to a manned Mountain Rescue Post, whichever is the quicker. Using a telephone the messenger should dial 999 and ask for police; they will then take charge of the situation and call out rescue teams.

Mountain Rescue Posts are marked on the Ordnance Survey Tourist Maps and on some of the 1 : 50 000 maps. A full list of Mountain Rescue Posts and Teams is given in 'Mountain and Cave Rescue'. This is the handbook of the Mountain Rescue Committee and is published bi-annually. Copies are available from Mr H. Worsdall, Treasurer MRC, 20 Heysbank Road, Disley, via Stockport, Cheshire, SK12 2BE.

International distress signal

This consists of six long blasts on a whistle at ten second intervals for one minute, followed by a pause of one minute before repeating. The reply signal is three long blasts on a whistle at twenty second intervals, followed by a pause of one minute before repeating. A flash on a torch, a shout or even the waving of a handkerchief may also be used.

An alternative signal, but less widely known, is the old SOS signal given in Morse Code as three short, three long, three short blasts or flashes.

It is very important not to use these signals or to make whistle blasts or torch flashes generally unless help is really required. They may result in rescue teams being called out unnecessarily.

INSURANCE

Most ramblers will probably feel that special insurance cover is unnecessary, but some should be considered particularly for winter fell-walking or walking holidays abroad.

1. Personal accident. Ordinary policies usually exclude mountaineering, (they may be more specific and refer to mountaineering with the use of ropes and guides). Fell-walking in summertime or mild winter conditions should not be excluded under this term, but doubt could possibly arise in the case of winter fell-walking, including the use of ice-axe, crampons and safety rope. In this case it would be advisable to confirm with the broker concerned that adequate cover was provided.
2. Loss of equipment. Home contents policies will not cover equipment whilst in use. Special cover can easily be arranged however, although an excess will usually be required and the premium may be high.
3. Public liability. A householder's comprehensive policy will already cover this within the UK and possibly abroad.
4. Mountain rescue and medical expenses. This insurance

will not be required within the UK but it is essential
abroad where rescue and medical expenses can be very
high.
5. Loss of travel and accommodation deposits. Important
   for booked holidays anywhere as deposits may be for-
   feited if holidays have to be cancelled.

In 1976 The British Mountaineering Council introduced a
comprehensive scheme of insurance intended for walkers
and climbers. This is available to BMC Member Clubs,
Associate Organizations and individual members. This provides some cover for all the cases above, both in the UK and
abroad.

British Mountaineering Council, Crawford House, Precinct
Centre, Booth Street East, Manchester, M13 9RZ.

CHAPTER 7

Walking Areas in the United Kingdom

THE NATIONAL PARKS

A National Park was defined by John Dower in 1945 as 'an extensive area of beautiful and relatively wild country in which, for the nation's benefit and by appropriate national decision and action, (*a*) the characteristic landscape beauty is strictly preserved, (*b*) access and facilities for public open-air enjoyment are amply provided, (*c*) wild life and buildings and places of architectural and historic interest are suitably protected, while (*d*) established farming use is effectively maintained'.

The first National Parks were established in other countries. In 1872 Yellowstone Park was designated in the United States, followed in 1885 by a similar park at Banff in Canada. Many other countries such as Argentina, South Africa and New Zealand and European countries such as Italy, Germany and Switzerland had created Parks before any were established in the United Kingdom.

Several Government reports between the wars recommended the formation of National Parks, and eventually John Dower, an architect, was asked to study the problems involved in their establishment. He reported in 1945 and a committee under Sir Arthur Hobhouse looked at the implementation of his recommendations.

Following the National Parks and Access to the Countryside Act of 1949 a National Parks Commission was established. This was responsible for the designation of the ten National Parks in England and Wales between 1950 and 1957. (About 9 per cent of land area.) In 1968 the Countryside Commission replaced the National Parks Commission and became responsible for conservation and countryside recreation on a much wider scale. The administration of National Parks was last changed again in 1974. With local

Figure 20. The National Parks. (For identification of areas see text)

government machinery each park has now a single executive committee or board which is responsible for planning. A National Park Chief Officer is appointed with a team of offices and wardens; most of the expenditure (i.e. about 75 per cent) being met directly by the government.

An important point is that within a National Park the land does not change ownership, whether that ownership is by private individuals or by an organization such as the Forestry Commission or National Trust. Neither have visitors any special rights to walk over the land.

Until quite recently National Park Authorities concentrated on development control and are still largely responsible for it. But increased attention is now being given to the management of the Parks. Each Park must produce a National Park Plan as a basis for action to protect the traditional character of the landscape and to provide services for visitors and their transport. Each has its own information service.

See note on page 65.

1. BRECON BEACONS NATIONAL PARK
(PARC CENEDLAETHOL BANNAU BRYCHEINIOG)

Designated in 1957, the Brecon Beacons National Park occupies an area of 519 square miles (1,344 sq km) in the Welsh counties of Dyfed, Powys, Mid Glamorgan and Gwent.

General description
The predominant feature is mountain and moor, but there is also a fair amount of cultivated valley land. The former may be divided into four areas:

1. Black Mountain in the west of the range consists of a ridge of peaks running towards the north-east.
2. Fforest Fawr. A broad area of rolling uplands with the main summits running from west to east.
3. The Brecon Beacons, which contains Pen y Fan (2,907 ft

or 886 m), the highest peak of the Park, is deeply indented by a series of impressive parallel cwms particularly on its north-eastern side.
4. The Black Mountains, with four parallel main ridges, in the north-east corner of the Park.

A narrow extension of the Park towards Pontypool includes Blorenge and the escarpment to the south. The best walking in the area is to be found on the great ridges of the four mountain groups which offer glorious views.

Guides

1. '30 Walks in the Abergavenny Area', Park Information Centres.
2. 'Information Sheet No. 25. Walking in the Beacons'. Park Information Centres.
3. 'Information Sheet No. 24. Some Short Walks around Brecon'. Park Information Centres.
4. 'The Welsh Peaks'. W. A. Poucher, Constable.

Other books

'Brecon Beacons'. National Park Guide No. 5. Ed. M. Davies, HMSO.

Maps

1. Ordnance Survey 1 : 25 000 Outdoor Leisure Map.
2. 146, 159, 160, 161, 171.

Further information

1. Wales Tourist Board, PO Box 151, WDO, Cardiff, CF5 1XS.
2. Brecon Beacons National Park, Glamorgan St, Brecon, Powys. Brecon 2763.

2. DARTMOOR NATIONAL PARK

An area of 365 square miles (945 sq km) lying entirely within the county of Devon. It was designated in 1951.

General description

The Park is approximately circular in shape and is mainly composed of rough, bare moorland more than 1,000 ft (305 m) high, topped by eroded outcrops of hard granite (tors). Unlike Exmoor the moor is crossed by few roads and offers long stretches of lonely walking. The eastern part of the Park has more roads however and also extensive areas of forest land. The moorland area, called Dartmoor Forest, rises to its maximum height in the north-west corner, the highest points being High Willhayes (2,039 ft or 621 m) and Yes Tor (2,028 ft or 619 m).

Rivers radiate out from the area, the most notable being the Dart, Bovey, Teign, Tavy, Plym and Avon.

The high moorland to the north of Princetown is an army training area and access may be forbidden (and dangerous) at certain times. Earlier users of the moor have left many hill-forts, hut-circles, barrows, clapper bridges and remains of tin-mines.

Guides

1. 'Read about Walks on Dartmoor and Exmoor'. Photo Precision Ltd.
2. 'Walks and Rides on Dartmoor'. H. D. Westacott, Footpath Publications.
3. 'Walks in the Dartmoor National Park'. Dartmoor National Park Dept. (3 guides).

Other books

'Dartmoor National Park'. National Park Guide No. 1. Ed. W. G. Hoskins, HMSO.

Maps

1. Ordnance Survey Dartmoor one-inch Tourist Map.
2. 191, 201, 202.

Further information

1. The Devon County Tourist Office, Trinity Court, 37 Southernhay East, Exeter. Exeter 55794.
2. The Information Officer, Dartmoor National Park Dept, Parke, Haytor Rd., Bovey Tracey, Devon, TQ13 9JQ. Bovey Tracey 832093.
   The National Park Department organizes a comprehensive programme of guided walks,

3. EXMOOR NATIONAL PARK

An area of 265 square miles (686 sq km) mainly in the north-west corner of Somerset but including part of Devon. Designated 1954.

General description

A region of grass and heather moors mainly more than 600 ft (183 m) high and with some extensive areas over 1,200 ft (365 m). The highest point is Dunkery Beacon (1,704 ft or 519 m). The uplands are broken by deep stream valleys (combes); these are often wooded, particularly on the outskirts of the Park. Some coniferous forests have been established by the Forestry Commission in the Brendon Hills in the eastern region. Part of the region is called the Exmoor Forest; this refers to its earlier use as a royal game reserve and is not afforested.

The northern boundary of the Park is formed by the coastline between Combe Martin and Minehead; a coast-line of high and spectacular cliffs and rivers falling steeply through wooded combes into the sea.

Guides

1. 'Exmoor Coastal Walks'. T. Abbott, Cider Press.
2. 'Exmoor Walks'. T. Abbott, Cider Press.
3. 'Read about Walks on Dartmoor and Exmoor'. Photo Precision.
4. 'Waymarked Walks. Exmoor National Park'. Park Information Centres. (3 booklets.) Other leaflets also available.

Other books

'Exmoor National Park'. National Park Guide No. 8. Ed. J. Coleman-Cooke, HMSO.

Maps

1. Ordnance Survey Exmoor One-inch Tourist Map.
2. 180, 181.

Further information

1. The Exmoor National Park Centre, Exmoor House, Dulverton, Somerset, TA22 9HL. Dulverton 23665.

4. LAKE DISTRICT NATIONAL PARK

The Park is a region of mountains and lakes lying entirely within the county of Cumbria. It has an area of 866 square miles (2,243 sq km) and was designated in 1951.

General description

The mountains may be divided into three main groups which are separated by wide valleys:

(1) The Skiddaw-Blencathra Group lying to the north of Keswick and approximately circular in shape. An area of smooth, rounded grassy slopes and ridges.

(2) A huge 'horse-shoe' of peaks about 17 miles (27 km) long around the southern end of Ullswater. The principal peak is Helvellyn (3,118 ft or 950 m) on the western side which contains the fine arête of Striding Edge.

(3) The main mass of mountains, slightly elongated in a NW–SE direction, occupy the western half. With the exception of the northern area, this region is composed of high rugged mountains with large cliffs and screes of igneous rock. The highest peak in England, Scafell Pike (3,210 ft or 977 m), lies near the centre of the group.

The dales and lakes are further attractive features; the largest lake being Windermere which is about 11 miles (18 km) in length.

Walking guides

1. 'Lake District Walks for Motorists.
   Central Area.
   Northern Area.
   Western Area'.
   John Parker, Warne Gerrard.
2. 'Lakeland Fells'. F. Goddard, *Dalesman*.
3. 'The Lakeland Peaks'. W. A. Poucher, Constable.
4. 'A Pictorial Guide to the Lakeland Fells'.
   1. The Eastern Fells.
   2. The Far Eastern Fells.
   3. The Central Fells.
   4. The Southern Fells.
   5. The Northern Fells.
   6. The North Western Fells.
   7. The Western Fells.
   A. Wainwright. *Westmorland Gazette*.
5. 'Read about Walks in the Lake District'. Photo Precision.
6. 'Walking in Central Lakeland'. B. and J. Greenwood.
   'Walking in Northern Lakeland'. P. Lewis and B. Porter.
   'Walking in Southern Lakeland'. B. and J. Greenwood.
   Dalesman.

Other books

1. 'Lake District'. National Park Guide No. 6. HMSO.
2. 'Cumbria'. J. Parker, Bartholomew.

Maps

1. Ordnance Survey Lake District One-inch Tourist Map.
2. Ordnance Survey The English Lakes 1 : 25 000 Outdoor Leisure Maps.
3. 85, 89, 90, 96, 97.

Further information

1. National Park Information Service, Bank House, High St, Windermere, Cumbria, LA23 1AF. Windermere 2498.
2. The Cumbria Tourist Board, 'Ellerthwaite', Windermere, Cumbria, LA23 2AQ. Windermere 4444.

5. NORTH YORK MOORS NATIONAL PARK

A well-defined area of 553 square miles (1,432 sq km) situated mainly in North Yorkshire but including a small part of Cleveland. The Park was designated in 1952.

General description

The Park boundary is defined in the east by the coastline from near Scarborough to Loftus omitting only the built-up area around Whitby. A fine coast of sandy bays and high cliffs which can be walked throughout its length.

Inland the boundary follows the edge of the high ground roughly about the 400 ft (122 m) contour, being bounded in the south by the Vale of Pickering, on the west by the Vale of York and in the north by Teesside. The great moorland of the Park reaches a maximum height of 1,489 ft (454 m) on Urra Moor and is deeply penetrated by numerous small green dales mostly running roughly parallel in a north to south direction. Roads run up the dales providing easy access to the main moorland area but there are few east-west roads within the Park.

The Park is rich in archaeological remains such as stone circles, barrows and crosses.

Guides

1. 'Exploring the North York Moors'. M. Boyes, *Dalesman.*
2. 'North York Moors Walks'.
   Two volumes: West and South, North and East. G. White, Warne Gerrard.
3. 'Walking on the North York Moors'. RA (North Yorkshire and South Durham Area), *Dalesman.*

Other reading

'North York Moors'. National Park Guide No. 4. A. Raistrick, HMSO.

Maps

1. Ordnance Survey North York Moors One-inch Tourist Map.
2. 93, 94, 99, 100, 101.

Further information

1. North York Moors National Park, The Old Vicarage, Bondgate, Helmsley, York, YO6 5BP. Helmsley 657/8.

6. NORTHUMBERLAND NATIONAL PARK

This is the most northerly of the National Parks lying wholly within the county of Northumberland and occupying 398 square miles (1,031 sq km) between Hadrian's Wall and the Scottish border. It was designated as a National Park in 1956.

General description

The Park is about 45 miles (72·5 km) long and varies in width from 3½ to 22 miles (5·6–35 km) running roughly N.N.E. It includes 15 miles (24 km) of the Roman Wall on its southern boundary and is bounded on the west by the Border Forest Park and further north by the Scottish border.

The main feature of the Park is the Cheviot Hills which rise to a height of 2,676 ft (815 m) at The Cheviot. Most of the area consists of rolling grassy hills, changing to peat and heather in places, and penetrated by the valleys of the College, Breamish, Coquet, Rede, Harthope Burn and North Tyne.

To the south lies the area of the Roman Wall. The wall runs east to west along the top of an outcrop of basalt, known as the Whin Sill. South of this outcrop is the green valley of the South Tyne which forms the southern boundary of the Park.

The area is rich in relics of the past, the outstanding feature being the Roman Wall which is seen at its best between Cawfields and the fort of Housesteads.

Guides

1. 'Ramblers' Tynedale'. RA (Northern Area). H. Hill, Newcastle.
2. 'Green and Heather Tracks', (2 parts). Wade Balmain, *Northumberland Gazette*.
3. 'Ramblers through Northumberland'. RA. B. Hiley, 44 Montagu Avenue, Newcastle on Tyne.

Other books

'Northumberland National Park'. National Park Guide No. 7. Ed. J. Philipson, HMSO.

Maps

74, 75, 80, 81, 86, 87.

Further information

1. Northumbria Tourist Board, Prudential Buildings, 140–150 Pilgrim St, Newcastle upon Tyne NE1 6TH.
2. Northumberland National Park Department, Bede House, All Saints Centre, Newcastle upon Tyne.

7. PEAK DISTRICT NATIONAL PARK

This was the first National Park, designated in 1950. It has an area of 542 square miles (1,404 sq km), situated mainly in Derbyshire but extending into the neighbouring counties of Cheshire, Greater Manchester, Staffordshire, West and South Yorkshire. The area of Buxton with its extensive limestone quarries is excluded. It is within easy reach of the great conurbations around Leeds, Manchester and Sheffield and is therefore probably the most popular of the Parks with an estimated 16 million day visitors each year.

General description

There are three main types of scenery:

(1) The dark, peat moors of the northern, western and eastern areas containing the huge plateaux of Kinder Scout, Bleaklow and Black Hill which rise to over 2,000 ft (610 m). This is the area of millstone grit, a hard rough rock which can be observed as long cliffs on the edges of the plateaux or as weathered outcrops. This area is sometimes called the Dark Peak.

(2) The limestone area between Buxton and Ashbourne in the southern region of the Park which is between 1,000 (305 m) and 1,500 feet (457 m) high. A gentler region of grassy hills and steep dales. This is known as the White Peak.

(3) The shale region which extends as a broad strip around the limestone area and is characterized by broad green valleys such as around Hope and Bakewell.

Access agreements have been negotiated for 76 square

miles (197 sq km) of moorland on Kinder Scout, Bleaklow and elsewhere which allow free access for walkers, apart from a few days of the grouse shooting season.

Walking guides

1. 'Peak District Walks. 1. Short Walks for the Motorist'. J. N. Merrill, *Dalesman*.
2. 'Peak District Walks. 2. Long Walks for the Rambler'. J. N. Merrill, *Dalesman*.
3. 'Peak District Walks for Motorists'. C. Thompson, Warne Gerrard.
4. 'Rambles in Peakland'. R. A. Redfern, Hale.
5. 'Read about Walks in the Peak District'. Photo Precision Ltd.
6. Peak District Walking Guides.
    1. Walks around Edale.
    2. Walks around Longdendale.
    3. Walks around Dovedale.
    4. Walks around Eyam and Hathersage.
    5. Walks around Bakewell.
   Peak Park Planning Board, National Park Office.

Other books

'Peak District National Park'. National Park Guide No. 3. HMSO.

Maps

1. Ordnance Survey Peak District One-inch Tourist Map.
2. 109, 110, 118, 119.

Miscellaneous information

1. National Park Office, Aldern House, Baslow Road, Bakewell, Derbyshire, DE4 1AE. Bakewell 2881.

8. PEMBROKESHIRE COAST NATIONAL PARK (PARC CENEDLAETHOL ARFORDIR PENFRO)

The Park as designated in 1952 covered the greater part of the Pembrokeshire coast from east of St Dogmael's to near Amroth. It is now part of the new Welsh county of Dyfed. With a total area of 225 square miles (583 sq km) it is the smallest of the National Parks.

General description

This Park is distinct in at least three respects. (1) Whereas the others consist of one compact area the Pembrokeshire Coast National Park is made up from three separated regions. (2) It consists in the main of a long thin coastal strip. (3) It includes only a small proportion of wilderness area, whereas the others consist largely of mountain or moorland.

The three regions of the Park are:

(*a*) The greater part of the coastline from Amroth to St Dogmael's, generally varying in width from about ½ mile to 2 miles (0·8–3·2 km). The neighbouring islands of Ramsey, Skomer, Grassholm, Skokholm and Caldey are also included.

(*b*) An inland area in the upper reaches of Milford Haven at the junction of the Eastern and Western Cleddau rivers.

(*c*) A further inland sector centred upon the Presely Hills (Brynian Presely). (Highest point 1,760 ft [537 m].)

Guides

1. 'Trails'. Pembrokeshire Coast National Park Information Leaflet.

Other books

1. 'Pembrokeshire Coast'. National Park Guide No. 10. Ed. D. Miles, HMSO.

2. 'Pembrokeshire Coast National Park Official Handbook'.
National Park Committee.

Maps

145, 157, 158.

Miscellaneous information

1. Pembrokeshire Coast National Park Department, Information Service, County Offices, Haverfordwest, Dyfed. Haverfordwest 3131. (Postal inquiries).
2. Wales Tourist Board, PO Box 151, WDO, Cardiff, CF5 1XS.

9. SNOWDONIA NATIONAL PARK (PARC CENEDLAETHOL ERYRI)

The Snowdonia National Park was designated in 1952 and covers an area of 840 square miles (2,176 sq km). It lies within the county of Gwynedd. The Lleyn peninsula, the coastline to Conwy, the coastal resorts of Porthmadog, Barmouth, Tywyn and the area around Blaenau Ffestiniog are all excluded. It should not be confused with the Snowdon National Forest Park which is Forestry Commission property and made up from the Gwydir and Beddgelert Forests.

General description

A splendid region of wild and rugged mountains, attractive valleys, forests and numerous lakes. The Park lies near to popular holiday resorts and fine beaches.

The main mountain areas are:

(1) Carneddau. A long range of mountains with outlying spurs, running approximately north-east to south-west and containing six peaks over 3,000 ft (914 m), the highest being Carnedd Llywelyn (3,484 ft or 1,062 m).

(2) Glyder-Elidyr Group. A group of mountains situated south of the Carneddau and between the Nant Ffrancon and

Llanberis passes. Some spectacular cliffs and fine scrambling ridges, particularly around Tryfan and Cwm Idwal.

(3) Snowdon. Contains the highest summit in England and Wales, Yr Wyddfa (3,560 ft or 1,085 m), which is surrounded by long ridges rising to subsidiary peaks. The summit contains a hotel reached by mountain railway from Llanberis. Several impressive crags such as the famous Clogwyn du'r Arddu. The Snowdon Horseshoe is the finest ridge walk south of the Cuillins.

(4) Moel Hebog Group. A group situated to the south-west of Beddgelert. Another fine walk, the Nantlle Ridge, lies to the north.

(5) Moelwyn-Moel Siabod Group. Situated to the east of Beddgelert and around the mining area of Blaenau Ffestiniog. Contains the impressive peak of Cnicht (2,265 ft or 690 m).

(6) Rhinog (The Harlech Dome). A range running north-south to the east of Harlech. The mountains to the north of Y Llethr contain some of the hardest walking in the Park.

(7) Cader Idris Group. Most southerly group of mountains with a maximum height at Cader Idris of 2,927 ft or 892 m).

(8) Arenig. A small group of peaks to the north of Llyn Celyn.

A number of rivers go out of the area. The Conwy, Owgen, Afon Gwyfrai and the Afon Llyfri to the north; the Dee to the east; the Dovey and Dysynni to the south and the Afon Dwyryd to the west.

Walking guides
1. 'The Ascent of Snowdon'. E. G. Rowland, Cicerone Press.
2. 'Glyder Range'. Snowdonia District Guide Book. Showell Styles, West Col.
3. 'Rambles in North Wales'. R. A. Redfern, Hale.

4. 'Snowdon Range'. Snowdonia District Guide Book. Showell Styles, West Col.
5. '20 Walks in North Wales'. Rambler (pseud), Philip, Son and Nephew.
6. 'Wales Walking'. Wales Tourist Board.
7. 'Walks in Gwydyr Forest'. Forestry Commission.
8. 'The Welsh Peaks'. W. A. Poucher, Constable.

Other books

'Snowdonia National Park'. National Park Guide No. 2. Ed. G. Rhys Edwards, HMSO.

Maps

1. Ordnance Survey Snowdonia National Park Half-inch Map.
2. Ordnance Survey Snowdonia 1 : 25 000 Outdoor Leisure Map.
3. 115, 116, 124, 125, 135.

Miscellaneous information

1. The National Park Information Officer, Yr Hen Ysgol, Maentwrog, Blaenau Ffestiniog, Gwynedd, LL41 4HW.
2. Wales Tourist Board, P.O. Box 151, WDO, Cardiff, CF5 1XS. Cardiff 27281.

10. YORKSHIRE DALES NATIONAL PARK

The Yorkshire Dales National Park occupies an area of 680 square miles (1,761 sq km) and is situated in Cumbria and North Yorkshire. The Park was designated in 1954.

General description

Three major divisions may be distinguished:

(a) Swaledale and Wensleydale, in the northern part, which contain rivers draining to the east. An area of smooth rounded valleys and fell-slopes with few rock outcrops.

(*b*) The Craven Pennines to the south of the Park. A region of limestone cliffs and scree slopes, large areas of flat limestone pavement, potholes, caves and streams which appear and disappear. The main rivers are the Ribble and Wharfe which flow to the south.

(*c*) The north-west region with the valleys of Garsdale and Dentdale. These are small narrow valleys with streams and stone walls running in parallel lines up the fell sides. Contains the attractive village of Dent.

Most of the land is above 600 ft (183 m) and there are many peaks over 2,000 ft (610 m).

Walking guides

1. 'Yorkshire Dales Walks for Motorists' and 'Further Dales Walks for Motorists'. Ramblers' Association, Warne Gerrard.
2. 'Walking in the Craven Dales'. C. Speakman, *Dalesman*.
3. 'Walking in the Northern Dales'. Ramblers' Association, *Dalesman*.
4. 'Walks in Limestone Country'. A. Wainwright, *Westmorland Gazette*.
5. A series of walking leaflets and footpath maps is published by the National Park Committee and can be obtained from the address below.

Other books

1. 'The Pennine Dales'. A. Raistrick, Eyre and Spottiswood.
2. 'The Yorkshire Dales'. M. Hartley and J. Ingilby, Dent.

Maps

1. Ordnance Survey 1 : 25 000 Outdoor Leisure Maps. (*a*) The Three Peaks, (*b*) Malham and Upper Wharfedale.
2. 92, 97, 98, 99, 103, 104.

Miscellaneous Information

National Park Office, 'Colvend', Hebden Rd, Grassington, Skipton, North Yorkshire, BD23 5LB. Grassington 752748.

AREAS OF OUTSTANDING NATURAL BEAUTY (AONB)

There are 33 such areas in England and Wales. In all they cover 5,589 square miles (14,476 sq km), but range enormously in size from the 22 sq mile (57 sq km) area of Dedham Vale to the 671 sq miles (1,738 sq km) of the North Wessex Downs. The latter is bigger than all but three of the National Parks.

The proposal that a new area be included is made jointly by the Countryside Commission and the local authority. The Commission then passes the proposal to either the Secretary of State for the Environment or the Secretary of State for Wales for ratification. No special administrative arrangements are made although some areas have advisory committees or standing conferences. The Countryside Commission must be consulted however by local authorities before any major developments take place within an AONB.

Below are details of all AONB's which have been ratified. Ratification usually took place in the same year as designation or the following year. The date given is that of designation.

1. *Anglesey (83 sq miles or 215 sq km) 1966*

This covers the entire coastline of the island except for a few miles of developed areas. Holy Island is also included. Lovely beaches and outstanding cliffs.

2. *Arnside and Silverdale (29 sq miles or 75 sq km) 1972*

An area bounded by the River Kent, Morecambe Bay and the A6 road from Carnforth to Milnthorpe. Situated just to the south of the Lake District National Park and easily reached from the Lancashire towns, it is made up of low limestone hills, pierced by woodlands, which give splendid views over the tidal flats to the Lake District.

Figure 21.   The Areas of Outstanding Natural Beauty.
(For identification of areas see text)

3. *Cannock Chase (26 sq miles or 67 sq km) 1958*

An area of high heathland and forest with many attractive valleys to the north of Birmingham and its satellite towns. Over 3,000 acres (12 sq km) of the Chase are open to the public.

4. *Chichester Harbour (29 sq miles or 75 sq km) 1963*

This area lies to the east of Portsmouth and is defined by the A27 road, the harbour mouth, Hayling Island and the village of Apuldram. It remains in a relatively undeveloped state being mainly tidal flats and sea creeks which support a rich birdlife. A very popular area for yachting.

5. *Chilterns (309 sq miles or 800 sq km) 1964*

About 50 miles (80 km) of chalk hills radiating from the large area of uplands around Marlborough and merging near Luton into the East Anglian Heights. Some bare wind-swept ridge at Ivinghoe Beacon but covered extensively with beautiful beechwood forests. Very easy to visit for a day's walking from the London area starting from such points as High Wycombe, Wendover, Amersham or Chesham. Many National Trust properties.

6. *Cornwall (360 sq miles or 932 sq km) 1959*

Includes most of the coast of Cornwall but also some inland areas such as Bodmin Moor. Among the best coastal areas are Dodman Point, Fal estuary, Helford River, the Lizard, the stretch from St Ives to Mousehole near Penzance, Tintagel and Boscastle. A very popular area in the summer. The main features are high cliffs and lovely coves.

7. *Cotswolds (582 sq miles or 1,507 sq km) 1966*

The second largest AONB consisting of limestone uplands running to the north-east from Bristol towards Evesham and

Moreton-in-Marsh. The highest point is just over 1,000 feet (305 m). An area of rolling wolds, narrow valleys, clear streams and beautiful villages.

8. *Dedham Vale (22 sq miles or 57 sq km) 1970*

The smallest AONB stretching from Nayland to near Manningtree on the Essex–Suffolk border. It is mainly flat country around the River Stour best known for its association with John Constable.

9. *East Devon (103 sq miles or 267 sq km) 1963*

The stretch from Exmouth to Lyme Regis along the Devon coast, with the exception of Sidmouth, Beer and Seaton; it extends to a depth of up to seven miles. Excellent cliff walking.

10. *North Devon (66 sq miles or 171 sq km) 1959*

The coast of North Devon from the eastern boundary to near Combe Martin, excluding the seaside resort of Ilfracombe. Particularly noteworthy are Hartland Point and Baggy Point.

11. *South Devon (128 sq miles or 332 sq km) 1959*

Runs along the coast from Plymouth to Tor Bay and includes stretches along several estuaries. The finest features of this coast are the large magnificent cliffs around Start Point and between Bolt Head and Bolt Tail, and the estuaries of the Dart, Avon, Erme and Yealm.

12. *Dorset (400 sq miles or 1,036 sq km) 1957*

This AONB covers the whole of West Dorset, the North Dorset Downs to Blandford and the area around Purbeck, altogether nearly 40 per cent of the county. The entire coast is included except for the Weymouth-Isle of Portland area.

Outstanding features are the Downs around **Cerne Abbas**
and Corfe Castle.

13. *Forest of Bowland (310 sq miles or 803 sq km) 1963*

An area of wild moorland in north Lancashire, which also
includes Pendle Hill (1,831 ft or 558 m) on the south side of
the Ribble. Easily reached from the towns further south.
Also includes some attractive dales and river valleys. Walking is fairly restricted at present.

14. *East Hampshire (151 sq miles or 391 sq km) 1961*

An area of chalk downs, which form an extension to the
South Downs; they stretch from Winchester to the Sussex
border. Beechwood 'Hangers', Gilbert White's Selborne,
and the village of Hambledon, famous for the origins of
cricket in this area.

15. *Gower (73 sq miles or 189 sq km) 1956*

The first AONB to be designated. A fairly isolated area on
the south Welsh coast near to Swansea it contains magnificent cliffs with attractive bays.

16. *Isles of Scilly (6 sq miles or 16 sq km) 1975*

A group of about 140 islands, of which only four are in-
habited, lying to the south-west of Cornwall. A rocky coast
with sandy beaches and areas of dune.

17. *Isle of Wight (73 sq miles or 189 sq km) 1963*

This AONB covers a large part of the coastline of the island
omitting only areas of urban development around Totland,
Cowes, Ryde, Sandown and Shanklin. The central areas of
downland are also included.

18. *Kent Downs (326 sq miles or 844 sq km) 1968*

This is a continuation of the Surrey Hills AONB and follows
the line of the North Downs for about 60 miles (97 m) to
end at Dover, reaching a maximum width of about 10 miles
(16 km) in its eastern section. Magnificent views southwards
from the Downs.

19. *Lincolnshire Wolds (216 sq miles or 559 sq km) 1973*

An area of rolling chalk hills and quiet villages running in a
north-westerly direction from around Horncastle.

20. *Lleyn (60 sq miles or 155 sq km) 1956*

The coast of the Lleyn peninsula in North Wales from
Pwllheli to Clynnog fawr, omitting only a small stretch near
Nefyn. A fairly flat but attractive area with beautiful head-
lands and good beaches. The island of Bardsey, now a bird
sanctuary, is also included.

21. *Malvern Hills (40 sq miles or 104 sq km) 1959*

A line of hills to the west of Great Malvern and running
north-south. The highest point is Worcestershire Beacon
(1,394 ft or 424 m). Steep sided hills with numerous paths
and magnificent views, particularly over the Vale of Severn
to the east.

22. *Mendip Hills (78 sq miles or 202 sq km) 1972*

A range of limestone uplands running from Bleadon Hill to
near Wells and rising to over 1,000 feet (305 m). A bare
plateau with fine views over the surrounding countryside.
Contains the spectacular gorge at Cheddar and numerous
caves.

23. *Norfolk Coast* (*174 sq miles or 451 sq km*) *1967*

Includes a large part of the Norfolk coast, to a maximum depth of about 5 miles (8 km). The main section extends from Hunstanton to Bacton (excluding the holiday resorts of Sheringham, Cromer and Mundesley) and two smaller sections are situated on the east side of the Wash south of Heacham and north of Winterton. The coast is very varied with the flats of the Wash, cliffs at Hunstanton and sand dunes at Winterton.

24. *Northumberland Coast* (*50 sq miles or 130 sq km*) *1958*

A stretch of coastline, 43 miles (69 km) long, from the mouth of the Coquet to near Berwick-upon-Tweed. A quiet, unspoilt length of coast with immense interest. The walled town of Berwick, Holy Island (reached by causeway at low tide), the Farne Islands (famous for seabirds and seals) and the magnificent castle of Bamburgh are some of the features of this area.

25. *North Wessex Downs* (*671 sq miles or 1,738 sq km*)

The largest AONB; it is an area of chalk uplands in the shape of an horseshoe around the meeting point of the county boundaries of Hampshire, Wiltshire and Berkshire. The highest point is Inkpen Beacon (974 feet or 296 m). Numerous sites of historical interest are to be found in this area, notably Avebury, Silbury Hill and the Uffington White Horse.

26. *Quantock Hills* (*38 sq miles or 98 sq km*) *1956*

This area, about 3 miles (5 km) wide and 12 miles (19 km) long, stretches from the sea near Watchet in Somerset in a south-easterly direction to Taunton. The highest point is at Will's Neck (1,261 feet or 384 m). Good walking on bare hills and in wooded valleys.

27. *Shropshire Hills (300 sq miles or 777 sq km) 1958*

An area around the small town of Church Stretton near Shrewsbury. A region of deep attractive valleys and steep sided hills which gives rugged walking and magnificent views. The maximum height is just over 1,700 ft (518 m).

28. *Solway Coast (41 sq miles or 106 sq km) 1964*

A narrow coastal strip from near the border with Scotland to the town of Maryport, excluding an area around the holiday town of Silloth. Particularly interesting for ornithologists as large flocks of wild duck and geese use the estuary in winter.

29. *South Hampshire Coast (30 sq miles or 78 sq km) 1967*

A 14-mile (23-km) strip of coast from Calshot Castle to Hurst Castle on the western end of the Solent, plus a narrow stretch up the estuary of the Beaulieu River. Salt-marshes and attractive woods are a feature of this coast, plus the castles and the Beaulieu Estate.

30. *Suffolk Coast and Heaths (151 sq miles or 391 sq km) 1969*

This AONB covers 38 miles (61 km) of the Suffolk coastline from Kessingland, near Lowestoft, to the banks of the Rivers Orwell and Stour, extending to a maximum width of about 7 miles (11 km) at the southern end. The town of Felixstowe is excluded. A remarkable feature is the shingle spit at Orford Ness.

31. *Surrey Hills (160 sq miles or 414 sq km) 1956*

An area crossing Surrey from west to east and joining the adjacent AONBs of the Sussex and Kent Downs. It follows the line of the North Downs but also includes the Greensand Hills to the south, attaining a maximum width of about 10 miles (16 km). The long ridge of the Downs with magnificent views to the south, the Greensand Hills and the lovely heaths around Hindhead are some features of an area very near to London.

32. *Sussex Downs (379 sq miles or 982 sq km) 1965*

This covers the area of the South Downs from the border with Hampshire to the cliffs near Eastbourne, but broadens in its western end to a width of about 15 miles (24 km) to meet the Surrey Hills AONB. The Downs give magnificent walking, with wonderful views to north and south, and include the spectacular cliffs around Beachy Head.

33. *Wye Valley (125 sq miles or 324 sq km) 1970*

The line of the River Wye is followed from Chepstow to near Hereford, reaching a maximum width of about 5 miles (8 km).

For a more detailed description of the National Parks and AONBs read 'The National Parks of England and Wales'. Roger Bush, Dent.

AREA WALKING GUIDES

A considerable number of guides have now been published, and first or revised editions are appearing at an average of about one per week. These vary enormously in quality, scope and price. The vast majority, however, cost less than one pound and deal with a relatively small area.

Below are listed over one hundred guides. These may be obtained through local bookshops or directly from the publisher. A more comprehensive list is given in Fact Sheet No. 4 issued by the Ramblers' Association. This comes in ten parts on a regional basis and is revised regularly.

Guides to the National Parks and long distance routes are given separately.

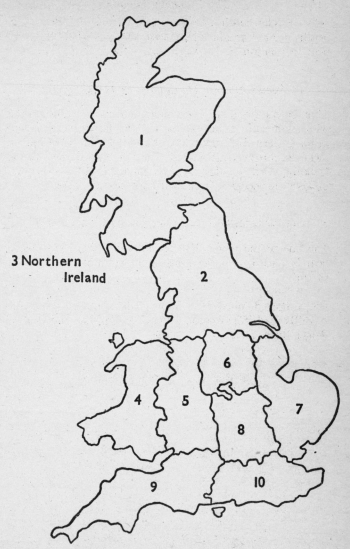

Figure 22. Regions for route-guide list

General

1. 'Along the Green Roads of Britain'. J. H. B. Peel, Cassell.
2. 'No Through Road'. Drive Publications.
3. 'Nicholson's Guides to the Waterways'. British Waterways Board.

1. Scotland and Northern Islands

4. 'Scottish Hill Tracks, Old Highways and Drove Roads'. Part 1. Southern Scotland, Part 2. Northern Scotland. D. G. Moir, Bartholomew.
5. 'The Scottish Peaks'. W. A. Poucher, Constable.
6. District Guide Books:
     The Scottish Highlands. W. H. Murray.
     The Western Highlands. G. S. Johnstone.
     The Southern Highlands. D. J. Bennet.
     The Northern Highlands. T. Strang.
     The Central Highlands. C. R. Steven.
     The Cairngorms. A. Watson.
     The Southern Uplands. Andrew and Thrippleton.
     The Island of Skye. M. Slesser.
     The Islands of Scotland. N. Tennent.
   Scottish Mountaineering Trust.
7. 'Scotland for Hillwalking'. Scottish Tourist Board, 23 Ravelston Terrace, Edinburgh, EH4 3EU.
8. 'West of Scotland Rambles'. Sydney Smith, Molendinar Press.
9. 'Pentland Walks'. D. G. Moir, Bartholomew.
10. 'Rambles in the Hebrides'. R. A. Redfern, Hale.
11. 'Walking in the Lochalsh Peninsula'. National Trust for Scotland.

2. Northern England

(Cleveland, Cumbria, Durham, Greater Manchester, Humberside, Lancashire, Merseyside, Northumberland, Tyne and Wear; South, North and West Yorkshire).

See also Lake District, Northumberland, North York Moors and Yorkshire Dales National Parks.

12. 'The Peak and Pennines from Dovedale to Hadrian's Wall'. W. A. Poucher, Constable.
13. 'Walking in Weardale'. T. R. Spedding, *Dalesman*.
14. 'Walks on the Howgill Fells and adjoining Fells'. A. Wainwright, *Westmorland Gazette*.
15. 'Walks in the Yorkshire Dales'. H. O. Wade, Spurbooks.
16. 'Pendleside and Brontë Country Walks for the Motorist'. G. Banks, Warne Gerrard.
17. 'East Yorkshire Rambles'. G. Eastwood, 60 Front St, Lockington, Driffield, North Humberside.
18. 'Rambles in the Dales'. RA, Warne Gerrard.
19. 'Walking in Central Lancashire'. C. Spiby, *Dalesman*.
20. 'Walking around Preston'. I. O. Brodie and P. Davy, *Dalesman*.
21. 'Ten Walks for Motorists in the Wirral'. Greenways, Belvidere Press.
22. 'Ramblers' Tynedale'. B. Fletcher, H. Hill.
23. 'Ramblers' Cheviot'. H. Hill.
24. 'Walks on the West Pennine Moors'. G. Sellers, Cicerone.
25. 'Walking in the Brontë Country'. RA, *Dalesman*.
26. 'Walking in South Yorkshire'. J. L. Ferns, *Dalesman*.
27. 'Walks in Swaledale'. G. White, *Dalesman*.
28. 'Walks in Wensleydale'. G. White, *Dalesman*.

3. Northern Ireland and Isle of Man

29. 'A Guide to Walking in the Mournes'. E. Stanley-Jones, *Mourne Observer*. (See 30).
30. 'Hill Walks in the Mournes'. J. S. Doran, *Mourne Observer*, Main St, Newcastle, Co. Down.
31. 'A Fell Walking and Climbing Guide to the Isle of Man'. J. W. Caine (Ed.), Cade.
32. 'Manx Hill Walks'. Footpath Group, Manx Conservation Council, Landsworth, Beach Rd, Port St Mary, Isle of Man.

4. Wales

See also Brecon Beacons, Pembrokeshire Coast and Snowdonia National Parks.

33. 'Wales Walking'. Wales Tourist Board, P.O. Box 151, WDO, Cardiff, CF5 1XS.
34. 'The Welsh Peaks'. W. A. Poucher, Constable.
35. 'Welsh Walks and Legends'. Showell Styles. John Jones Cardiff.
36. 'Walks in Gwent. Nos. 1 and 2'. Information Section, Gwent County Council, County Hall, Cwmbran, Gwent, NP4 2XH. (And others).
37. 'Walks in the Taff Valley'. David Rees, H. J. Lear.
38. 'From Offa's Dyke to the Sea through Picturesque Mid Wales'. C. D. Ehrenzeller, St Christopher's, Ithor Road, Llandrindod Wells, Radnorshire.
39. 'Walking North Wales'. Showell Styles, John Jones Cardiff.
40. 'Rambles Round Radnorshire'. C. D. Ehrenzeller (See 38).

5. Western England

(Cheshire, Gloucestershire, Hereford and Worcester, Salop.

41. 'Walking around Painswick', etc. Gloucestershire County Council.
42. 'Cheshire Walks for Motorists'. J. F. Edwards, Warne Gerrard.
43. 'Sandstone Trail'. Cheshire County Council, County Hall, Chester.
44. '20 Walks in Mid-Cheshire'. Rambler (pseud.), Philip, Son and Nephew.
45. 'Walking in Cheshire'. J. Baker and J. Hanmer, *Dalesman*.
46. 'Cotswolds Walks for Motorists'. (2 volumes, northern and southern areas). P. A. Price, Warne Gerrard.
47. 'Cotswold Rambles'. P. Drinkwater and H. Hargreaves, Thornhill.

48. 'Discovering Walks in the Cotswolds'. R. Kershaw and B. Robson, Shire.
49. 'Tracking through Mercia'. (3 volumes). D. Baker, Express Logic.
50. 'Walks in the Cotswolds'. R. Hodges, Spurbooks.

6. North Midlands

(Derbyshire, Leicestershire, Nottinghamshire, Staffordshire, West Midlands). See also Peak District National Park.

51. 'Staffordshire Moorlands Footpath Guides'. Staffordshire Moorlands District Council, Leek.
52. 'Walking in Derbyshire'. J. Haworth (Ed.), *Derbyshire Countryside*.
53. 'Walks in the Derbyshire Dales'. J. Haworth (Ed.), *Derbyshire Countryside*.
54. 'Walks in Leicestershire'. Leicestershire Footpath Association, Leicestershire Libraries and Information Service.
55. 'Nottinghamshire Walks'. J. Brock, BBC Publications.
56. 'Walks in Nottinghamshire'. Nottinghamshire County Council.
57. 'Midland Walks'. E. J. Schatz, Spurbooks.

7. Eastern England

(Cambridgeshire, Essex, Lincolnshire, Norfolk, Suffolk)

58. 'Walks and Rides around Cambridge'. Cambridgeshire and Ely County Council.
59. 'The Footpaths of Linton District'. Linton District Amenity Society, The Village College, Linton, Cambridgeshire.
60. 'Walks on the Hertfordshire and Essex Border'. Bishop's Stortford and District Footpaths Association, 144 Barrell's Down Rd, Bishop's Stortford, Herts.
61. 'Harlow Trail'. Harlow Development Corporation.
62. Several leaflets from Lincolnshire County Council.
63. 'Walking around Hadleigh'. A. O'Reilly, Keith Avis (Hadleigh).

64. 'Short Walks in London's Epping Forest and its Immediate Surroundings'. F. Matthews and H. Bitten (See 65).

65. 'Short Walks in West Essex'. F. Matthews and H. Bitten. From F. Matthews, Glen View, London Rd, Abridge, Essex.

66. 'London Countryside Walks for Motorists. North East'. W. A. Bagley, Warne Gerrard.

67. 'Rambles in North Norfolk'. J. Le Surf, North Norfolk District Council.

68. 'Six Waymarked Routes'. South Norfolk District Council.

8. South Midlands

(Bedfordshire, Buckinghamshire, Hertfordshire, Northamptonshire, Oxfordshire, Warwickshire).

69. 'Walks in the Chilterns'. Colourmaster International.

70. 'Discovering Walks in Buckinghamshire'. R. Pigram, Shire.

71. 'Walks in Buckinghamshire'. Vera Burden, Spurbooks.

72. 'Walks in Oxfordshire'. N. Hammond, Spurbooks.

73. 'London Countryside Walks for Motorists. North West'. W. A. Bagley, Gerrard.

74. 'Afoot in Hertfordshire'. D. Veall, Spurbooks.

75. 'Walking around Oxford'. Oxford Fieldpaths Society, Oxford Illustrated Press.

76. 'Walks along the Ridgeway'. E. Cull, Spurbooks.

9. South-West Peninsula

(Avon, Cornwall, Devon, Dorset, Somerset, Wiltshire). See also Dartmoor and Exmoor National Parks.

77. A number of pamphlets have been issued by the Western National Omnibus Co., Exeter, Devon.

78. 'Walks in Devon'. C. Green, Spurbooks.

79. 'Read about Walks in South Devon'. Photo Precision.

80. 'Discovering Hardy's Wessex'. A.M. Edwards, BBC Publications.

81. 'Coastal Rambles'. North Devon Printing Works.
82. 'Severnside'. S. Taylor, Croom Helm.

10. Southern England

(Berkshire, Hampshire, Kent, London, Surrey, Sussex, Isle of Wight).

83. 'Chalkways of the South and South-east England'. E. C. Pyatt, David and Charles.
84. 'Climbing and Walking in South-east England'. E. C. Pyatt, David and Charles.
85. 'Country Walks'. Several books from London Transport Board.
86. 'South-east England: a Guide to Family Walks'. I. Campbell (Ed.), Croom Helm.
87. 'Walks in Sussex'. Norman Willis, Spurbooks.
88. 'Rambling for Pleasure around Maidenhead'. P. Nevell, Donnybrook, 25 Altwood Rd, Maidenhead, Berks, SL6 4PB.
89. 'Discovering Country Walks in North London'. M. Lundow, Shire.
90. 'Walks in Berkshire'. V. Burden, Spurbooks.
91. 'Walks in the Hills of Kent'. J. Spayne and A. Krynski, Spurbooks.
92. 'Walks around the Downs: Ten Country Rambles near Reading, Newbury, Andover and Basingstoke'. R. Chapman, Countryside Books.
93. 'Discovering Walks in West Kent'. M. Crouch, Shire.
94. 'New Forest Walks'. A.-M. Edwards, BBC Publications.
95. 'Walks in the New Forest'. W. Wenban-Smith, Spurbooks.
96. 'Green London Walks'. W. A. Bagley, Warne Gerrard.
97. 'London Countryside Walks for Motorists'. W. A. Bagley, Warne Gerrard. (South west and south east volumes).
98. 'Walks in the Surrey Hills'. J. Spayne and A. Krynski, Spurbooks.
99. 'Walks in Hampshire'. D. Knowlton, Spurbooks.
100. 'South Sussex Walks'. C. Teviot, BBC Publications.

101. 'Walks along the South Downs Way'. C. Teviot, Spurbooks.
102. 'Long Distance Trails'. Pamphlets from Isle of Wight County Council, County Hall, Newport, Isle of Wight, PO30 1UD.

CHAPTER 8

Long Distance Routes

One of the outstanding developments since 1965 has been the establishment of long distance walking routes in England and Wales. Many of these are 'official' routes which have been established by the Countryside Commission, but others are the work of organizations such as the Ramblers' Association and County Councils or enthusiastic individuals.

The inspiration for this activity can be traced back to a newspaper article in June 1935 in which Tom Stephenson, the first full-time secretary of the Ramblers' Association, suggested the creation of a Pennine Way. As a result, representatives of open-air organizations met at Hope, Derbyshire in February, 1938 and formed the Pennine Way Association. A survey of the route showed that about 180 miles (290 km) of existing footpath could be utilized, but that 70 miles (113 km) of new paths would have to be established.

In 1942 the Committee on Land Utilization in Rural Areas recommended the opening of a Pennine Way and also the old coastguard path around the coast of England and Wales. The Dower Report on National Parks in England and Wales went further in 1945 when it recommended that long distance routes, such as the Pennine Way, should be established as soon as possible. A special Committee on Footpaths and Access to the Countryside, under the chairmanship of Sir Arthur Hobhouse, specifically recommended the creation of six long distance footpaths: the Pennine Way, Chilterns to Devon Coast, Pilgrim's Way, South Downs to Salisbury Plain, Offa's Dyke and the Thames Towpath.

The National Parks Commission was established by Act of Parliament in 1949 and was made responsible for submitting proposals for the creation of long distance routes. When the Countryside Act became law in 1968 the Countryside Commission replaced the National Parks Commission.

A route is created in four stages. First, the Commission prepares a report proposing a new route which is then submitted to either the Secretary of State for the Environment or to the Secretary of State for Wales or Scotland. Second, the Secretary of State then approves the report, or otherwise, modifying the route as he thinks fit. Third, the Secretary of State asks local authorities to create any new rights of way which are required. Fourth, the route is waymarked where necessary and a guide book is issued. The Commission is responsible for any expenditure incurred by local authorities in the construction, maintenance and improvement of approved routes. These routes are known as National Long Distance Routes. At present all of these routes are in England and Wales, none existing in Scotland or Northern Ireland. A 92-mile (148-km) route from Glasgow to Fort William to be called the West Highland Way, a Southern Uplands Way and the Speyside Way have now been approved however.

Nevertheless, there is no reason whatsoever why any organization or individual should not plan a long distance walking route using existing rights of way. Several have already done so and, as a result, some fine routes have been described. Presumably others will follow.

The routes included here are 20 (32 km) or more miles in length, have been given a name and have been described in detail in a guide book available to the general public. Many other long distance routes have been described in magazines and club journals.

Long distance routes can therefore be divided into three categories depending upon their origin:

1. National Long Distance Routes
2. Routes planned by organizations other than the Countryside Commission
3. Routes organized by individuals

The descriptions following are arranged in alphabetical order. Some suggestions for long distance routes in Scotland are included at the end of the chapter. See note on page 77.

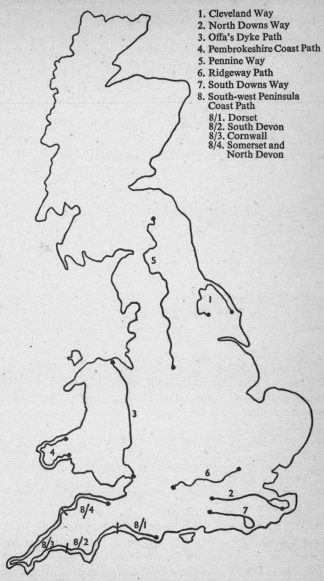

1. Cleveland Way
2. North Downs Way
3. Offa's Dyke Path
4. Pembrokeshire Coast Path
5. Pennine Way
6. Ridgeway Path
7. South Downs Way
8. South-west Peninsula Coast Path
   8/1. Dorset
   8/2. South Devon
   8/3. Cornwall
   8/4. Somerset and North Devon

Figure 23. National Long Distance Routes

1. ACROSS WALES FROM NORTH COAST TO SOUTH COAST

History. Devised by Showell Styles in 1977. The Countryside Commission has approved, in principle, a high-level long distance route from Cardiff to Conwy to be called the Cambrian Way. At the time of writing however there is considerable debate both on the concept and on the line of the route.

Distance. 183 miles (295 km).

Starting point. Penmaenmawr, Gwynedd (115–718766).

Finishing point. Pwll du Head, West Glamorgan. (159–570864).

Route. Runs almost due south to the region of Llandovery, Dyfed, where it turns roughly south-west towards the Gower peninsula.

Main interests. The route avoids all the high mountain areas but gives grand walking along valleys, through forests and over wild stretches of moorland.

Accommodation. Youth hostels at Penmaenmawr (115–737780), Capel Curig (115–726579), Ffestiniog (124–704427), Corris (124–753080), Ystumtuen (135, 147–735786), Blaencaron (146, 147–713608) – 3 miles off route, Bryn Poeth Uchaf (146, 147, 160–796439) and Llanoldeusant (160–776245) – 4 miles off route.

Guides. 'Backpacking in Wales'. Showell Styles, Hale.

Maps. 115, 124, 135, 146, 159.

2. BAY TO BAY WALK

History. Devised by Showell Styles in 1977.

Distance. 128 miles (206 km).

Starting point. Point of Ayr, near Prestatyn, Clwyd. (116–127852).

Finishing point. Llwyngwril, Gwynedd. (124–587101).

Route. A long curve of a route between Liverpool Bay and Barmouth Bay which crosses the Clwyd range, Llantisilio mountain, the Berwyns, the Arans and finally Cader Idris.

Main interests. Long stretches of fine ridge walking with splendid views; away, in the main, from the more popular and hence busy areas of North Wales.

Accommodation. Youth hostels at Maeshafn (117–208606), Cynwyd (125–058408), Plas Rhiwaedog (125–947348), Kings-Dolgellau (124–683161), but these are all 3–5 miles off the route. As the search for accommodation necessitates dropping off the ridge backpacking should be considered as an alternative.

Guides. 'Backpacking in Wales'. Showell Styles, Hale.

Maps. 116, 124, 125.

3. CALDERDALE WAY

History. Created by Civic Trusts, Civic Societies and Todmorden Conservation Group of the Metropolitan Borough of Calderdale, it was the first Recreation Footpath of the Countryside Commission. Opened by Lord Winstanley at Halifax on 21 October 1978. A Calderdale Way Association has been formed to look after the general interests of the Way.

Distance. 50 miles (80 km).

Starting and Finishing point. Clay House, Greetland, West Yorkshire. (104–097214).

Route. An approximately oval route around the steep-sided valley of the Calder between Brighouse and Todmorden. Woodland, field paths and open moor. There are 15 link paths joining the Way with parking and public transport facilities in the valley.

Waymarking. Waymarked throughout with yellow arrows and Calderdale Way emblems (CW in the shape of a tree).

Main interests. Good views over the Calder valley. Clay House (17th century), Wainhouse Tower, Ripponden Farm museum, Hinchliffe Arms (counterfeit coins), TeDeum stone, Stoodley Pike, Heptonstall village, Lumb Falls, Hardcastle Crags.

Accommodation. Youth hostel at Mankinholes (103–

960235). The South Pennines Information Service, 1 Bridge Gate, Hebden Bridge, HX7 1JP supply accommodation and camping lists.

Guides. 'The Calderdale Way'. The Calderdale Way Association, available from H. C. Morris, 7 Trinity Place, Halifax, HX1 1BD.

Maps. 103, 104, 110 (very small section).

4. CLEVELAND WAY

History. Opened in 1969, it was the second National Long Distance Route to be created.

Distance. 93 miles (150 km) in the shape of a horseshoe.

Starting point. Helmsley, North Yorkshire (100–613839).

Finishing point. Near Filey, North Yorkshire (101–115807).

Route. Divided into two parts of different character; the first part over the North York Moors (highest point reached 1,489 feet or 454 m), and the second part along the cliffs of the East Coast. The route coincides approximately with the boundary of the North York Moors National Park.

Waymarking. Signposts with the words 'Cleveland Way' where the path leaves or joins roads. Acorn markers away from the roads.

Main interests. Fine scenery over the moors and the Vale of York followed by high and spectacular cliffs along the east coast. Also Helmsley Castle, Rievaulx Abbey, Mount Grace Priory, monument to Captain Cook, Whitby Abbey.

Accommodation. Youth hostels at Helmsley (100–616840), Westerdale Hall (94–662059) off route, Saltburn-by-the-sea (94–662206), Whitby (94–902111), Boggle Hole (94–954040), Scarborough (101–026907). Guest houses and inns are available in the coast towns, but inland it may be necessary to descend to the valleys to find accommodation. The Bed and Breakfast Guide (Ramblers' Association) marks suitable accommodation.

Books and Guides
1. 'The Cleveland Way'. Long Distance Footpath Guide No. 2. Alan Falconer, HMSO.
2. 'The Cleveland Way'. Bill Cowley, Dalesman Publishing Co. Ltd.
3. 'A Guide to the Cleveland Way and Missing Link'. M. Boyes, Constable.

Maps. Tourist Map for North York Moors. 93, 94, 99, 100, 101.

5. COAST TO COAST WALK

History. Devised and described by A. Wainwright in June 1972.

Distance. 190 miles (306 km).

Starting point. St Bees Head, Cumbria. (89–970108).

Finishing point. Robin Hood's Bay, North Yorkshire. (94–953048).

Route. The walk commences on the western sea-cliffs and proceeds approximately eastwards across England. It crosses the heart of the Lake District, via Ennerdale, Helvellyn, Striding Edge and Patterdale and then on to the limestone plateau east of Shap. The Pennines are crossed in the area of Swaledale followed by the Vale of Morbray to the Cleveland Hills and the North York Moors. The route ends on the sea-cliffs overlooking the North Sea. Some choice of route is offered in certain areas, such as the Lake District.

Main interests. Magnificent scenery in all mountain and moorland areas. Exhilarating crossing of Striding Edge, Shap Abbey, Seventeenth-Century Market Hall at Shap, Giant's Graves near Smardale Bridge, waterfalls near Keld, Marrick Priory, Richmond Castle, Mount Grace Priory, old crosses at Rosedale Head, steam trains on North York Moors, Falling Foss (waterfall) and sea-cliffs at each end.

Accommodation. Youth hostels at Ennerdale (89–142141),
Black Sail (89, 90–194123), Honister Hause (89, 90–
224135), Longthwaite (90–254142), Grasmere (90–331084/
336077), Patterdale (90–399156), Kirkby Stephen (91–
773082), Keld (91–892009), Grinton Lodge (98–048976),
Westerdale Hall (94–662059), Wheeldale (94–812983), and
Boggle Hall (94–954040). Accommodation in farms and
villages but this will be popular in some areas in holiday
periods. The Bed and Breakfast Guide (RA) marks
suitable accommodation.

Guides. 'A Coast to Coast Walk'. A. Wainwright, *Westmorland Gazette.*

Maps. 89, 90, 91, 92, 93, 94, 98, 99. (Some contain only
small sections of the route).

6. COTSWOLD WAY

History. Suggested by Antony J. Drake (Footpath Secretary, RA, N.E. & W. Gloucestershire) and designated
by Gloucestershire County Council in 1970.

Distance. 100 miles (161 km).

Starting point. The Old Market Hall, Chipping Campden,
Gloucestershire. (151–152391).

Finishing point. Roman baths, Bath, Avon. (172–750646).

Route. The Way follows the western boundary of the Cotswold escarpment in an approximately south-west direction.

Main interests. Extensive views from the escarpment, the
characteristic architecture of the Cotswolds, Jacobean
Market Hall at Chipping Campden, Hailes Abbey, Belas
Knap (restored Neolithic long barrow), hill forts, Roman
remains at Bath and a host of interesting houses, churches
and relics.

Accommodation. Youth hostels at Stratford-upon-Avon
(151–231562) – 10 miles (16 km) north of start, Cleeve Hill
(163–983267), Duntisbourne Abbots (163–970080) – 5
miles (8 km) off-route, Slimbridge (162–730043) – 5 miles
(8 km) off-route, Bath (172–766644).

The Bed and Breakfast Guide (Ramblers' Association) marks suitable accommodation.

Waymarking. Special markers have been placed throughout the route.

Guides. 'The Cotswold Way'. Mark B. Richards, Thornhill.

Maps. 150, 151, 162, 163, 172.

7. CUMBRIA WAY

History. Devised by John Trevelyan during 1975–1977 with help from members of the Lake District Area of the Ramblers' Association.

Distance. 70 miles (113 km).

Starting point. Ulverston, Cumbria (97–284785).

Finishing point. Carlisle, Cumbria (85–402556).

Route. Runs approximately due north through the Lake District National Park keeping, in the main, to the valleys although some high ground can be crossed on one of the alternatives north of Keswick.

Main interests. Good walking through the valleys. Grand views in the Lake District. Beautiful Coniston Water and Derwent water. Monument to Sir John Barrow, grave of John Peel at Caldbeck, Carlisle Castle and Cathedral.

Accommodation. Youth hostels at Coniston Coppermines 96, 97–289986), Coniston Holly How (96, 97–302980), Elterwater (90–327046), High Close (90–338052), Longthwaite (90–254142), Derwentwater (89, 90–268200), Keswick (89, 90–267235) and Carlisle (85–386569). Information on other accommodation along the way can be obtained from Cumbria Tourist Board, Ellerthwaite, Windermere, Cumbria.

Guides. 'The Cumbria Way'. John Trevelyan, *Dalesman*.

Maps. 85, 90, 97.

8. DALES WAY

History. Suggested by Tom Wilcock and Colin Speakman and created by members of the West Riding Area of the Ramblers' Association.

Distance. 73 miles (118 km).

Starting point. Ilkley, West Yorkshire. (104–117480).

Finishing point. Bowness on Windermere, Cumbria (97–402968).

Route. Follows the course of Wharfedale through Grassington, Kettlewell and Buckden. The Way crosses the Pennine Way in the neighbourhood of Cam Fell and descends into Dentdale. The last few miles are due east towards Windermere. Some high level walking but mostly along the valleys.

Waymarking. White arrows on some sections.

Main interests. Seventeenth-century bridge at Ilkley, Bolton Abbey, the Strid, rapids at Loup Scar, ancient cultivation terraces, Quaker Meeting House at Brigflatts, sixteenth-century Crook of Lune bridge, fourteenth-century pele tower at Burneside Hall. Interesting villages.

Accommodation. Youth hostels at Linton (98–998627), Kettlewell (98–971724), Dentdale (98–774850), Kendal (97–512911), Windermere (90–405013).

The Bed and Breakfast Guide (Ramblers' Association) marks suitable accommodation.

Guides

1. 'Across Northern Hills'. Geoffrey Berry, *Westmorland Gazette*.
2. 'The Dales Way'. Colin Speakman, *Dalesman*.
3. 'The Dales Way'. The Ramblers' Association, Warne Gerrard.

Maps. 97, 98, 104.

9. DERWENT WAY

History. Devised in 1977 by Richard Kenchington, Footpath Secretary for the East Yorkshire and Derwent Area of the Ramblers' Association.

Distance. 80 miles (129 km).

Starting point. Barmby on the Marsh, Humberside. (106–690285).

Finishing point. Lilla Howe, North Yorkshire. (101–889987).

Route. Follows the River Derwent from its meeting-point with the Ouse to its source on the North York Moors, passing through the Vale of York, Howardian Hills and the Vale of Pickering.

Main interests. Stretches of quiet and very pleasant walking along the banks and towpaths of the Derwent, followed by the Forestry Commission forests on the southern edge of the North York Moors National Parks. Wressle castle, site of the Battle of Stamford Bridge, Kirkham Abbey, Malton Priory (twelfth century) and Ayton Castle.

Accommodation. Malton (100–778710) is the only youth hostel actually on the route. Wheeldale (94, 100–812983), Boggle Hole (94–954040), Scarborough (101–026907), Thixendale (100–843610) and Selby (105–620319) are 5–6 miles off-route.

Guides. 'The Derwent Way'. Richard C. Kenchington, *Dalesman.*

Maps. 100, 101, 106.

10. EBOR WAY

History. The idea and route are due to J. K. E. Piggin, who completed the inaugural walk in September/October 1975 with Tony Cronin, a fellow member of the Ebor Acorn Rambling Club. The Route description was published in 1978. The name of the Way was derived from the Roman name for York which was Eboracum.

Distance. 70 miles (113 km).

Starting point. Helmsley, North Yorkshire. (100–613839).

Finishing point. Ilkley, West Yorkshire. (104–117480).

Route. Joins the Cleveland Way with the Dales Way via the cathedral city of York. Uses footpaths throughout except for $3\frac{1}{2}$ miles of road. The route goes due south to York, then swings west towards Ilkley.

Waymarking. Wooden signs and painted waymarks throughout the route.

Main interests. Pleasant views over the Vale of York; castles at Helmsley, Sheriff Hutton and Newton Kyme; York with Minster, wall, museums, gardens, National Railway Museum and much else; Bishopthorpe Palace; beautiful stretch of the Wharfe at Boston Spa; Harewood House; the Cow and Calf rocks at Ilkley.

Accommodation. Youth hostels at Helmsley (100–616840) and York (105–589528). There is much accommodation in the main towns on the route, but this is in great demand in the holiday season.

Guides. 'The Ebor Way'. J. K. E. Piggin, *Dalesman.*

Maps. 100, 104, 105.

Badges and certificates for successful completions can be obtained from J. K. E. Piggin, 95 Bishopthorpe Road, York, YO2 1NX.

11. EDEN WAY

History. First suggested and described by Geoffrey Berry in 1975.

Distance. 55 miles (89 km).

Starting point. Cotter Riggs, near Hawes, North Yorkshire. (98–838923).

Finishing point. Wetheral, Cumbria. (86–468544).

Route. The route goes north-west from the A684 over the limestone hill of Cotter End and crosses the Ure and Eden. It meets the Eden again at Outhgill and remains near to the river until Wetheral.

Main interests. Pot-holes on Cotter End, Hell Gill gorge, Hell Gill Foss, Pendragon Castle, Kirkby Stephen, sixteenth-century Warcop Bridge and the prehistoric monument of Long Meg and her daughters. But the main attraction is the long and beautiful stretch of the Eden with its woods, shingle beds and bridges.

Accommodation. Youth hostels at Hawes (98–867897). Garsdale Head (98–796947), Kirkby Stephen (91–773082), Dufton (91–688252), Carlisle (85–386569).

Guides. 'Across Northern Hills'. Geoffrey Berry, *Westmorland Gazette.*

Maps. 86, 90, 91, 98.

12. ESSEX WAY

History. Prepared as a project by the pupils of the Chelmsford Technical High School and adopted by The Council for the Protection of Rural England as a long distance footpath. Opened 3 June 1972 at Stonards Hill, Epping.

Distance. 70 miles (113 km).

Starting point. Epping, Essex. (167–465025).

Finishing point. Dedham, Essex. (168–058332).

Route. Gentle route in agricultural countryside.

Waymarking. Route marked with small plastic waymarkers on trees, etc.

Main interests. Church at Greensted-juxta-Ongar (wooden Saxon church), Norman baronial castle at Pleshey, old barns at Cressing, Paycocke's House at Coggeshall (National Trust), the Constable country around Dedham. Pleasant but not spectacular views.

Accommodation. Youth hostels at Epping Forest (167, 177–408983) 4 miles (6 km) south of Epping, Colchester (168–006252) 6 miles (10 km) from Dedham.

Books and Guides. 'The Essex Way'. East Anglia Tourist Board, 14 Museum St, Ipswich.

Maps. 167, 168.

13. FOREST WAY

History. Designated, described and waymarked by the Essex County Council to mark European Conservation Year. Opened 1972.

Distance. 20 miles (32 km).

Starting point. Epping Forest near Woodredon Farm, Essex. (167–420995).

Finishing point. Hatfield Forest near Woodside Green, Essex. (167–530187).

Type of walking. Gentle country. Field footpaths, green lanes, commons and a few miles of road. The walk starts and ends in very attractive forest areas but does not include much on the route.

Waymarking. The entire route is well marked with (*a*) tall oak signposts, and (*b*) small posts with plastic waymarkers.

Main interests. The beautiful forest areas at each end.

Accommodation. Youth hostels at Epping Forest (167, 177–408983) about 1 mile (1·6 km) from southern end, Harlow (167–450109) about 2½ miles (4 km) off-route, near mid-point.

Books and Guides. 'Forest Way. A Cross Country Walk'. Essex County Council, County Hall, Chelmsford, Essex.

Map. 167.

14. GLYNDŴR'S WAY (FFORDD GLYNDŴR)

History. Devised by the Planning Information Service of Powys County Council in 1977–8. It was named after Owain Glyndŵr who led an uprising of the Welsh against the English in the fifteenth century.

Distance. 122 miles (196 km).

Starting point. Knighton, Powys. (148–283724).

Finishing point. Welshpool, Powys. (126–216076).

Route. Passes close to the sites of many incidents of the uprising. From Knighton it goes in an irregular manner north-west to Machynlleth and then swings north-east towards Welshpool. The Way joins with the Offa's Dyke Path at Hope near Welshpool.

Waymarking. Blue and yellow arrows.

Main interests. Knucklas Castle, Short Ditch (C15 rampart), Bronze Age and Iron Age remains, Castell Tinboeth, Market Hall at Llanidloes, Fan (lead) and Bryntail (lead Barytes) mines, Owen Pugh's House at Machynlleth, Dyfnant forest, Powys Castle at Welshpool. Grand views with good walking on high moorland, footpaths and forest tracks.

Accommodation. Youth hostels at Knighton (148–285725), Nant-y-Dernol (136–903754) – 5 miles off-route and Corris (124–753080) – 5 miles off-route.

Guides. A set of 16 pamphlets describing the route and points of interest with O.S. strip map, published by the

Planning Department of Powys County Council, County
Hall, Llandrindod Wells, Powys.
Maps. 125, 126, 135, 136, 148.

15. HADRIAN'S WALL

History. The wall was built on the instructions of the Em-
peror Hadrian in A.D. 122 to form the northern frontier
of the Roman Empire. An army of 5,500 cavalry and
13,000 infantry guarded the wall against attacks from the
north. The wall itself was about 73 miles (118 km) long
but a series of watchtowers extended down the western
coast for a further 7 miles (11 km). The wall was abandoned temporarily and overrun several times before the
occupation finally ceased in the fourth century. The wall
remains the finest Roman relic in the British Isles.

Distance. The total distance of the wall is 73 miles (118 km)
from Wallsend on Tyne to Bowness but part does not give
attractive walking (e.g. along the B6318), and the footpath
is restricted to about 28 miles (45 km).

Starting point. By Sewing Shields Farm, near Hexham,
Northumberland. (87–823706).

Finishing point. Wallfoot, near Carlisle, Cumbria. (85–
428593).

Main interests. The magnificent remains of the wall with its
forts, mile castles, turrets, quarries, signal stations and
vallum.

Accommodation. Youth hostels at Newcastle (88–259644),
Acomb (87–934666), Once Brewed (86–752668), Greenhead (86–659655) and Carlisle (85–386569). Other
accommodation in the villages along the A69 a few miles
to the south of the wall.

Guides
1. 'Across Northern Hills'. Geoffrey Berry, *Westmorland
   Gazette*.
2. 'Hadrian's Wall'. A. R. Birley, HMSO. For description
   of remains.

Maps
1. 85, 86, 87.
2. O.S. Hadrian's Wall, 2 inches to 1 mile.

16. ISLE OF WIGHT COASTAL PATH

History. The path was devised by the County Surveyor and
 Planning Officer, Mr J. E. Reed, using existing rights of
 way and was opened in 1971.

Distance. 60 miles (97 km).

Starting and Finishing points. The circular route may be
 joined at any point, but visitors from the mainland will
 probably join at a ferry terminus, i.e. Yarmouth, East
 Cowes, Fishbourne or Ryde.

Route. The Way makes a complete circuit of the island
 staying generally within about one half-mile (0·8 km)
 from the sea. A substantial detour is necessary however
 around the estuary of the Newtown River and to the east
 of East Cowes. Some stretches of road are included but
 mainly footpath. Some holiday resorts have also to be
 crossed.

Waymarking. Waymarked throughout with red trail flashes
 (also used for trails on the island) and blue signposts.

Main interests. Osborne House, Quarr Abbey, sea forts
 (constructed 1860–80), Earl of Yarborough monument,
 Bembridge Fort, Sandown zoo and geological museum,
 Shanklin Chine, Tennyson monument, the Needles light-
 house. Splendid views over cliff and sea. Most of the
 coastal area has been designated as an Area of Outstanding Natural Beauty.

Accommodation. Permanent youth hostels at Sandown
 (196–597843), Whitwell (196–521776) and Totland (196–
 324865), with 'Summer only' hostels at Yarmouth,
 Wootton Bridge and Shorwell. Much accommodation in
 guest houses and hotels but this will be heavily booked in
 the holiday period.

Guides. Four brochures, each covering about 15 miles (24

km) of the path, are available from the Isle of Wight
County Council, County Hall, Newport, Isle of Wight,
PO30 1UD.
Map. 196.

17. LLEYN COAST

History. Devised by Showell Styles in 1977.
Distance. 51 miles (82 km).
Starting Point. Pwllheli, Gwynedd. (123–375350).
Finishing point. Nanhoron, Gwynedd. (123–284316).
Route. Around the coastline of the peninsula, finishing with
a short section inland from Porth Ysgadan. The peninsula
has been designated as an Area of Outstanding Natural
Beauty.
Main interests. In the holiday season some popular tourist
areas have to be crossed, but in the main the route lies
along quiet and beautiful stretches of the peninsula coast.
Accommodation. There are no Youth Hostels on the route.
Some holiday accommodation is available but there will
be a heavy demand for this in the season.
Guides. 'Backpacking in Wales'. Showell Styles, Hale.

18. LONDON COUNTRYWAY

History. Suggested by B. K. Chesterton in 1973 and planned
by him with help from fellow members of the Long
Distance Walkers Association. Completed in 1976.
Distance. 205 miles (330 km).
Starting and Finishing point. Stepping stones over River
Mole near Box Hill, Surrey (187–173513).
Route. Follows a circular path around London running
between 15 and 30 miles (24–48 km) from the centre. Good
radial transport facilities are available to points on the
route. There is a surprising number of steep hills in the
southern and western sections. The northern and eastern
parts traverse flatter country. Most people, who are

visiting for the first time, will be surprised at the quietness
and beauty of the countryside which is so near to London.

Main interests. Good views over the Kent, Surrey and
Chiltern Hills; Epping Forest; the Thames towpath; the
Lea, Wey and Basingstoke canals; Windsor Castle and
Park; Cathedral and Roman remains at St Albans;
Waltham Abbey; Churchill's home at Chartwell;
National Rose Society gardens and Royal Horticultural
Society gardens at Wisley.

Accommodation. Youth hostels at Tanners Hatch (187–
140515), Windsor (175, 176–955770), Bradenham (165–
828972), Lee Gate (165–893055), St Albans (166–139076),
Epping Forest (167, 177–408983), Kemsing (188–555588)
and Crockham Hill (187, 188–441504). There are also
hotels, but the eastern part is rather lacking in accommodation.

Guides. 'A Guide to the London Countryway'. B. K.
Chesterton, Constable.

Maps. 165, 166, 167, 175, 177, 186, 187, 188. Nos. 167 and
186 only cover small sections.

19. LOWER WYE VALLEY WALK

History. Provided by Gwent County Council with co-
operation from the Forestry Commission and local landowners. Opened February 1975.

Distance. 21 miles (34 km).

Starting point. Outskirts of Chepstow, Gwent. (162–531942).

Finishing point. Symonds Yat Station (disused), Gwent.
(162–561159).

Route. Follows generally the valley of the Wye.

Waymarking. Posts with white arrows and orange dots.

Main interests. A walk in part of the Wye Valley Area of
Outstanding Natural Beauty. Excellent views, e.g. Eagle's
Nest on the Wyndcliff 700 ft (213 m) above the river,
Tintern Abbey, woodlands, Wye Bridge at Monmouth.

Guides. Brochure from County Planning Officer, County
Hall, Cwmbran, Gwent, NP4 2XF.

Map. 162.

It is the intention to extend this walk to Hereford.

20. NAVIGATION WAY

History. Devised by Peter Groves in 1978.

Distance. 100 miles (161 km).

Starting point. Worcester Bar basin, Gas Street, Birmingham, West Midlands. (139–063867).

Finishing point. Chasewater, near Chasetown, West Midlands. (139–041073).

Route. A very irregular route along the towpaths in the extensive canal system of the Birmingham area. Includes the Netherton tunnel, 3,027 yards (2,768 m) long.

Main interests. Canal towpaths are often delightfully quiet places even near to the centre of large towns. This route goes through built-up areas (e.g. the centre of Birmingham), but there are also sections in beautiful countryside. Twelve canals are visited which abound in interesting items of canal architecture: aquaducts, viaducts, locks, old bridges, pumping stations, disused wharves, toll houses, etc. associated with Brindley, Smeaton, Telford and other famous eighteenth- and nineteenth-century figures.

Accommodation. No Youth Hostels in the area, but there is ample public transport to take you to other types of accommodation.

Guides. 'The Navigation Way'. Peter Groves; Tetrado Publications Ltd, Bridge House, Shalford, Guildford, Surrey.

Maps. 138 (very small section only), 139.

21. NORTH BUCKINGHAMSHIRE WAY

History. Developed by members of the Ramblers' Association and the North Bucks Rambling Club. Opened at

Addington, 8 April 1972 by Mr C. Hall, Secretary, The Ramblers' Association.

Distance. 30 miles (48 km).

Starting point. Chequers Knapp, Buckinghamshire. (165–829054).

Finishing point. Wolverton, Buckinghamshire (152–821415).

Route. The Way runs from the Chiltern Ridgeway at Chequers Knapp on the northern scarp of the Chiltern Hills and through the Vale of Aylesbury. Mainly footpaths in pleasant farming country. Highest point Quainton Hill (613 ft or 187 m).

Waymarking. Standard Buckinghamshire County Council footpath signposts at most points where the Way crosses roads, with additional signposts at selected points on the route. Orange arrows painted on gateposts at frequent intervals.

Main interests. Many good viewpoints. Chequers Court (not open to public), Hartwell House, Waddesdon Manor (National Trust), Claydon House (National Trust), fine villages.

Accommodation. No youth hostels close to the route, the nearest being Ivinghoe (165–945161), Lee Gate (165–893055) and Greens Norton (152–670500).

The Bed and Breakfast Guide (Rambler's Association) marks suitable accommodation.

Books and Guides. 'The North Buckinghamshire Way'. The Ramblers' Association.

Maps. 152, 165.

Note: Two 'Country Paths' were established and waymarked by the County Highways and Transportation Department of the Northamptonshire County Council in 1975, which provide an extension to the North Buckinghamshire Way. These are: The Grafton Way, Wolverton to Greens Norton, 12½ miles (20 km). The Knightley Way, Greens Norton to Badby, 12 miles (19 km). Route descriptions prepared by the Footpaths Committee of the Northampton Group of the Ramblers' Association obtainable from: County Leisure and Amenities Officer, Northampton House, Northampton, NN1 2JP.

22. NORTH DOWNS WAY

History. The North Downs, stretching from the Straits of Dover to the early settlements in Hampshire and Wiltshire, were probably much used as a natural highway from these settlements to the Continent. In the Middle Ages they also had importance as an obvious line of travel between the political capital at Winchester and the great centre of Christianity at Canterbury. This was enhanced by the murder of Thomas Becket, Archbishop of Canterbury, and regular pilgrimages along the North Downs to his shrine were held each year, reaching their height towards the end of the C14.

The North Downs Way long distance route was opened by the Archbishop of Canterbury, Dr Coggan, near Ashford on 30 September 1978.

Distance. 141 miles (227 km).

Starting point. Farnham, Surrey (186–844465).

Finishing point. Dover, Kent. (179–319417).

Route. The North Downs run roughly east-west and are cut by five rivers: the Stour, Medway, Darent, Mole and Wey. They form a well-defined ridge of chalk with a fairly steep slope to the south. Walking in the main is dry and across grassy slopes keeping as close as possible to the crest of the Downs.

Waymarking. Very extensive.

Main interests. Many fine views to the south.

Accommodation. Youth hostels on or near the route are Hindhead (186–892368), Ewhurst Green (187–094398), Holmbury St Mary (187–104450), Tanners Hatch (187–140515), Crockham Hill (187, 188–441504), Kemsing (188–555588), Doddington (178–925552), Canterbury (179–157570), Dover Central (179–312421), and Dover Town (179–318421).

Many railway lines run radially from London and cut the line of the Downs giving easy access to various points. The Bed and Breakfast Guide (Ramblers' Association) marks suitable accommodation.

Books and Guides
1. 'A Guide to the Pilgrim's Way and North Downs' Christopher John Wright, Constable.
2. 'The Pilgrim's Way'. Sean Jennett, Cassell.
Maps. 178, 179, 186, 187, 188, 189.

23. OFFA'S DYKE PATH

History. Offa was King of Mercia in the latter part of the C8 A.D. It is thought that the Dyke was built as a boundary between Britons and Saxons, rather than as a fortification. It cannot be traced along the entire length of the boundary; about 81 miles (130 km) being recognizable between the Bristol Channel and the north coast. The Dyke is a simple earthwork, consisting normally of a ditch with an earth wall on its east side. The path was formally opened on 10 July 1971 by Lord Hunt at Knighton.

Distance. 168 miles (270 km).

Starting point. Near Chepstow, Gwent. (162–548931).

Finishing point. Prestatyn, Clwyd. (116–064830).

Route. Varied with river banks, meadow footpaths, mountain ridges, moorlands and woods. The path follows the 81 miles (130 km) of the Dyke closely for about 60 miles (96 km) of its distance.

Waymarking. Signposts throughout.

Main interests. The main interest is the Dyke itself, but its state varies. Some parts have suffered from road-building; in other areas it has become almost obliterated by time or ploughing, but some stretches are still very impressive with banks 20 ft (6 m) high. Also magnificent scenery, Monmouth, White Castle at Llanvetherine, ridge walks in the Black Mountains, Llanthony Abbey (off-route), Telford's aqueduct over the Dee, prehistoric hill-forts.

Accommodation. Youth hostels at Severn Bridge (162–523934), St Briavels (162–558045), Monmouth (162–508130), Capel-y-ffin (161–250328), Glascwm (148–158532) – about 4 miles (6 km) off-route, Knighton (148–

285725), Clun (137–303812) – about 2½ miles (4 km)
off-route, Llangollen (117–231413) – 2½ miles (4 km)
off-route, Maeshafn (108, 117–208606) – 4½ miles (7 km)
off-route.

The Bed and Breakfast Guide (Ramblers' Association)
indicates suitable accommodation. Also accommodation
list from Offa's Dyke Association.

Books and Guides

1. 'Walks along Offa's Dyke'. E. and K. Kay, Spurbooks.
   (Circular walks along the Way).
2. 'The O.D.A. Book of Offa's Dyke Path'. Frank Noble,
   Offa's Dyke Association.
3. 'Through Welsh Border Country following Offa's Dyke
   Path'. M. Richards, Thornhill.
4. 'A Guide to Offa's Dyke Path'. C. J. Wright, Constable.
5. 'Offa's Dyke'. Long Distance Footpath Guide No. 4.
   HMSO.

Maps. 116, 117, 126, 137, 148, 161, 162. Also set of strip
maps from Offa's Dyke Association.

24. OXFORDSHIRE WAY

History. First suggested by Mr Roland Pomfret of Wood-
stock. The route was devised by him and members of the
Council for the Protection of Rural England (Oxfordshire
Branch).

Distance. 65 miles (105 km).

Starting point. Bourton-on-the-Water, Gloucestershire.
(163–170209).

Finishing point. Henley-on-Thames, Oxfordshire. (175–
761826).

Route. Runs in an easterly direction from Bourton in the
Cotswolds to north of Oxford before turning south-east
towards Henley. Highest ground is nearly 800 ft (244 m).

Main interests. Churches at Bledington, Wheatfield and
elsewhere; sixteenth-century toll house at Burford – 4

miles (6 km) off-route, Ditchley Park, Blenheim Park and Palace for magnificent mansion and gardens; Oxford for museums, botanic gardens, cathedral, churches and colleges – 4 miles (6 km) off-route; the Thames at Henley.

Waymarking. Specially designed signposts and waymarks provided by Oxfordshire County Council.

Accommodation. Youth hostels at Stow-on-the-Wold (163–191258) – 4 miles (6 km) from start, Charlbury (164–361198), Oxford (164–533074) – 5 miles (8 km) off-route and Henley (115–759831).

Books and Guides. Three strip maps may be obtained from Branch Secretary, CPRE Oxfordshire, Sandford Mount, Oxford. (1 : 25 000). Also 'The Oxfordshire Way'. Alison Kemp, CPRE.

Maps. 163, 164, 165, 175.

25. PEAKLAND WAY

History. The idea and route are due to John N. Merrill of Sheffield who completed the inaugural walk 10–15 August 1973.

Distance. 96 miles circular (154 km).

Starting and Finishing point. Ashbourne, Derbyshire is suggested. (119–180464).

Route. The Peakland Way goes through the two types of country that make up this region, the limestone dales and the gritstone moorlands. The route is recommended in a clockwise direction and is along rights of way with a total of about 5 miles (8 km) of road. Riverside walks; quiet, beautiful limestone dales; rough moorland walking over Kinder Scout; walking along the characteristic gritstone edges of the Peak. The route finishes along the High Peak and Tissington Trails which are disused railway lines converted into footpaths.

Main interests. Magnificent scenery. But also a wide variety of churches, halls and ancient monuments. Many interesting items of industrial archaeology.

Accommodation. Youth hostels at Ilam Hall (119–131506),

Hartington (119–131603), Buxton (119–062722), Raven-
stor (119–152732), Castleton (110–150828), Edale (110–
139865), Hathersage (110–226814), Bakewell (119–215685)
Elton (119–224608). Many inns and villages offer accommodation and there are also camp sites available. Many
farmers will also allow occasional campers.

Guides. 'The Peakland Way'. John N. Merrill, *Dalesman.*
Maps. 110, 119.

26. PEDDARS WAY

History. Built as a wide and substantial road by the
Romans during the late first century, A.D. probably for
military purposes after the rise of the Iceni under Bou-
dicca, but also to connect with Lincolnshire via a ferry
over the Wash. Probably remained in some more local
use until a few hundred years ago. The present route was
devised by Bruce Robinson in 1978. The Countryside
Commission and Norfolk County Council have commenced work on a Norfolk Paths Long Distance Route
which will consist of Peddars Way and the coast to
Cromer, 76 miles (120 km).

Distance. 50 miles (80 km).

Starting point. Holme next the Sea, Norfolk. (132–695440).

Finishing point. Knettishall, Norfolk. (144–938795).

Route. Runs in a straight line to the SSW before bending
southwards in the last few miles near Thetford. Generally
follows the line of Peddars Way except for sections where
the original line is uncertain or goes over private ground.

Waymarking. Signposts at most main roads.

Main interests. Footpaths, green lanes, heath, Forestry
Commission plantations and some stretches of road.
Eleventh-century castle at Castle Acre, market at Swaff-
ham, Army battle ground, Thetford museum, barrows
and other ancient sites. Beautiful, lonely sections away
from towns in deepest Norfolk.

Accommodation. Youth hostels at Hunstanton (132–
674406) and Brandon (144–788864) – 9 miles off-route.

The East Anglia Tourist Board, 14 Museum Street, Ipswich (Ipswich 214211) will help with accommodation.

Guides. 'The Peddars Way'. Bruce Robinson, Weathercock Press Ltd, Gunton Hall, Lowestoft, Suffolk.

Maps. 132, 144.

27. PENNINE LINK

History. First suggested about ten years ago. Description by Geoffrey Berry in 1975.

Distance. 70 miles (113 km).

Starting point. Old Ing, farmhouse 3 miles (5 km) north of Horton in Ribblesdale, North Yorkshire. (98–804773).

Finishing point. Keswick, Cumbria. (90–265235).

Route. The way joins the Pennine Way with the Lake District. The route starts in a north-westerly direction over the northern slopes of Whernside into Dentdale. Beyond Sedbergh the Lune is followed to the M6 motorway, followed by the valley of the Borrow Beck and on to Ambleside. The remainder of the route is NNW towards Keswick, passing Rydal Water, Grasmere and Thirlmere.

Waymarking. None.

Main interests. Limestone country with potholes and caves, God's Bridge, packhorse bridge at Thorns Gill, Force Gill waterfalls, Dentdale, Lune Valley, Borrowdale, C14th pele tower at Kentmere Hall, lovely stretches of moorland and beautiful views in the Pennines and Lake District.

Accommodation. Youth hostels at Stainforth (98–821668) 7 miles (11 km) south of start, Dentdale (98–774851), Ambleside (90–377031), Grasmere (90–336077, 331084), Thirlmere (90–318190), Keswick (90–267235). Other accommodation in villages but heavily booked in the summer.

Guides. 'Across Northern Hills'. Geoffrey Berry, *Westmorland Gazette*.

Maps. 90, 91, 97, 98.

28. PENNINE WAY

History. See earlier. Opened officially 24 April 1965 on Malham Moor.

Distance. 250 miles (403 km).

Starting point. Edale, Derbyshire. (110–123859).

Finishing point. Kirk Yetholm, Roxburghshire, Scotland. (74–826282).

Route. Very varied, consisting of roads, meadow footpaths, green lanes, riverside walks, moorland and scrambling. But mainly a high-level route over rough and lonely moorlands. Only approximately 15 miles (24 km) of hard road in the entire journey, the longest continuous stretch being about 2 miles (3 km).

Waymarking. Most people start from Edale and walk northwards and guide books usually assume this. The Way is extensively marked by oak signposts, white painted acorns on gates and rocks, etc., and stakes and cairns on some moorland stretches, but this is not consistent and the sections vary considerably. Large information boards with map sections are also placed at intervals of about 10 miles (16 km). The route is in any case becoming more marked with use, and therefore is easier to follow.

Main interests. Magnificent scenery throughout the walk. Many points of interest including the Roman road at Blackstone Edge, Stoodley Pike, Top Withens, (Wuthering Heights of Emily Brontë), Malham Cove, Gordale Scar, pot-holes in limestone area of Yorkshire Dales, Hardraw Force (highest waterfall in British Isles), Tan Hill Inn (highest inn in England), God's Bridge (natural rock bridge), High Force (largest waterfall in British Isles), Cauldron Snout (rapids), Hadrian's Wall, Roman fort at Housesteads, the Border forests.

Accommodation. Youth hostels at Edale (110–139865), Crowden-in-Longdendale (110–073993), Marsden (110–048112), Mankinholes Hall (103–960235), Earby (103–915468), Malham (98–901629), Stainforth (98–821668),

Hawes (98–867897), Keld (91–892009), Langdon Beck (92–860304), Dufton (91–688252), Alston (86–717461), Greenhead (86–659655), Once Brewed (86–752668), Bellingham (80–843834), Byrness (80–764027), Kirk Yetholm (74–826282, Scottish YHA).

A few simple bothies have now been established for an overnight stop in emergency; these are situated on Cross Fell and in the Cheviots.

The Bed and Breakfast Guide (Ramblers' Association) marks suitable places. But usually these are limited and all accommodation should be booked in advance, particularly at Easter and in the summer months. Some farmhouses are now providing light refreshments but this is not to be relied upon. Note particularly:

1. Keld YH to Middleton in Teesdale (21 miles [34 km]). Keld YH to Langdon Beck YH is even further (29 miles [47 km]). But alternative route may be used to break the stretch at Bowes.

2. Byrness to Kirk Yetholm (29 miles [47 km]).

Books and Guides

1. 'The Pennine Way'. Long Distance Footpath Guide No. 1. Tom Stephenson, HMSO. Description of route with photographs, and including all relevant sections of Ordnance Survey maps.

2. 'Along the Pennine Way'. J. H. B. Peel, Cassell. Good book about the main points of interest on the Way. Photographs.

3. 'A Guide to the Pennine Way'. Christopher John Wright, Constable. Excellent guide book with many photographs, good description of route and all relevant sections of O.S. maps.

4. 'Pennine Way Companion: a pictorial guide'. A. Wainwright, *Westmorland Gazette*. Excellent guide book with route instructions, detailed maps and drawings. The most detailed guide available.

The walking of the Pennine Way in one expedition should not be undertaken lightly. It is undoubtedly the hardest of the long distance routes so far established. On some sections, for example Kinder Scout, Bleaklow and the

Cheviots, the walking is particularly hard. In mist or rain, route finding in some areas can be difficult and map and compass and the ability to use them are essential. Most of all perhaps there is the danger of underestimating the effort and organization needed for a walk of 250 miles (403 km) over rough country. Many more people start than finish. The 'drop-out' rate in the early stages from Edale is very high.

Guides. A combination of guide books 1 and 4 will probably be sufficient.

Maps. 74, 80, 86, 91, 92, 98, 103, 109, 110.

29. PEMBROKESHIRE COAST PATH

History. This was the third long distance footpath to be created by the Countryside Commission, and the first for Wales. Opened 16 May 1970.

Distance. 167 miles (269 km).

Starting point. Amroth, Dyfed. (185–173072).

Finishing point. St Dogmaels, Dyfed. (145–163469).

Route. The route follows the coast of Pembrokeshire making a considerable detour at Milford Haven. Detours have also to be made at Penally, Manorbier and Castlemartin to avoid Ministry of Defence areas.

Main interests. Magnificent cliff walk with beautiful and impressive views. Submerged forest at low tide near Amroth, Manorbier Castle, Pembroke Castle, twelfth-century cathedral at St David's, many Iron Age forts. The coastline is one of the richest areas in the British Isles for sea-birds and seals. Six Pembrokeshire National Park information centres are on the route, and there is a special Countryside Unit established by the Countryside Commission at Broad Haven.

Accommodation. Youth hostels at Pentlepoir (158–116060), Marloes Sands (157–778080), St David's (157–739176) Trevine (157–840324), Pwll Deri (157–891387) and Poppit Sands (145–144487). Inn and guest house accommo-

dation is available along the coast but will tend to
be booked at holiday times. The Bed and Breakfast Guide
(Ramblers' Association) marks suitable accommodation.

Books and Guides. 'Pembrokeshire'. Long Distance Footpath Guide No. 3. John H. Barrett, HMSO. Contains all
relevant O.S. map sections as well as detailed notes and
illustrations.

Maps. 145, 157, 158.

30. RIDGEWAY PATH

History. As other chalk ridges in the south this provided a
dry and safe route for prehistoric man, in this case part of
the route from Devon to East Anglia. The long distance
footpath was officially opened on 29 September 1973 by
Lord Nugent at Coombe Hill, near Wendover, Bucks.

Distance. 85 miles (137 km).

Starting point. Overton Hill, near Avebury, Wiltshire. (173–
119681).

Finishing point. Ivinghoe Beacon, Buckinghamshire. (165–
960169).

Route. The route is noted particularly for its broad green
lanes running along the high ground of chalk hills. In the
west it runs over the North Wessex Downs and is also
open to cyclists and horse-riders, whilst in the east it runs
along the Chilterns and is restricted to walkers. The surface tends to be heavily rutted in places. The Thames is
followed for about 6 miles (10 km) in the middle section
after Streatley-on-Thames. There are many car-parks
throughout the length of the Ridgeway.

Waymarking. Acorn signs, wooden and stone markers
throughout the route.

Main interests. The scenery is pleasant, particularly in the
neighbourhood of Ivinghoe Beacon. The area however is
particularly rich in remains from the Bronze and early
Iron Ages. The main features are: Avebury Circle, Bar-

bury Castle, Liddington Castle, Wayland Smith's Cave, Uffington Castle, Alfred's Castle, Segsbury Camp, Ivinghoe Beacon.

Accommodation. There is a scarcity of youth hostels on or near the route. Possible ones are: Inglesham (163–204964) about 8 miles (13 km) off-route, Streatley-on-Thames (174–591806), Henley-on-Thames (175–759831) about 6 miles (10 km) off-route, Bradenham (165–828972) about 3 miles (5 km) off-route, Lee Gate (165–893055) and Ivinghoe (165–945161). There are few villages on route but several nearby. The Bed and Breakfast Guide (Ramblers' Association) marks suitable accommodation.

Books and Guides

1. 'The Ridgeway Path'. Long Distance Footpath Guide No. 6. Sean Jennet, HMSO.
2. 'The Oldest Road'. J. R. L. Anderson and Fay Godwin, Wildwood House Ltd.
3. 'Discovering the Ridgeway'. V. Burden, Shire.
4. 'A Practical Guide to Walking the Ridgeway Path'. H. D. Westacott, Footpath Publications, Adstock Cottage, Adstock, Buckingham, MK18 2HZ.

Maps. 165, 173, 174, 175.

31. ROMAN WAY

History. Suggested and described by Geoffrey Berry, secretary of the Friends of the Lake District, in 1975.

Distance. 48 miles (77 km).

Starting point. Brougham Castle, near Penrith, Cumbria. (90–537290).

Finishing point. Ravenglass, Cumbria. (96–084962).

Route. The route lies almost entirely within the Lake District National Park and joins the Roman forts of Brougham, Ambleside, Hardknott and Ravenglass using old Roman roads. The river Eamont is followed for about four miles (6 km) before the Way turns southwards and follows the Roman road of High Street over several

mountain summits to Troutbeck. The Way then turns
easterly and goes via the Wrynose and Hardknott Passes
to Ravenglass.

Main interests. The Roman forts, Brougham Castle, ancient
monument at Mayburgh, stone circle on Moor Divock,
fine fell walking over High Street, the Wrynose and
Harknott Passes, the estuary at Ravenglass. Magnificent
views.

Accommodation. Youth hostels at Patterdale (90–399156) 3
miles (5 km) off-route, Ambleside (90–377031), Elterwater
(90–327046), Eskdale (90–195010). Other accommodation
is available but must be booked beforehand in the holiday
season.

Guides. 'Across Northern Hills'. Geoffrey Berry, *Westmorland Gazette.*

Maps. 90, 96.

32. ROSEDALE CIRCUIT WALK

History. Devised by the members of the Blackburn Welfare
Society Rambling Club.

Distance. 37 miles (60 km).

Starting and Finishing point. Rosedale Abbey, North Yorkshire. (94–723959).

Route. A circular route taken clockwise through the dales of
the central region of the North York Moors National
Park: Rosedale, Farndale, Bransdale, Baysdale, Westerdale, Danby Dale, Great Fryup Dale, Glaisdale, Rosedale.

Main interests. Old mill at Bransdale, Fryup Dale Head,
Farndale Valley (for daffodils), Botton village for
architecture.

Accommodation. Youth hostels at Westerdale Hall (94–662060) and Wheeldale (94–812983) 3 miles (5 km) off-route.

Books and Guides. Duplicated sheets giving details of the
route may be obtained from The Rosedale Circuit
Secretary, Blackburn Welfare Society (Rambling Club

Section), Hawker Siddeley Aviation Ltd, Brough, North
Humberside, HU15 1EQ.

Maps. North York Moors Tourist Map. 94.

Certificates and Badges. A certificate and badge may be
obtained in Botton village from either the cafe or from the
secretary of the Camphill Trust.

33. SAMARITAN WAY

History. Created by R. T. Pinkney under the auspices of the
Teesside Samaritans; the Way was opened in 1978.

Distance. 40 miles (64 km).

Starting and Finishing point. Guisborough, North Yorkshire. (94–615160).

Route. A circular route around Esk Dale, Little and Great
Fryup Dales, Farndale, Westerdale and Baysdale designed
to give great variety of walking.

Waymarking. Some yellow arrows have been provided in
the Westerdale section.

Main interests. Grand views over the dales of the North
York Moors National Park, Fat Betty, Ralphs Cross,
Captain Cook's Monument. The route coincides with the
Cleveland Way and the Lyke Wake Walk over short
distances.

Accommodation. Youth hostel at Westerdale Hall. (94–
662059).

Guides. Duplicated sheets from R. T. Pinkney, 5 Wake
Street, North Ormesby, Middlesbrough.

Maps. North York Moors Tourist Map. 93, 94.

Walkers who have completed the route may have their
names entered into the official record book and obtain
certificates and badges for a small fee from R. T. Pinkney
(address above). All money received is forwarded to the
Teesside Samaritans.

34. SOUTH DOWNS WAY

History. Officially opened by Lord Shawcross 15 July 1972 at Beachy Head, near Eastbourne.

Distance. 80 miles (129 km).

Starting point. Eastbourne, East Sussex. (199–598983).

Finishing point. The Hampshire border at Buriton, near Petersfield. (197–740201).

Route. The South Downs are a range of chalk hills running approximately east-west. The Way follows the line of the Downs, mostly above 600 ft (183 m), but it is necessary to descend and then ascend again where they are cut by four rivers, the Cuckmere, Ouse, Adur and the Arun. The Way lies in the main along the northern escarpment but there is an alternative route at the start from Eastbourne to Alfriston along the coast. The highest points are just over 800 ft (244 m).

Waymarking. The Way is designated as a bridlepath as well as a walking route, except for the first section along the coast. Waymarking is by special oak signs, small stone plinths or stencil painted acorns.

Main interests. The unspoilt cliffs at Beachy Head and the Seven Sisters, the dewpond and the Long Man of Wilmington, Clergy House at Alfriston, windmills, Devil's Dyke, Arundel Castle, (off-route). Also magnificent views northwards over the Weald and southwards over the Downs with occasional glimpses of the sea.

Accommodation. Youth hostels at Beachy Head (199–588990), Alfriston (199–518019), Telscombe (198–405033), Patcham (198–300088), Truleigh Hill (198–220105), Arundel (197–033074). Those at Patcham and Arundel are about 2–3 miles (3–5 km) off-route. There is a gap of about 20 miles (32 km) without a hostel from Arundel to the western end. It is possible to descend into villages off the Downs and obtain accommodation. The Bed and Breakfast Guide (Ramblers' Association) marks suitable accommodation.

Books and Guides
1. 'The South Downs Way'. Ernest G. Green, Ramblers' Association.
2. 'The South Downs Way'. Sean Jennett, HMSO.
Maps. 197, 198, 199.

35. SOUTH-WEST PENINSULA COAST PATH

History. Old coastguard paths existed around the peninsula but had fallen into disuse. It was recommended as long ago as 1942 that these should be available to walkers. The Cornwall Coast Path was opened by Lord Caradon at the Barrow fields, Newquay on 19 May 1973.
The South Devon and Dorset Coast Paths were opened by Lord Amory on 14 September 1974.
The Somerset and North Devon Coast Path was opened by Denis Howell, Minister for Sport and Recreation, on 20 May 1978.

Distances.
Section 1. Dorset Coast Path. 72 miles (116 km).
Section 2. South Devon Coast Path. 93 miles (150 km).
Section 3. Cornwall Coast Path. 268 miles (431 km).
Section 4. Somerset and North Devon Coast Path. 82 miles (132 km).
Total = 515 miles (829 km).

Starting point. Studland, Dorset. (195–037867).
Finishing point. Minehead, Somerset. (181–975464).
Route. The object is to keep as near to the sea as possible, but in some places it has been necessary to deviate inland. Most of the route lies along the top of the cliffs and offers rugged walking as the path is far from level and frequently descends into and then rises out of gullies. Major resorts such as Paignton, Torquay and Weymouth have to be crossed as well as estuaries by ferry.
Waymarking. Fairly good throughout, but this varies greatly from one region to another.

Main interests. Magnificent cliff scenery and very good walking. Also lovely bathing beaches, delightful fishing villages and estuaries. The mild climate produces a lush vegetation with semi-tropical plants. Numerous sea-birds, seals and even basking sharks can be seen from the path. Also King Arthur's Castle at Tintagel, Doyden Castle, ruined tin mines, Minnack open-air theatre, St Michael's Mount, Plymouth, Chesil Beach and others.

Accommodation. Youth hostels at:

Section 1. Swanage (195–030785), Litton Cheney (194–548900) about 5 miles (8 km) off-route, Bridport (193–462930).

Section 2. Beer (192–223896), Start Bay (202–839469), Salcombe (202–728374), Bigbury (202–650445), Plymouth (201–461555).

Section 3. Golant (200–118556), Boswinger (204–991411), Pendennis Castle (204–823319), Coverack (204–783181), Penzance (203–457302), Land's End (203–361304), Hayle (203–562381), Newquay (200–818619), Treyarnon Bay (200–859741), Tintagel (200–047881), Boscastle (190–096915).

Section 4. Elmscott (190–231217), Instow (180–482303), Lynton (180–720487), Minehead (181–973442).

There is also much accommodation in farms, inns and guest houses, but this is the most popular holiday area in England and will probably be heavily booked in season. The Bed and Breakfast Guide (Ramblers' Association) marks accommodation.

Books and Guides

1. 'The South-West Peninsula Coast-Path'. Ken Ward and John H. N. Mason, Charles Letts. (Book 1, Minehead to St Ives; Book 2, St Ives to Plymouth; Book 3, Plymouth to Poole).

2. The South-West Way Association produce an annual guide to the Way, 'South West Way. Guide to the Coastal Path' (Chapter 11).

Maps

Section 1. 193, 194, 195.

Section 2. 192, 193, 201, 202.

Section 3. 190, 200, 201, 203, 204.
Section 4. 180, 181, 190.

36. STAFFORDSHIRE WAY

History. A route of 90 miles from Mow Cop to Kinver
 Edge is being created by the Staffordshire County Council. The first section to Rocester was opened in 1977, and
 it is intended that the second section to Cannock Chase
 will be completed during 1979.
Distance. 32 miles (52 km).
Starting point. Mow Cop, Staffordshire. (118–857574).
Finishing point. Rocester, Staffordshire. (128–110394).
Route. Approximately north-east from Mow Cop over the
 gritstone ridges of Congleton Edge and The Cloud, before
 turning south-east to Rudyard Lake. The route then
 follows the wooded valley of the Churnet to its junction
 with the Dove near Rocester.
Waymarking. Painted yellow and blue arrows (Countryside
 Commission method) each with a white paint outline of
 the Staffordshire Knot.
Main interests. Mow Cop Castle (a sham built in 1754),
 Beautiful Rudyard Lake, James Brindley's mill at Leek,
 the Caldon Canal (re-opened in 1974 after restoration),
 Hawksmoor Reserve (National Trust), Alton Castle.
 Grand views from Old Man of Mow, The Cloud, Cliffe
 Park, Toothill Rook and several other points on the route.
 Beautiful woods.
Accommodation. Youth hostels at Meerbrook (118–986608)
 – 3 miles off-route and Dimmingsdale (119, 128–052436).
 Tourist Information Centres at 18 St Edward Street,
 Leek and 13 Market Place, Ashbourne will supply
 information.
Guides. 'The Staffordshire Way – Mow Cop to Rocester'.
 Planning Department, Staffordshire County Council,
 County Buildings, Martin Street, Stafford, ST16 2LE.
Maps. 118, 119 (very small section), 128.

37. ST PETER'S WAY

History. A route to this area of the Essex coast was proposed by the Council for the Protection of Rural England in 1970 as an alternative to the Essex Way. The present route based upon this idea was prepared by members of West Essex Group of the Ramblers' Association and the Epping Forest Holiday Fellowship. The Inaugural Walk was held 26–28 August 1978 by the West Essex.

Distance. 45 miles (72 km).

Starting point. Chipping Ongar, Essex. (167–551035).

Finishing point. St Peter's Chapel, Essex. (168–032083).

Route. Runs in west to east direction across Essex, with a final stretch of about 2–3 miles northwards along the coast. Generally low-lying country, but with some surprisingly steep hills around Purleigh.

Main interests. Castle and old buildings at Ongar, windmill at Stock, Hanningfield Water, views of the Blackwater estuary, the sea wall, St Peter's Chapel.

Accommodation. The only convenient youth hostels are Epping Forest (167, 177–408983) and Harlow (167–450109) at the western end.

Guides. 'The St Peter's Way'. Fred Matthews and Harry Bitten, from Fred Matthews, 'Glen View', London Road, Abridge, Essex.

Maps. 167, 168.

38. SUSSEX BORDER PATH
(WEST SUSSEX SECTION)

History. The idea of a path along the border of Sussex is due to Aeneas Mackintosh and Ben Perkins, who completed the first section around West Sussex (including the West and East Sussex dividing line) in 1978. Work is now progressing on the second section around East Sussex.

Distance. 122 miles (196 km).

Starting point. Emsworth, Hampshire. (197–753058). The starting point is just inside West Sussex.

Finishing point. Mile Oak, near Brighton, West Sussex. (198–250066).

Route. Runs around and near to the border of West Sussex, deviating from it where more attractive routes are to be found close at hand.

Main interests. A complete circuit of Thorney Island is followed by good walking across the South Downs and through the Weald. The South Downs are crossed for a second time near to Patcham. These are areas of fine scenery.

Accommodation. Youth hostels at Portsmouth (196–649055) – 6 miles from start, Hindhead (186–892368) – 3 miles off-route, Ewhurst Green (187–094398) – 3 miles off-route and Patcham (198–300088).

Guides. 'Sussex Border Path. Part 1 – West Sussex'. Aeneas Mackintosh and Ben Perkins. From Dr B. A. W. Perkins, 11 Old London Road, Patcham, Brighton, Sussex.

Maps. 186, 187, 197, 198.

39. THAMESDOWN TRAIL

History. Created in 1978 by Laurence Main, Footpaths Secretary of Swindon Group of the Ramblers' Association.

Distance. 54 miles (87 km).

Starting and Finishing point. Cricklade, Wiltshire. (173–101936).

Route. A circular route around Swindon; keeping within 10 miles of the town centre, it crosses the Marlborough and Berkshire Downs, the western end of the Vale of the White Horse and the upper Thames valley.

Waymarking. Waymarking of the route is being carried out using the Countryside Commission's recommended method.

Main interests. Ringsbury Camp, Little Town White Horse, Bincknoll Castle, Barbury Castle, part of the Ridgeway long distance route, site of the Battle of Beranburgh (556 A.D.) and a section along the River Thames.

Accommodation. Youth Hostel at Inglesham (163–204964) 2½ miles off-route. Bed and Breakfast accommodation lists may be obtained from Thamesdown Information Centre, 32 The Arcade, David Murray John Building, Brunel Centre, Swindon, SN1 1LN.

Guides. 'The Thamesdown Trail'. Laurence Main, 14 Fanstones Road, Eldene, Swindon, SN3 6DX.

Maps. 173, 174.

40. THREE FORESTS WAY

History. Devised by the West Essex Group of the Ramblers' Association to commemorate the Silver Jubilee of Queen Elizabeth II. The Inaugural Walk was held during August 1977.

Distance. 60 miles (97 km).

Starting and Finishing point. Loughton, Essex. (167–423956).

Route. A circular route joining the three Essex forests of Epping, Hatfield and Hainault.

Main interests. Lovely deciduous forests seen at their best in spring and autumn, Loughton Camp (ancient earthworks), pleasant views over the Lea Valley.

Accommodation. Youth Hostels at Epping Forest (167, 177–408983) and Harlow (167–450109).

Guides. 'The Three Forests Way'. Fred Matthews and Harry Bitten, from Fred Matthews, 'Glen View', London Road, Abridge, Essex. Badges available for sale to successful walkers.

Maps. 166, 167, 177.

41. TWO MOORS WAY

History. Suggested jointly by Tom Stephenson of the Ramblers' Association, Sylvia Sayer of the Dartmoor Preservation Society and John Coleman-Cooke of the Exmoor Society. Work commenced in 1965 and the route was finally described in 1976.

Distance. 103 miles (166 km).

Starting point. Ivybridge, Devon. (202–637562).

Finishing point. Lynmouth, Devon. (180–725494).

Route. A very varied route. It commences on the southern edge of the Dartmoor National Park and crosses the open moor over the first stretch of its journey. A small section of the Mariners' Way is followed (an old route between Bideford and Dartmouth supposedly used by seamen) and then a stretch in the Teign valley. The central section is in agricultural country and the route finishes over high ground in the Exmoor National Park.

Waymarking. Some in the mid-Devon section provided by the Devon County Council.

Main interests. Good walking on the open moor sections of Dartmoor and Exmoor. The wooded valleys of the Dart, West Webburn, Teign and Barle. A wealth of antiquities particularly on Dartmoor. Cob-built houses in mid-Devon. Disused tin mines and china clay workings.

Accommodation. Youth hostels at Bellever (191–654773), Exford (181–853383), Gidleigh (191–670884) and Lynton (180–720487). Much accommodation at Lynmouth and some hotels in villages on route. The Bed and Breakfast Guide (Rambler's Association) marks suitable accommodation.

Guides. 'Two Moors Way'. A very well-written guide published by the Devon Ramblers' Association and obtainable from J. R. Turner, 'Coppins', The Poplars, Pinhoe, Exeter, Devon.

Maps. 180, 181, 191, 202.

42. VIKING WAY

History. The idea of a long distance footpath south of the Humber was first suggested by the Ramblers' Association in the 1950s, and a route was proposed by the Kesteven and Lindsey County Councils in the late 1960s. After the local government reorganization of 1974 the County Councils of Humberside, Lincolnshire and Leicestershire continued the work. The Bigby-Woodhall Spa section was officially opened on 5 September 1976, at Tealby, by Councillor W. C. Hall and the next section to Woolsthorpe on 10 September 1977.

Distance. Approx. 112 miles (180 km) – excluding spur and loop.

Starting point. The Humber Bridge, Barton-upon-Humber, Humberside. (112–032219).

Finishing point. Oakham, Leicestershire. (141–862089).

Route. It uses existing rights of way with the exception of two sections near Market Rasen and Horncastle. The route goes approximately south-east along the Lincolnshire Wolds to Horncastle, then south-west over flat country to the Lincolnshire county boundary near Grantham before moving southwards to Oakham. An alternative loop through Lincoln and a linking spur to Grantham are provided.

Waymarking. Posts marked with a Viking head shield.

Main features. The Lincolnshire Wolds. Flat, black fenland. Fine churches at Barton-upon-Humber, Bigby, Caistor and elsewhere; houses at Belton, Scrivelsby Court and Woolsthorpe (home of Isaac Newton); site of iron-age fort at Honington, Roman town at Ancaster and many deserted medieval villages; Lincoln, Grantham and Oakham also have much of interest.

Accommodation. Youth hostels at Woody's Top (122–332786) – 4 miles (6 km) off-route, Lincoln (121–980700) – on alternative route and Grantham (130–919356).

Guides. Director of Technical Services, Humberside County

Council, Eastgate, Beverley, North Humberside. Humber
Bridge – Bigby (1 leaflet).
Lincolnshire County Council, County Offices, Lincoln,
LN1 1YL. Bigby – Woolsthorpe (6 brochures).
Maps. 112, 113, 121, 122, 141.

43. WEALDWAY

History. Proposed in the 1960s as a continuous route from
the Thames to the English Channel. The final part from
Uckfield to Eastbourne has not yet been completed.

Distance. 81 miles (130 km).

Starting point. Gravesend, Kent. (177–647745).

Finishing point. Eastbourne, East Sussex. (199–615990).

Route. The Way runs in an approximately north to south
direction through Tonbridge and Uckfield. It crosses the
North and South Downs and the Weald.

Main interests. Thirteenth-century castle gatehouse at Tonbridge, Penshurst Place and Royal Tunbridge Wells – both
3 miles (5 km) off-route, Buckhurst Park at Withyham,
Buxted Park, Michelham Priory, Clergy House at Alfriston, Wilmington Old Man, Towner Art Gallery at Eastbourne. Several old and attractive inns. Fine views over
the Weald. Ashdown Forest. The North and South
Downs.

Accommodation. Youth hostels at Blackboys (199–521215),
Alfriston (199–518019) and Beachy Head, Eastbourne
(199–588990). The South East England Tourist Board
office at Royal Tunbridge Wells may also be able to help
with accommodation.

Guides. 'The Wealdway, Section 1. Gravesend to Ton-
bridge'. Meopham Publications Committee, 'Wrexbury',
Wrotham Road, Meopham, Kent, DA13 0HX.
A set of six cards in a clear plastic map case with route
description, illustrations and maps (4½ inches to 1 mile).
Geoffrey King. Independent Design Executive, Tonbridge,
Kent. These cover the route from Tonbridge to Uckfield.

Maps. 177, 188, 198, 199.

44. WEY-SOUTH PATH

History. The Wey and Arun Canal, opened in 1816, linked
the navigable rivers Wey and Arun to form a water link
between London and the South Coast. The canal was
closed in 1868, but still remains largely intact and restoration work is being undertaken by the Wey and Arun
Canal Trust. The Path follows the line of the canal to
link the North Downs Way with the South Downs Way.

Distance. 36 miles (60 km).

Starting point. Guildford, Surrey. (186–994494).

Finishing point. Amberley, West Sussex. (197–026118).

Route. Follows the Wey Navigation for three miles to its
junction with the canal. The Path then goes near or along
the route of the canal to join the Arun Navigation at
Pallingham, ending where the Navigation cuts through
the line of the South Downs.

Main interests. The lovely countryside of the Surrey Hills,
the Weald and the South Downs. The canal with old
locks, aqueducts, bridges, etc. Amberley Wild Brooks.

Accommodation. Youth hostels at Ewhurst Green (187–
094398) – 3 miles off-route and Arundel (197–032074) –
3 miles from end.

Guides. 'Wey-South Path'. Aeneas Mackintosh, The Wey
and Arun Canal Trust Ltd, 24 Griffiths Avenue, Lancing,
West Sussex, BN15 0HW.

Maps. 186, 187, 197.

45. WHITE ROSE WALK

History. Devised by the Yorkshire Wayfarers in 1967, and
first completed in June 1968.

Distance. Three alternative routes are offered in the middle
section giving different total distances: Scarth Nick route
40 miles (64 km) and 4,900 ft (1,494 m) climbing; Carlton
Moor route 37 miles (60 km) and 4,900 ft (1,494 m)
climbing; Chop Gate route 34 miles (55 km) and 3,700 ft
(1,128 m) climbing.

Starting point. South of Newton-under-Roseberry, Cleveland. (93–571128).

Finishing point. The White Horse, North Yorkshire. (100–514813).

Route. Runs entirely within and approximately parallel to the western boundary of the North York Moors National Park along an escarpment of the Hambleton and Cleveland Hills.

Waymarking. None, but some sections of the Cleveland Way are used and these are waymarked with acorn and other signs.

Main interests. Roseberry Topping, Captain Cook's Monument, ancient drove roads, unusual sign at Cheques Farm ancient earthworks, White Horse. Extensive views.

Accommodation. No youth hostels on the route but Westerdale Hall (94–662059) and Helmsley (100–616840) may be used for the start and finish, although some distance away.

Guides. 'The White Rose Walk'. Geoffrey White, *Dalesman*.

Maps. North York Moors One-inch Tourist map. 93, 94, 100.

Badges. Badges and cards of congratulation may be obtained for a small fee by successful walkers from the White Rose Recorder of the Yorkshire Wayfarers, F. G. White, 14 Trentholme Drive, York, YO2 2DG. No time limit is stipulated.

46. WOLDS WAY

History. A. J. Brown, in his book 'Tramping in Yorkshire' (1932), referred to a Wolds Way which was a general ramble across the Yorkshire Wolds. In 1968 however the East Riding Area of the Ramblers' Association proposed a specific route to be known by this name. The East Riding County Council approved this plan in principle, as did the Countryside Commission, and surveyed a possible route. Negotiations on this route are still in progress.

Distance. 67 miles (108 km).

Starting point. Filey Brigg, North Yorkshire. (101–132815).

Finishing point. North Ferriby, Humberside. (106–983251).

Route. The Yorkshire Wolds have the general shape of a crescent with the concave side towards Spurn Head in the south-east. With a broad northern end and gradually becoming narrower they reach a maximum height at Garrowby Hill (807 ft or 246 m). The route follows the line of the Wolds mainly on the northern and eastern edges. Mainly heavily cultivated, open countryside.

Main interests. The sea at Filey Brigg, many 'lost' villages such as Cleaving and Wauldby, ancient dykes and earthworks, fine views towards the North York Moors, the Humber.

Accommodation. Malton (100–778711), Thixendale (100–843611). The Bed and Breakfast Guide (Ramblers' Association) marks suitable accommodation.

Guides. 'The Wolds Way'. David Rubinstein, *Dalesman.*

Maps. 100, 101, 106.

The end of the Wolds Way at Filey Brigg may be reached by public footpath from the end of the Cleveland Way. In addition it will be possible to continue at the southern end over the Humber Bridge on to the Viking Way.

47. YORKSHIRE DALES CENTURION WALK

History. Devised and described by Jonathan E. Ginesi in 1976.

Distance. 100 miles (161 km).

Starting and Finishing point. Horton-in-Ribblesdale, North Yorkshire. (98–808725).

Route. A circular route lying largely within the Yorkshire Dales National Park. It crosses seven main peaks over 2,000 ft (610 m), visits nine dales, and includes long stretches of rough moorland walking (total 16,000 ft or 4,877 m climbing).

Main interests. The beauty of the Yorkshire Dales, glorious views from mountain ridges and summits, pot-holes, Dent with its narrow cobbled streets, and other attractive villages, Tan Hill Inn (the highest inn in England), Aysgarth Falls.

Accommodation. Youth hostels at Stainforth (98–821668) – 4 miles (6 km) south of start, Dentdale (98–774850), Kirkby Stephen (91–773082), Grinton (98–048976), Aysgarth Falls (98–012884), Kettlewell (98–971724).

Guides. 'Official Guide Book to the Yorkshire Dales Centurion Walk'. Jonathan E. Ginesi, John Siddall (Printers) Ltd.

Maps. 91, 92*, 97*, 98. (*Very small sections only.)

This walk must not be confused with the regular events organized to enable walkers to join the Centurions. This is a walking club, membership being restricted to those who have walked 100 miles (161 km) within 24 hours.

Long distance routes in Scotland

Some suggestions are given in two excellent books: 'Scottish Hill Tracks, Old Highways and Drove Roads'. Part 1. Southern Scotland, Part 2. Northern Scotland. D. G. Moir, Bartholomew.

A. Kielder to Edinburgh.
B. Rochester to Dunbar.
C. Edinburgh to Newton Stewart.
D. Glasgow to Elgin.
E. Glasgow to Inverness.
F. Glasgow to Skye via Fort William.
G. Glasgow to Skye via Glen Affric.
H. Fort William to Tonque.

CHAPTER 9

Challenge Walks

Rambling is generally regarded as an essentially non-competitive outdoor activity, and this is the case for the vast majority of ramblers. Nevertheless, competition has never been entirely absent from the walking scene. There have always been individuals who wanted to walk and tried to walk further or faster than anybody else, or who tried to improve upon their own best time over a set route.

The Three Peaks Walk of Yorkshire, for example, has been the subject of record attempts since the first known walk in 1887. In the Lake District in the 1920s and 1930s there were several attempts to climb as many peaks as possible within 24 hours, and long distance feats such as the 70-mile (113-km) Colne to Rowsley Walk and the 120-mile (193-km) Tan Hill to Cat and Fiddle Walk were accomplished in the Pennines before and after the Second World War.

These were 'Challenge Walks' which could be attempted at any time. During the past twenty years or so, however, a new form of activity has arisen; this is the Organized Event. These are held on a particular day and over a fixed distance, which is usually not less than twenty miles (32 km). The walker is either (1) given a detailed route description, or (2) required to choose his own route between certain points. He has to report at checkpoints along the route, usually in a fixed order. His time of finishing is noted and it is usual to publish a results list after the event giving the order of finishing with the individual time for each walker. Each participant who finishes within the time limit set is given a certificate to mark his performance. In a few cases trophies are awarded for 'First Man Home' or 'First Lady Home'.

About sixty events of this type are now held each year and the number is growing with well-established events usually attracting large numbers of participants. Tanners Marathon, a 30-mile (48-km) event held annually in July, usually attracts about 750 walkers with a record 908 in 1967. The Fellsman Hike in Yorkshire is now so over-subscribed that a draw has to be held each year for starting places.

It must be emphasized that these are not 'sponsored walks'. Walkers do not raise money for a charity, they are there essentially for the walking. It should also be emphasized that these events are not organized as races; in fact organizers usually emphasize the opposite. As a result many walkers enter these events who have no ambitions beyond finishing the route within the time allowed and so earning a certificate. But these are treated very seriously by other walkers who try to improve on their own previous performances or who try to finish as high as possible in the results list.

Events are organized by various organizations such as the local groups of the Ramblers' Association, Scout Association and Youth Hostels Association. The most active body in this field however is the Long Distance Walkers Association (Chapter 11). The LDWA publishes a regular newsletter which gives details of past and future events, and membership is a 'must' for any walker seriously interested in challenge walking.

Organized events are sometimes called Marathons, e.g. the Chiltern Marathon, but this is misleading as events are hardly ever over the official marathon distance of 26 miles 385 yards which is used in modern athletics. Usually the distance is greater. The greatest distance covered in the United Kingdom at the moment is 100 miles (161 km).

A. ORGANIZED EVENTS

Events vary somewhat in their organization but the following notes are general and should be useful to walkers interested in entering for the first time.

(1) Write to the organizer for details of the event, enclosing a *stamped, addressed envelope*. Some events will accept entries on the day, but where entry is limited some may fill

up long before. Generally it is as well to write about five months beforehand to ensure a place.

(2) The organizers will send a full description of the event and an entry form. The entry form has to be completed, the entrant usually having to sign a declaration that he will not hold the organizers in any way responsible for accidents that occur during the course of the event. The entry fee has to be included with the entry form. This varies from about 25 p to several pounds for more ambitious events. Once again enclose a stamped, addressed envelope.

(3) The entry is acknowledged and final details are sent. Each entrant is given a number.

(4) On the day have a high carbohydrate meal before you start (not less than two hours before). Arrive at the start in plenty of time. For most events one hour should be sufficient, but the organizers may insist on equipment checks and specify a particular time. Try to avoid a long, tiring journey beforehand. If the starting time is early then make sure that you have a good sleep the night before and preferably for several nights previously.

(5) There will be an official checking-in point. Report your arrival giving name and number. You will be provided with a checkcard or tally and route details. It is advisable to carry a compass and a 1 : 50 000 Ordnance Survey map of the district. Some organizers insist upon this.

(6) Change and gather your equipment. It is a good idea to carry your route description and map in a transparent map case or polythene bag as these sheets rapidly disintegrate with rain or sweat.

(7) About ten minutes before the start proceed to the starting point which is sometimes a short distance away.

(8) Do not rush off madly at the start, pace yourself so that you finish in reasonable time and condition. Do not run unless you are trained and equipped for it. Remember that your first priority is to pass through all checkpoints and to finish within the time stated. You will usually be disqualified if you miss a checkpoint or finish outside time. It is advisable not to follow other entrants unless you are sure that they are on the right route. They may get you lost.

(9) Be courteous to all checkpoint officials even if there is a delay in booking you in and however hot and tired you may feel. Remember that they are doing the job voluntarily and would probably prefer to be walking with you.

Ensure that your card is signed or punched or stamped at each checkpoint. It is easy, particularly if refreshments are provided, to omit this.

(10) Eat little but often. Except on the longer events most people do not stop for meals as you would on an ordinary ramble. (Chapter 13).

(11) There will be a finishing point at the end. Book in immediately, making sure that your name is on the check-card.

(12) Refreshments will usually be available at the end and sometimes showers or washing facilities. You will probably have to address an envelope for your results list.

A number of factors must be taken into account when judging the severity of an event:

1. Distance.
2. Amount of ascent and descent.
3. The roughness of the ground.
4. Time of year.
5. Equipment to be carried.
6. Time allowed.

Do not start with one of the more ambitious events. It will probably be far harder than you imagine. Start with an easy one and work up.

Details of most of the more popular and well-established events are given on pages 199–221. It should be appreciated that arrangements change from time to time. The descriptions are given therefore to help the reader make an initial choice. The final details for events should always be checked with the organizers. In most cases the events are open to all.

See note on page 77.

Figure 24. Location of principal organized challenge walks.
(For identification of walks see text)

1 Across Wales Walk

A walk of 45 miles (72 km) organized by the West Birmingham YHA Group and held each September since 1964. The route starts near Clun and finishes near Aberystwyth, the object being to cross the Principality from the east border to the coast. A certificate is awarded to all walkers who complete within 18 hours. Entry limited by accommodation at each end. A good stretch is over hard roads but Plynlymon (2,468 ft or 752 m) must be crossed. Entrants must be YHA members.

West Birmingham YHA Group, Quinborne Community Centre, Ridgacre Road, Quinton, Birmingham, B32 2TW.

2 Berkshire 25

First held in 1974 this event is organized annually in May by the Thatcham Walkers. The 25-mile (40-km) route lies over the chalk downs around the Berkshire Ridgeway. Manned checkpoints and certificates to all finishers under nine hours.

Roy Chapman, 10 Beverley Close, Thatcham, Newbury, Berkshire, RG13 4AB.

3 Blackwater Marathon

First held in 1976, repeated in 1977 and then every other year in November; this event is organized by the Essex-Herts Group of the Long Distance Walkers Association. The circular route from Maldon, Essex is about 25 miles (40 km) long over generally flat country and includes an attractive stretch along the Essex sea-wall.

Mike Powell Davies, 13 The Avenue, Witham, Essex, CM8 2DN.

4 Bullock Smithy Hike

First organized in 1976 by the 3rd Hazel Grove Scout Group and since then annually in September. The 56-mile (90-km) route commences at Hazel Grove, Stockport and involves over 7,000 feet (2,134 m) of climbing mainly in the Peak District. Participants must carry a specified amount of equipment and are formed into groups of three during the night. Certificates to all who finish within 24 hours and several trophies for the best performances.

Fielding Lord, 89 Bramhall Moor Lane, Hazel Grove, Stockport, Cheshire.

5 Chevy Chase

A walk of 17 miles (27 km), held annually in May–June, starting and finishing at Wooler Youth Hostel, Northumberland (75–992278), and involving 4,000 feet (1,219 m) of climbing in the Cheviots. Participants must choose their own route between the four checkpoints. Time limit eight hours. Certificates to all finishers and an annual Challenge Cup to the winner. Organized by the Border and Dales Regional Group of the YHA.

Honorary Secretary, B & D Regional Group, YHA, 30 Baliol Square, Durham, DH1 3QH.

6 Chiltern Marathon

A 25-mile (40-km) circular route over the Chiltern Hills starting from Marlow, Buckinghamshire, which has to be completed in 9 hours. This is organized by the Middle Thames Ramblers and has been held annually in September since 1970. Certificates to successful individuals and teams of six or more.

Vince Smith, Glencairn, Green Road, Thorpe, Egham, Surrey, TW20 8WT.

7 The Crosses Walk

This tough event of 53 miles (85 km) over the North York Moors, starting and finishing at Goathland, has been held each July since 1972. It is an open event organized by the Scarborough and District Search and Rescue Team on behalf of the North York Moors Rescue Teams. The route visits ancient crosses on the moors and in some areas crosses private land for which special permission has to be obtained. Certificates to all finishing, with special awards for the first man (Moorcock Trophy), first woman (Moorhen Trophy), oldest finisher (Old Man of the Moors Trophy), youngest finisher (Ruth Russell Trophy) and for the team with the lowest aggregate time.

For an account of the early walks read 'The Crosses Walk'. Malcolm Boyes, *Dalesman*.

Mrs A. E. Hood, 21 St Peter's Street, Norton, Malton, Yorkshire, YO17 9AL.

8 Dalesman Hike

An event held annually since 1960 in the Yorkshire Dales. Entry is restricted to teams of young people between the ages of 15 and 20 inclusive. The event lasts two days with a compulsory overnight camp and involves tests of initiative as well as walking speed and skill.

Dalesman Hike, 5 St Andrew's Close, Southowram, Halifax.

9 Dorset Doddle

33 miles (53 km) and 5,000 feet (1,524 m) of ascent along a fine stretch of the South West Peninsula Coast Path from Weymouth to Swanage. Organized under the auspices of the Bournemouth Youth and Community Council in August each year since 1976.

Fred Daldry, YMCA, Westover Road, Bournemouth, BH1 2BS.

10 Downsman Hundred

This event, first held in 1973, was the forerunner of the ultra long distance walks arranged by the LDWA. The 100 miles (161 km) route starts in Winchester and finishes in East-bourne, including almost the whole of the South Downs in its length. A full route description and sketch maps are issued to those who take part. The time limit is 48 hours and on the last two promotions to date, held during the Spring Bank Holiday, over 100 walkers have successfully completed the challenge.

A. Blatchford, 11 Thorn Bank, Onslow Village, Guildford, Surrey, GU2 5PL.

11 Fellsman Hike

A very tough event of 59 miles (95 km) organized by the Keighley District Scout Service Team. The event has taken place every year since 1962. It is very popular and applications greatly outnumber places so that a draw is held in February or March. The route is over a series of mountains and stretches of moorland in the Yorkshire Dales National Park. A minimum amount of equipment must be carried and walkers are arranged into groups of four for the night. Walkers work out their own route between manned checkpoints. Successful participants receive a certificate and several trophies are awarded.

The Fellsman Hike, PO Box 30, Keighley, West Yorkshire, BD21 3EP.

12 Guildford Boundary Walk

An open event organized by the Guildford and Godalming Athletic Club since 1971 and held on alternate years in September. The event was inspired by the ancient custom of 'Beating the Bounds' and the route follows the 1933 boundary of Guildford, suitably modified to avoid private property and to make the walk more interesting. (22 miles or 35 km). Certificates are awarded to all individuals who finish within nine hours.

A. Blatchford, 11 Thorn Bank, Onslow Village, Guildford, Surrey, GU2 5PL.

13 High Peak Marathon

A very strenuous event of 40 miles (64 km) and 5,000 ft

(1,542 m) of climbing around the Derwent watershed in the High Peak of Derbyshire, commencing at Edale. The route consists mainly of wild and rough moorlands. The first recorded completion of the route was by Eustace Thomas, Norman Begg, Alf Schaanning, William Walker and Bill Humphrey in 1918. The organized event was first held in 1972 and now takes place annually during the winter months. Teams of four walkers must carry certain items of personal and team equipment which are checked before and during the event. A formidable list of manned checkpoints must be reached and time limits are set for specified points on the route. Teams are started at intervals after dark and must complete by dusk on the following day giving a maximum time of about 18 hours. A trophy is awarded to the fastest team and certificates to all walkers who complete.

Dr H. J. Prosser, 94 Green Drift, Royston, Hertfordshire.

14 Karrimor International Two Day Mountain Marathon

A very challenging event, first held in 1968, and staged annually in October in various areas of wild mountain country in England, Scotland or Wales. The exact location is not disclosed until near to the event. Entrants must carry all food and equipment for two days of walking and for a compulsory overnight camp on a high exposed site. In 1976 there were four classes:

1. Elite	40–50 miles (72–80 km)	10,000–15,000 ft (3,048–4,572 m) ascent
2. 'A' course	35–40 miles (56–64 km)	8,000–12,000 ft (2,438–3,657 m) ascent
3. 'B' course	30–35 miles (48–56 km)	up to 10,000 ft (3,048 m) ascent
4. Expedition course		

The first three events were highly competitive and prizes were awarded for the fastest performance, whilst certificates of competence were given to all in the fourth class who completed the course.

Karrimor International Ltd, Avenue Parade, Accrington, Lancashire.

15 Lake District Four 3000s

A very tough event held since 1965 and organized annually in June by the Ramblers' Association. The 46-mile (74-km) walk commences and finishes at Keswick, Cumbria, and involves the ascent of the four peaks over three thousand feet (914 m). A time limit of 22 hours is set with certificates to all who finish within that time.

C. H. Ford, 21 Hallsenna Road, Seascale, Cumbria, CA20 1JJ.

16 Long Mynd Hike

A tough event of 50 miles (80 km), organized by the 2nd Long Mynd Scout Group, and held annually in October since 1966. The route commences and finishes at Church Stretton in Shropshire and passes over a series of hills including Stiperstones, Long Mynd, Corndon, Black Rhadley, Ragleth and Caer Caradoc. The highest point is 1,731 ft (529 m) but the hills are steep-sided and give rough walking, much of which is at night. Each walker must carry certain items of equipment and determine his own route between manned checkpoints. Before dark all walkers are grouped into parties of three, which must be kept during the night. Certificates are given to all successful walkers, and a number of special trophies and prizes are also awarded.

Mrs Todd, 'Penshurst', Crossways, Church Stretton, Salop.

17 Mallerstang Marathon

An event first held in 1972, and now organized annually in June. The marathon starts and finishes at Garsdale Head Youth Hostel and follows a circular route to the north. Walkers, who must be YHA members and equipped with suitable clothing, must complete the 25 miles (40 km) within twelve hours to gain a certificate.

The route can also be completed at any time (see later).

Mr P. G. Gilks, c/o YHA Regional Office, 96 Main Street, Bingley, West Yorkshire, BD16 2JH.

18 Malvern Midsummer Marathon

A 35-mile (56-km) event organized by the Bristol and West Group of the Long Distance Walkers Association since 1977 and held each year on the Saturday nearest to midsummer day. The circular route is based on the Malvern Hills which rise to a height of 1,394 ft (425 m). A certificate to each walker who finishes within 14 hours.

A. Rowley, 17 Western Grange, Glebelands Road, Filton, Bristol, BS12 7BA.

19 Manx Mountain Marathon

Although primarily a fell race, this marathon now contains a separate Walkers' Class; participants must cover the 30 miles (48 km) in a maximum of eleven hours. The route involves 9,000 feet (2,743 m) of climbing.

A. C. Jones, Hon. Sec. Manx Mountain Marathon, 97 Silverburn, Ballasalla, Isle of Man.

20 Masters Hike

A tough walk of approximately 45 miles (64 km) over the moorlands of the Peak District organized by the Holme Valley District Scout Fellowship. The event is restricted to teams of four who must be members of the Scout or Guide movement and over 15 years of age. Each person and team must carry certain items of equipment. Certificates to all finishers.

P. Lenton, 35 Deercroft Crescent, Salendine Nook, Huddersfield.

21 Mid-Wales Mountain Walk

First held in 1963, and now annually in April, the route

involves 22 miles (35 km) and 7,000 ft (2,133 m) ascent, including the climbing of Cader Idris (2,927 ft or 893 m). The walk commences at Dinas Mawddwy Youth Hostel (124, 125–858139) and ends at Kings (Dolgellau) Youth Hostel (124–683161). Walkers must find their own route between checkpoints. Certain items of equipment must be carried.

Neville Tandy, 47 Lightwoods Road, Pedmore, Stourbridge, West Midlands, DY9 0TR.

22 Mourne Wall Walk

This event is organized by the Youth Hostel Association of Northern Ireland and has been held in County Down, Northern Ireland, each June since 1957. The route of 22 miles (35 km), involving 10,000 ft (3,048 m) climbing, is along the boundary wall of the Belfast Water Commissioners' catchment area and must be completed in twelve hours for the award of certificate and badge.

YHANI, 93 Dublin Road, Belfast, BT2 7HF.

23 One-Day International Walk

Held each September since 1975 this event is organized by the International Walking Section of British Airways Clubs. Two circular routes of 15½ and 25 miles (25 and 40 km) are followed by means of waymarks within Windsor Great Park, Berkshire. Participants who complete the route within the maximum times of six and ten hours respectively are awarded a medal.

International Walking Section, British Airways Engineering Base, PO Box No. 6, London Heathrow Airport, Hounslow, Middlesex.

24 Punchbowl Marathon

First held in 1962, and since then in alternate years, this event of 30 miles (48 km) starts and finishes at Witley, near

Godalming, Surrey. It is now organized by the Surrey Group
of the Long Distance Walkers Association. The route varies
but always includes the Devil's Punchbowl. Certificates to
all individuals and teams of six who complete the route
within ten hours.

Jeff Ellingham, 76 Church Road, Milford, Godalming,
Surrey.

25 Purbeck Plod

A challenge walk over 25 miles (40 km) first held in 1971
which, after a difficult start, is now popular. Starting from
Swanage the first nine miles of the walk are along the coast
which has been designated as an Area of Outstanding
Natural Beauty; the route then turns inland over the South
Dorset Downs and returns to Swanage. Normally held in
June.

Fred Daldry, YMCA, Westover Road, Bournemouth.

26 Reservoir Roundabout

An event of 17–20 miles (27–32 km) held over the wild moors
of the Elenith in central Wales, the route being circular and
around the Elan and Claerwen reservoirs. Held annually in
January since 1967. Walkers must find their own route between manned checkpoints and a limit is placed on the
number of entrants. Certificates to all finishers.

Neville Tandy, 47 Lightwoods Road, Pedmore, Stourbridge
West Midlands, DY9 0TR.

27 Ridgeway Walk

This walk has been held since 1962 and is now organized by
the Ridgeway Group, which mainly consists of ex-members
of the disbanded Reading YHA Group who were the original organizers. Normally held in May, and open to YHA,
RA and LDWA members only, the event commences near
Marlborough and follows the Ridgeway Path for 40 miles
(64 km) to the finish at Streatley-on-Thames Youth Hostel

(174–591806). A generous time limit of 14 hours is allowed.

Norman Griffin, 618 Wokingham Road, Earley, Reading, RG6 2HN.

28 Rodings Rally

Organized by the Walthamstow and Chingford Youth Hostel Association Local Group, teams of two to four walkers complete a course of approximately twelve miles (19 km) during the night. This event has been held annually each October–November in the Roding valley area of Essex since 1957. Participants must deduce the position of each checkpoint from the information given and then find them in numerical order. Checkpoints are usually well-hidden. Members of teams who find all checkpoints within eight hours receive a certificate. Special trophies are awarded to the fastest team and the YHA Group/Club with the three highest performing teams.

Cliff Hendon, 179 Peterborough Road, Leyton, E10 6HH.

29 Sevenoaks Circular Walk

A 30-mile (48-km) circuit around Sevenoaks organized annually since 1975 by the Kent Group of the Long Distance Walkers Association. Normally held in March. Participants have a maximum of ten hours to complete the course through a series of manned checkpoints.

Peter Rickards, 26 Childsbridge Lane, Kemsing, Sevenoaks, Kent.

30 South Wales 7 Peaks Marathon Walk

A tough event of about 45 miles (72 km) and 18,000 feet (5,490 m) ascent held each year normally in May. The route is between Capel-y-Ffin Youth Hostel, Abergavenny (161–250328) and Llanddeusant Youth Hostel (160–776245), crossing the Black Mountains, Brecon Beacons and Carmarthen Fans. Plaques to all successful finishers.

R. J. Barber, 2 Casba Terrace, Llanfoist, Abergavenny, Gwent.

31 Surrey Summits 100 km Walk

Organized by the Surrey Group of the Long Distance Walkers Association this event has been held each year in April since 1976. The 62 miles (100 km) route commences at Guildford and involves 16 summits and 1,000 ft (2,134 m) of ascent; it must be completed within 28 hours for award of a certificate.

The route can also be attempted at any time, a certificate being awarded for a completion under two days. Description of route, certificates and event details from Jeff Ellingham, 76 Church Road, Milford, Godalming, Surrey.

32 Tanners-Hindhead Walk

Normally held on a Saturday in February. Participants may either walk a fixed route or choose their own way between checkpoints from Tanners Hatch Youth Hostel, Surrey (187–140515), to Hindhead Youth Hostel (186–892368). The distance of 25–30 miles (40–48 km) must be covered in a maximum time of ten hours for the award of a certificate. A similar walk in the opposite direction may be undertaken on the following day.

G. Peddie, Tanners Hatch Youth Hostel, Polesden Lacey, Dorking, Surrey, RH5 6BE.

33 Tanners Marathon

Probably the most popular event in Britain. It is now organized by the Tanners Marathon Association (formerly by the Epsom and Ewell YHA Group) and has been held on the first Sunday in July since 1960. The route of 30 miles (48 km), starting at Leatherhead or Tanners Hatch Youth Hostel and finishing at the former, includes the North Downs and the hills further to the south. Certificates to all finishers within ten hours. Team certificates, YHA Group Trophy and School's Trophy are also awarded.

In 1969, 1970 and since then on alternate years, a 50-mile (80-km) event has also been run on the same day (Tanners Fifty). This must be accomplished within 15 hours for a certificate. A further event of ten miles (16 km) was added in 1974.

Alan Blatchford, 11 Thorn Bank, Onslow Village, Guildford, Surrey.

34 Teesdale Marathon

Organized by the Tyne-Tees Group of the Long Distance Walkers Association in September each year since 1977. The route is 25 miles (40 km) long over rough moorland starting and finishing at Middleton-in-Teesdale.

Tony Cresswell, 23 Burnopfield Gardens, Newcastle, Tyne and Wear.

35 Ten Tors Expedition

A very popular event held on Dartmoor each May since 1960 and restricted to teams of six persons between the ages of 14 and 19. The event takes place over two days with an overnight camp and involves routes of 35, 45 and 55 miles (56, 72 and 89 km) depending on age. Medals to all who finish by a certain time limit. A one-day special event is included for physically and mentally handicapped walkers.

The Co-ordinating Secretary, Ten Tors Expedition, HQ South West District, Beacon Barracks, Bulford Camp, Salisbury, SP4 9NY.

36 Three Peaks Trial

Held about March each year since 1963 and organized by the Cardiff YHA Group. The route starts from Abergavenny Gwent, and involves the ascent of the three main peaks of the area: Sugar Loaf (1,956 ft or 596 m), Skirrid Fawr (1,596 ft or 486 m) and Blorenge (1,834 ft or 559 m). The distance is about 18 miles (29 km) with approximately 4,500 ft (1,371 m) climbing.

R. J. Barber, 2 Casba Terrace, Llanfoist, Abergavenny, Gwent.

37 Vectis 30 Marathon Walk

A 50-kilometres route in the Isle of Wight held annually in October since 1969 and organized by the Hampshire/Berkshire Sub-regional Group of the YHA. The starting point, finishing point and route are varied each year. A time limit of ten hours for award of a certificate.

Hampshire/Berkshire Sub-regional Group, c/o South Region Youth Hostels Ltd, 58 Streatham High Road, London, SW16.

38 Welsh 1,000 Metres

First held in 1971 this event is really a fell race, but also includes Mountaineers' Classes which are suitable for walkers. The start is at Aber and the participants must reach the summits of the four peaks over 1,000 metres, i.e. Carnedd Llewelyn, Carnedd Dafydd, Crib-y-ddysgl and Yr Wyddfa. Normally held in June. The distance is about 20 miles (32 km).

Mrs J. H. Jones, Rhandirmwyn, Llandegai, Bangor, Gwynedd, LL57 4LD.

B CHALLENGE WALKS WHICH MAY BE ATTEMPTED AT ANY TIME

(Include a stamped, addressed envelope with any inquiries).

Colne to Rowsley

A walk of 70 miles (113 km) from Colne, Lancashire to Rowsley, Derbyshire which was first completed as a single walk in 1926 by Fred Heardman and John Firth Burton. It follows the high moorlands of the Pennines in a SW direction commencing over Boulsworth Hill and along the Pennine Way to Black Hill, then over Britland Edge Hill to the A628 before commencing the traverse of the eastern side of the Derwent watershed. The final section is along Stanage, Froggatt and Baslow Edges.

Lyke Wake Walk

History. Suggested by Bill Cowley in 1955 in *The Dalesman* magazine and first walked the same year. It is now completed by approximately 8,000 walkers each year, a total of 72,000 crossings having been recorded by end 1976.

Distance. 40 miles (64 km) with about 5,000 ft (1,524 m) climbing.

Starting point. Beacon Hill triangulation pillar, Scarth Wood Moor, near Osmotherley. (99–459997).

Finishing point. Raven Hall Hotel, Ravenscar, North York shire. (94–980018).

Route. Essentially a rough moorland walk almost due east over the North York Moors. Can be very wet after bad weather. Includes only about one mile of road.

Waymarking. Some have been provided, e.g. black discs marked LWW and other types. But the route is now well marked by the passage of many walkers.

Main interests. Fine views particularly in the early stages, old drove roads, prehistoric entrenchments, ancient stones and crosses, flagged causeways, Fylingdales Early Warning Station.

Accommodation. Youth hostels at Wheeldale (94–812983) and Boggle Hole (94–954040) but none near the start.

Guides. 'Lyke Wake Walk'. Bill Cowley, *Dalesman*.

Maps. North York Moors one-inch Tourist map. 93, 94, 99.

Badges. Walkers who complete the walk within 24 hours may apply for membership of the Lyke Wake Club. A Badge and Card of Condolence are provided for a small fee from Bill Cowley, Chief Dirger, Potto Hill, Swainby, Northallerton, Yorkshire. Members are known as Dirgers (males) or Witches (females) and higher orders exist for those who have completed several crossings! Send for circular before attempt.

Mallerstang Marathon

Although organized as an annual event this walk may also be attempted at any time for the award of a certificate. Walkers must stay at Garsdale Head Youth Hostel, North Yorkshire (98–796947) and complete the 25-mile (40-km) route within twelve hours.

The circular route offers very attractive scenery and follows high ridges and edges for most of its way, traversing the summits of High Seat (2,328 ft or 710 m), Nine Standards Rigg (2,171 ft or 662 m), Wild Boar Fell (2,324 ft or 708 m) and Swarth Fell (2,234 ft or 681 m).

Further details can be obtained from Garsdale Head Youth Hostel, Shaws, Lunds, Sedbergh, Cumbria, LA10 5PY.

Marsden-Edale Walk

First suggested by Ross Evans and developed by Cecil Dawson in 1902. Originally the tradition was to complete the 24-mile (39-km) route within a day by using a morning train to Marsden from Manchester and returning by a late train from Edale, but it may, of course, be completed in a longer or shorter time. The double journey was completed by Fred Heardman in 1923 and the triple journey by Don Morrison and Harry Gillot in 1968.

The route starts at Marsden station, West Yorkshire (110–047119), crosses Black Hill, Bleaklow and Kinder and finishes at Edale, Derbyshire (110–123858). Walkers may choose their own route.

North-South Surrey Walk

Approximately 39 miles (63 km) long from the most northerly to the most southerly points of Surrey; these are Laurel Close, Colnbrook (176–030771) and Chase Lane, on the edge of Black Down (186–914312) respectively. Other points nearby will be accepted however. Walkers may choose their own route. Originated by the Surrey Group of the LDWA.

Certificate and details from Keith Chesterton, 'Firle', Chestnut Avenue, St Catherines, Guildford, Surrey.

Saddleworth Five Trig Points Walk

A strenuous walk of about 20 miles (32 km) over the Saddleworth Moors and linking the triangulation points on Broadstone Hill, West Nab, Black Hill, Featherbed Moss and Alphin Pike. The route starts and finishes at the Clarence Hotel, Greenfield (110–002040) and consists mainly of rough, high moorland. The Pots and Pans obelisk and the Wessenden Reservoir must also be included.

Certificates and badges are awarded for successful completions (SAE and report required) from R. Tait, Physical Education Department, Oldham College of Technology, Rochdale Road, Oldham.

Six Shropshire Summits Walk

The six summits are Titterstone Clee, Brown Clee, Caer Caradoc, Long Mynd, Stiperstones and Corndon. The objective of the walk is to reach all six summits in one walk, commencing at Horseditch Cottages (129–594771) and finishing at Corndon (129–305969) or in the opposite direction. Walkers may devise their own routes but a total distance of about 35 miles (56 km) is involved. The walk was first completed by Vivian Bird and Philip Sharp in 1962.

Further information and certificates for successful completions may be obtained from V. Bird, *Sunday Mercury*, Colmore Circus, Birmingham 4.

Surrey Hills Walk

A 50-mile (80-km) walk traversing the county of Surrey from its Western border at Frensham Great Pond (186–842402) to the 'Old Ship' Public House at Tatsfield (187–418567) on the eastern border. This was first completed by walkers from the Surrey Constabulary on 17 March 1972. The route largely follows the Pilgrim's Way along the North Downs.

A 'Surrey Hills' Card is awarded to all who complete the route in a continuous walk of under 24 hours. Details of the walk should be sent to Bob Ball, c/o Surrey Police Headquarters, Guildford.

Tan Hill to Cat and Fiddle

A long distance walk of nearly 120 miles (193 km) between Tan Hill Inn, Cumbria (92–897067) and the Cat and Fiddle Inn, near Buxton, Cheshire (119–002719), which was devised by the Rucksack Club to celebrate their jubilee. It was completed by Vin Desmond, Frank Williamson and Ted Courtney during 5–7 June 1952, the shortest time being 54 hours 10 minutes. Any route can be chosen but it should be kept as far as possible upon high moorland. The original route included Great Shunner Fell, Great Whernside, Grassington, Todmorden, Black Hill and Edale.

Ten Reservoirs Walk

A circular walk of 22 miles (35 km) around the reservoirs of the Saddleworth Moors, starting and finishing at Dove Stone Reservoir (110–014034). Devised, like the Saddleworth Five Trig Points Walk, as a training exercise for members of the Oldham Mountain Rescue Team.

Information, certificates and badges from R. Tait, Physical Education Department, Oldham College of Technology, Rochdale Road, Oldham.

Three Peaks Walk of Yorkshire

The three peaks are Ingleborough (2,373 ft or 723 m), Whernside (2,419 ft or 736 m) and Pen-y-ghent (2,273 ft or 694 m) situated in the Yorkshire Dales National Park. The walker must reach the summits of the three mountains and return to the starting point within twelve hours. No particular route or starting point is specified, although an anti-clockwise route from Horton-in-Ribblesdale commencing with Pen-y-ghent is most used. Strictly speaking, there is no right of way to the summit of Whernside although the walk is very popular. The first record of the walk was in July 1887 by J. R. Wynne-Edwards and D. R. Smith, who completed the route in ten hours.

Guides

1. 'Walks in Limestone Country'. A. Wainwright, *Westmorland Gazette*.
2. 'Yorkshire's Three Peaks'. *Dalesman*.
3. 'Three Peaks Walk'. A. Gemmell. Route map.

A Three Peaks of Yorkshire Club exists for those who have completed the route. The membership fee includes a cloth badge and certificate of achievement. Before attempting the route, write for details to: Pen-y-ghent Stores, Horton-in-Ribblesdale, Yorkshire, BD24 0HE.

PEAK-BAGGING

Mountain climbing has a particular fascination of its own and there are almost endless opportunities for 'challenges' in the mountain areas. Some may take virtually a whole lifetime to accomplish, e.g. the ascent of all British mountains over 3,000 ft (914 m), whilst in other cases the objective is much more limited, e.g. the climbing of all mountains in a given area in one expedition or in the fastest time possible.

A difficulty is immediately encountered. How does one define a mountain? It is necessary not merely to specify some minimum height, but also to distinguish between a separate peak and a mere undulation on a long ridge.

It is fairly generally accepted that within the British Isles a mountain is any height of 2,000 ft (610 m) or more. Separate peaks of 3,000 ft (914 m) or more are usually called 'Munros', although the term should strictly be applied only to mountains in Scotland. The term is derived from Sir Hugh

Thomas Munro who prepared in 1891 a list of all peaks of 3,000 ft, or more in Scotland. This list was later published in the journal of the Scottish Mountaineering Club. It is now revised regularly (after re-surveys) and published as a separate volume (see below). It lists 279 Munros and 262 other Tops (1974).

Munro's tables accept a peak as a 'Munro' if it is separated from another peak by a drop of at least 500 ft (152 m) or by a considerable distance or by some notable obstacle. A 'Munro Top' must be separated by a drop of at least 75 ft (23 m) from another peak and must have 'some kind of individuality'. Nick Wright in his book 'English Mountain Summits' used a somewhat different system; he included all summits marked on the one-inch Ordnance Survey maps which were 2,000 ft or more in height and which were enclosed by an individual contour line (contour lines were at 50 ft intervals).

The 1974 edition of Munro's tables is the first metric edition and gives the height of each Top in both feet and metres. Metrication is already resulting in yet more ingenious 'challenges'.

Some of the best-known challenge walks are:

1 *Climbing the Munros*

The climbing of all the Munros of Scotland was first completed by A. E. Robertson in 1901. A. R. G. Burn was the first person to complete both Munros and Tops finishing in 1923. By 1972 one hundred and seven people had completed all the Munros. They have also been climbed in one expedition. This astonishing feat was accomplished by Hamish Brown who climbed the 279 summits between 4 April and 24 July 1974; the journey involving 449,000 ft (136,855 m) of ascent and 1,639 miles (2,639 km) of walking.

2 *Local groups of Munros*

The climbing of convenient groups of Munros in one expedition. Examples are the Arrochar Munros, the Glen Nevis Munros, the Munros of the Mamores and so on.

3 *The Welsh 3,000s*

A classic walk which involves the ascent of the 14 peaks of
Wales which are over 3,000 ft (914 m) in one expedition.
Most attempts start at Pen-y-Pass (115–647557) and finish
at Aber (115–655727), involving nearly 30 miles (48 km) of
walking and 12,000 ft (3,657 m) ascent. The peaks are
usually taken in the order:

1	Crib Goch	3,023 ft (921 m)	8	Tryfan	3,010 ft (917 m)
2	Crib-y-ddysgl	3,493 ft (1,065 m)	9	Pen-yr-ole-wen	3,210 ft (979 m)
3	Yr Wyddfa	3,560 ft (1,085 m)	10	Carnedd Dafydd	3,426 ft (1,044 m)
4	Elidir Fawr	3,029 ft (924 m)	11	Carnedd Llewelyn	3,484 ft (1,062 m)
5	Y Garn	3,104 ft (946 m)	12	Yr Elen	3,152 ft (961 m)
6	Glyder Fawr	3,279 ft (999 m)	13	Foel Grach	3,195 ft (974 m)
7	Glyder Fach	3,262 ft (994 m)	14	Foel Fras	3,091 ft (942 m)

An account of one attempt is included in the best-selling
book 'I Bought a Mountain'. Thomas Firbank, George G.
Harrap: New English Library.

4 *English 3,000s or Lake District 3,000s*

The four mountains over 3,000 ft (914 m) can be reached in
a single expedition:

1	Scafell	3,162 ft (964 m)	3	Helvellyn	3,118 ft (950 m)
2	Scafell Pike	3,210 ft (977 m)	4	Siddaw	3,053 ft (931 m)

There are also 3 subsidiary Tops.

5 *The Four Thousands*

There are eight Munros (13 Tops) over 4,000 ft (1,220 m); four in Lochaber and the remaining four in the Cairngorms. These have all been climbed in a single expedition using a car between the two principal mountain masses. In 1954 members of the Rucksack Club also climbed the peaks but walked the entire distance, 98 miles (158 km) and 13,000 ft (3,962 m) of ascent.

The traverses of the 4,000 ft peaks of either group also make attractive challenges. The four Cairngorm Munros in a round trip from Glenmore Lodge (36–986095), for example.

6 *The Cuillin Ridge*

The main mountain mass of the Island of Skye, off the west coast of Scotland, is termed the Cuillin and is made up of two areas, separated by Glen Sligachan, which are very different in character. The Red Cuillin is composed of reddish granite and the mountains are steep but rounded, whilst the Black Cuillin is mainly formed from black gabbro and the mountains are rock peaks with great crags and screes. Unlike most other British mountains the first ascent of many of the peaks of the Black Cuillin have been recorded, the last as recently as 1898.

The main ridge of the Black Cuillin is in the form of a 19-mile horseshoe around Loch Coruisk and comprises twenty peaks, many of them with several minor summits or pinnacles. The first traverse of the ridge in a single expedition was completed in 1911 by L. G. Shadbolt and A. G. MacLaren. Later climbers have added the peaks of Blaven and Clach Glas to the traverse of the main ridge, this being termed the Greater Traverse.

The complete traverse of the Black Cuillin in summertime offers the finest ridge walk in the British Isles with rough scrambling and spectacular views. It is not a proposition, however, for the pure walker as four recognized rock climbs have to be negotiated:

     1. The Thearlaich-Dubh gap
     2. King's Chimney on Sgurr Mhic Coinnich
     3. The Inaccessible Pinnacle
     4. The Bhasteir Tooth

Route finding on the ridge can be difficult in mist and compasses are unreliable. There is also a complete absence of drinking water which must therefore be carried. In winter conditions the ridge is a very hard climb, only possible to experienced mountaineers.

For excellent descriptions read:

1. 'Long Days in the Hills'. A. H. Griffin, Robert Hale.
2. 'Scottish Climbs: Volume 2'. Hamish MacInnes, Constable.

7 *The highest peaks*

In England, Wales and Scotland these are Scafell Pike, Snowdon and Ben Nevis respectively and these have all been climbed within 24 hours using fast car transport between the three mountain groups. This has also been achieved (but not within 24 hours!) as a walk without transport.

8 *County tops*

The highest points in the counties of the United Kingdom are listed in the 'Guinness Book of Records'.

Records have now been claimed for a majority of these challenges, but these are held mostly by very fit and hardy fell-runners and walkers stand no real chance of approaching their performances.

For lists of British mountains consult:

1. 'Munro's tables of the 3,000-feet mountains of Scotland and other tables of lesser heights'. Ed. J. C. Donaldson, Scottish Mountaineering Trust: West Col Productions. 1974 (1st Metric Edition).
   This also includes lists of the 2,500-feet summits with a

re-ascent of 500 feet on all sides (Corbett's tables) and
2,000-feet hills in the Lowlands (Donald's tables).
2. 'English Mountain Summits'. Nick Wright, Hale.
3. 'The Mountains of England and Wales'. George Bridge,
West Col.

CHAPTER 10

Walking Abroad

It is obviously impossible to deal adequately with a subject of this magnitude within the space of one chapter. In fact it would be necessary to devote at least three chapters (say, the equivalent of Chapters 7, 8 and 9) to each country to begin to do justice to the subject. This has therefore been restricted to a brief description of some of the possibilities that exist, indicating where further information can be obtained.

It is possible to spend a lifetime walking within the British Isles and never tire of the wonderful variety of its scenery. At the same time it must be recognized that some really magnificent walking country exists elsewhere and most of it is still comparatively unknown to the vast majority of British walkers. France, for example, has a network of over 12,000 miles (19,311 km) of long distance footpaths; the most spectacular of which is probably The Great Crossing of the French Alps which runs for 250 miles (403 km) from the Lake of Geneva to the Mediterranean coast. The Federal Republic of Germany has 52 National Parks which contain approximately 25,000 miles (40,250 km) of waymarked trails with 1,500 mountain refuges or huts. Further afield are the ultra-long distance trails of the United States: for example the Appalachian Trail (2,000 miles [3,220 km]) and the Finger Lakes Trail (650 miles [1,047 km]). Even a far-away place such as Nepal, which was virtually closed to visitors until 1954, is now visited by many trekking parties which reach, for example, the site of the Everest base camps or the Annapurna Sanctuary.

You may find that there are some special problems in rambling abroad. It can be difficult to obtain information on walking areas and routes, particularly as brochures and guide-books are not usually written in English. This is one reason, among several, why organized walking holidays are so popular, and these probably provide the best way to start your walking overseas. But, however you go, I hope that you will be attracted by those far-away places; they are waiting for *you*.

ORGANIZED WALKING HOLIDAYS

Some national organizations and travel agents offer organized walking holidays in Europe and elsewhere. These tend to fall into two classes: (*a*) holidays at fixed centres from which optional walking excursions are arranged, and (*b*) treks using guest houses, mountain huts and camp sites. They vary enormously in length, cost and difficulty.

An example of one of the easier walking holidays is a fortnight's stay in the Alpbach Valley of the Tyrol. Members stay at a hotel which is well-provided with facilities such as tennis courts and heated swimming pool. Easy rambles of less than five hours duration are arranged in the hills surrounding the village. An example of a very demanding holiday is a high altitude trek in the Himalayas, for example to Rolwaling Himal. These last normally from three to four weeks and are suitable only for very fit walkers who have had previous experience in the use of ropes, ice-axe and crampons under winter hill-walking conditions. To secure a place it is necessary to obtain a doctor's certificate and to supply details of previous experience. A large number of graded holidays are offered between these two extremes.

Some of the organizations which offer holidays are:

The Countrywide Holidays Association (Chapter 11).

The Holiday Fellowship Ltd (Chapter 11).

Ramblers' Holidays Ltd, Longcroft House, Fretherne Rd, Welwyn Garden City, Hertfordshire. Welwyn Garden 31133.

Sherpa Expeditions, 3 Bedford Road, Chiswick, London, W4. 01 994 7668.

Thomas Cook Ltd, PO Box 36, Peterborough, PE3 6SB. Peterborough 63200.

Waymark Holidays Ltd, 295 Lillie Road, London, SW6 7LL. 01 385 5015.

NATIONAL TOURIST OFFICES

National Tourist Offices are excellent sources of information on travel, accommodation and the more popular tourist attractions. Usually, however, they will be able to provide little information on walking routes, maps and guide-books, although there are some exceptions to this. But they are worth consulting for the more general information.

Austrian National Tourist Office, 20 St George Street, London, W1. 01 629 0461.

Belgian National Tourist Office, 66 Haymarket, London, SW1. 01 930 9618.

Bulgarian National Tourist Office, 126 Regent Street, London, W1. 01 437 2611.

Czechoslovak Travel Bureau Cedok (London) Ltd, 17 Old Bond Street, London, W1. 01 629 6058.

Cyprus High Commission, Tourist Information Office, 211 Regent Street, London, W1. 01 734 2593.

Danish Tourist Board, Sceptre House, 169 Regent Street, London, W1. 01 734 2637.

Danube Tourist Agency, 6 Conduit Street, London, W1. 01 493 0263.

Egyptian Tourist Information Centre, 62a Piccadilly, London, W1. 01 493 5282.

Finnish Tourist Board, Finland House, 56 Haymarket, London, SW1. 01 839 4048.

French Tourist Office, 178 Piccadilly, London, W1. 01 491 7622.

German Tourist Information Bureau, 61 Conduit Street, London, W1. 01 734 2600.

Iceland Tourist Information Bureau, Icelandair, 73 Grosvenor Street, London, W1. 01 499 9971.

Irish Tourist Office, 150 New Bond Street, London, W1. 01 493 3201.

Israel Government Tourist Office, 59 St James's Street, London, SW1. 01 493 2431.

Luxembourg National Trade and Tourist Office, 66 Haymarket, London, SW1. 01 930 8906.

Moroccan Tourist Office, 174 Regent Street, London, W1. 01 437 0073.

National Tourist Organization of Greece, 195 Regent Street, London, W1. 01 734 5997.

Netherlands National Tourist Office, 143 New Bond Street, London, W1. 01 499 9367.

Norwegian National Tourist Office, 20 Pall Mall, London, SW1. 01 839 6255.

Polish Travel Office (ORBIS), 313 Regent Street, London, W1. 01 580 8028.

Portuguese National Tourist Office, 1 New Bond Street, London, W1. 01 493 3873.

Rumanian National Tourist Office, 98 Jermyn Street, London, SW1. 01 930 8812.

Spanish National Tourist Office, 57 St James Street, London, SW1. 01 499 0901.

Swedish National Tourist Office, 3 Cork Street, London, SW1. 01 437 5816.

Swiss National Tourist Office, Swiss Centre, 1 New Coventry Street, London, W1. 01 734 1921.

Tunisian National Tourist Office, 7a Stafford Street, London, W1. 01 499 2234.

Turkish Tourism Information Office, 49 Conduit Street, London, W1. 01 734 8681.

Yugoslav National Tourist Office, 143 Regent Street, London, W1. 01 734 8714.

An excellent book is the 'Youth Hosteller's Guide to Europe' from YHA Services Ltd. This book is a mine of information on 22 countries, describing the geography, history, climate, people, etc. of each as well as some useful information on walking areas.

MAPS

Maps can be obtained within the United Kingdom for most European and Mediterranean countries. The style and scale of these will vary considerably however from country to country.

In general most western European countries have official survey organizations which have produced maps at scales of 1 : 25 000 and/or 1 : 50 000 (or similar) for the whole or a substantial part of their region. In some countries private companies have produced similar series, e.g. Freytag and Berndt for Austria. Maps at these scales can be obtained for Austria, Belgium, Denmark, France, West Germany, Holland, Iceland, Italy, Luxembourg, Norway, Portugal, Spain and Switzerland. In other countries the largest scale available will be 1 : 100 000 or higher. Finland and some areas of North Africa have been covered at 1 : 100 000; whilst Greece, Sweden and eastern European countries are generally at 1 : 200 000. Small areas, of particular interest to tourists, may be mapped in more detail however at larger scales; e.g. some of the mountain areas of Sweden have maps at 1 : 100 000. Footpaths are usually marked on the larger scale maps.

A wide variety of maps may be obtained or ordered through Edward Stanford Ltd, 12 Long Acre, London, WC2. 01 836 1321.

LONG DISTANCE FOOTPATHS

Long distance routes have been developed in a number of countries. Within Europe those of France and Germany are particularly good.

In France approximately 20,000 km of footpaths have now been waymarked. This is the work of Le Comité National des Sentiers de Grande Randonnée (National Committee for Long Distance Footpaths) which was established in 1947. Generally, these footpaths are created from public rights-of-way and are well waymarked with painted red and white flashes and square metal plaques bearing the number of the path. The Committee has prepared a series of 'Topo-guides' which cover most of the routes. These are written in French and give a detailed description of the route as well as useful information such as accommodation, places of interest, transport, etc. A quarterly journal is published which provides information on changes to the footpath system.

In addition to the routes created by national associations The European Ramblers' Association has established six European Long Distance Footpaths. These are:

1. 2,402 km North Sea-Lake of Constance–Gotthard–Mediterranean.
2. 2,089 km Holland–Mediterranean.
3. 2,292 km Atlantic–Ardennes–Forest of Bohemia.
4. 2,150 km Pyrenees–Jura–Neusiedlersee.
5. 600 km Lake of Constance–Adriatic Sea.
6. 2,776 km Baltic Sea–Wachau–Adriatic Sea.

Guide-books to these paths have been published which give route descriptions and sketch maps.

Topo-guides can be obtained from: Edward Stanford Ltd. (See Maps.)

Comité National des Sentiers de Grand Randonnée, 92 Rue de Clignancourt, 75883 Paris Cedex 18.

Sekretariat, European Ramblers' Association, Hospitalstrasse 21B, D-7000 Stuttgart 1.

Guides for European Long Distance Footpaths obtainable from J. Fink Verlag, Gebelsbergstrasse 41, D-7000 Stuttgart 1.

THE INTERNATIONAL YOUTH HOSTEL FEDERATION

The Youth Hostels Association (England and Wales) is responsible for the management of all youth hostels within England and Wales. All European countries and many others further afield have similar national associations which manage the hostels within their own regions. These national associations work together through the International Youth Hostel Federation. A member of any national Youth Hostel Association is automatically eligible to use the hostels in any other country throughout the world. At present there are more than 4,000 hostels in nearly 50 countries.

Hostels are run on very similar lines in all countries, but the rules may differ in details from one to another. The table below gives some information on the hostel situation in Europe and the Mediterranean area. It is for general guidance only as special rules may apply in some countries.

With some exceptions advance bookings must be made directly to the youth hostel concerned, but requests for information about youth hostels in other countries should be made initially to the inquirer's own association.

The general information below regarding hostels and the rules of each national association was taken from:

'The International Youth Hostel Handbook'. 1977.
Volume 1, Europe and Mediterranean countries.
Volume 2, Africa, America, Asia, Australasia.

Country	Number of Hostels	Age Limits Min./Max.		Normal Maximum Length of Stay (nights)	Hostel Density (sq. miles/ hostel)
Austria	96	5	—	3	337
Belgium					
(a) Vlaanderen	20	5	—	3 ⎫	280
(b) Wallonie	22	5	—	3 ⎭	
Bulgaria	30	5	—	3 or 5	1,428
Cyprus	6	5	—	3	595
Czechoslovakia	44	10	—	3	1,112
Denmark	80	5	—	3	207
Egypt (UAR)	12	6	—	3	32,176
Finland	90	5	—	3	1,446
France	177	7	—	3	1,234
Germany (West)	546	6	—	3	176
Greece	30	5	—	5	1,698
Hungary	21	15	—	3	1,710
Iceland	6	5	—	3	6,600
Ireland (Eire)	47	5	—	3	553
Israel	29	5	—	3	276
Italy	52	5	—	3	2,336
Luxembourg	10	8	35	3	100
Morocco	8	5	—	3	20,750
Netherlands	50	10	—	3	316

Country	Number of Hostels	Age Limits Min./Max.		Normal Maximum Length of Stay (nights)	Hostel Density (sq. miles/ hostel)
Norway	99	5	—	3	1,264
Poland	236	10	—	3	511
Portugal	12	7	—	3	2,875
Spain	75	10	—	3	2,622
Sweden	176	5	—	5	984
Switzerland	98	6	—	—	163
Syria	8	—	—	3	8,850
Tunisia	17	17	—	3	2,646
Yugoslavia	34	7	—	—	2,904
England & Wales	253	5	—	3-4	231
Northern Ireland	12	5	—	3	454
Scotland	77	5	—	—	378

Notes on Table

1. It should be noted that some countries, e.g. Austria and Poland, have many simple refuges or huts available for overnight stay in addition to the hostels listed.

2. Age limits. The minimum age limits given are for children accompanied by an adult relative, but unaccompanied children under 14 may not use hostels outside their own country. In some countries preference is shown to younger hostellers.

3. Hostel density. Obtained by dividing the total area of a country by the number of hostels within it. It should be appreciated, of course, that the distribution of hostels within a country is not necessarily (or usually) uniform. In the case of certain Mediterranean countries the data given is based upon the boundaries prior to 1967.

ORGANIZED WALKS (MARCHES)

Organized group walks, attracting large numbers of participants, are a popular feature of the walking scene in many European countries.

They originated in Holland over sixty years ago when a small organization, the Netherlands League for Physical Culture, began to hold group walks over a four day period each year starting from various centres. This grew enormously in popularity and eventually became established at Nijmegan. The four-day event, held in July each year, now attracts up to 18,000 walkers, of which many are from the armed forces and police, and enormous crowds of spectators. Each participant enters one of several classes and is required to cover a fixed distance on each day of the event. The route lies almost entirely along hard roads. A medal is awarded on the successful completion of the four walks. The event is essentially non-competitive, the main feature being the spirit of friendliness which is generated.

Similar events, usually called Marches, are now held in many other countries throughout Europe. One of this type held within the United Kingdom is the One-day International Walk (Chapter 9). A similar event is the International Four-Days' Walks held in June each year at Castlebar in Eire.

Many events are advertised only locally and it may be difficult to obtain information.

Nijmegan Marches Secretariat, 18 Valkenbosplein, The Hague, Netherlands.

The Secretary, International Four-Days' Walks, Castlebar, Co. Mayo, Eire.

CHAPTER 11

Useful Organizations

BACKPACKERS CLUB

Formed in 1972 by Peter Lumley and Michael Marriott to promote and protect the interests of the lightweight walker-camper. The President is John Hillaby.

It aims to protect rights of access to footpaths and areas of countryside, to encourage the use of long distance footpaths, National Parks and open areas, to campaign for the establishment of similar areas both in the UK and in Europe generally and to encourage and aid the development of lightweight camping, walking and camping equipment.

The Club has a comprehensive advisory and information service on back-packing and will also provide information on routes. A Back-packers Club Confidential Farm Pitch Directory is supplied on joining the Club and the newsletter 'Backchat' is published bi-monthly. A special discount service for use at specialized retailers and an insurance scheme are available to members. Camping week-ends are held monthly in various parts of the country for most of the year and an annual general meeting held centrally in May.

Mr E. R. Gurney, Honorary National Organizing Secretary, Backpackers Club, 20 St Michael's Road, Tilehurst, Reading, Berkshire, RG3 4RP. Reading 28754.

BRITISH NATURALISTS' ASSOCIATION (BENA)

The Association was formed in 1905 by E. Kay Robinson and was originally known as the British Empire Naturalists' Association.

It is concerned with the study and protection of wild life and the preservation of the countryside. The Association has 18 local branches which arrange their own programme of meetings, lectures, exhibitions, one-day and week-end rambles and field weeks. It also publishes literature on natural history.

Membership is open to the public on payment of an annual subscription, branches charging a small additional subscription. Members may take part in all activities and also receive a copy of 'Country-Side', three times per year, and the Bulletin which contains details of branch activities.

Hon. Secretary, The British Naturalists' Association, 'Willowfield', Boyneswood Road, Four Marks, Alton, Hampshire, GU34 5EA.

BRITISH ORIENTEERING FEDERATION

Orienteering is basically a competitive sport in which participants are required to navigate through a series of control points using map and compass. Generally, the total distance involved is between one and eight miles and the emphasis is on speed, accuracy of map-reading and the ability to select the best route. It is however a sport for all ages and abilities regardless of how fast they want to travel.

A good book for the beginner is:

'Orienteering'. B. M. Henley, EP Publishing.

British Orienteering Federation, National Office, Lea Green, Near Matlock, Derbyshire, DE4 5GJ. Dethick 628.

THE CAMPING CLUB OF GREAT BRITAIN AND IRELAND

Formed in 1901 by a group of cyclists, who also had an interest in camping, it has grown considerably both in membership and in the scope of its activities.

It represents the interests of 'campers' in the widest sense from the backpacker to the family using a large frame tent on holiday and even the users of motor or trailer caravans.

The main authority is the National Council, but membership is divided into region and district organizations who organize their own programme of activities. There is a staff of full-time officials. There are also a number of subsidiary groups which cater for specialist interests such as boating, folk dancing and mountaineering.

Membership is currently about 175,000. Each member receives a monthly magazine and a Sites List and Handbook every two years which lists among many others all camp-sites either owned by the Club or run by them in conjunction with local authorities. Special foreign touring and limited free insurance facilities are also offered.

The Camping Club of Great Britain and Ireland Ltd, 11 Lower Grosvenor Place, London, SW1W 0EY. 01 828 1012.

THE CHILTERN SOCIETY

The Chiltern Society was the inspiration of Christopher Hall and Lord Castle and was formally established at a public meeting at High Wycombe on 8 May 1965.

The object of the Society is to stimulate public interest in and care for the beauty, history and amenities of the area of the Chiltern Hills. The work is carried out by eight largely autonomous groups which arrange their own programmes and deal with all matters arising within their defined areas. These groups cover waymarking and maintenance of rights of way, restoration and protection of historic works and buildings, threats to natural resources, protection of trees and woodlands, clearance of litter, surveillance of planning applications, local transport and the preservation of com-mons. The Rights-of-Way group also organizes week-end walks and has prepared a series of local footpath maps. The society magazine is the Chiltern News.

Currently there are over 3,000 individual members with 230 affiliated organizations.

Membership Secretary, The Chiltern Society, Miss P. M. Watt, 9 Kings Road, Berkhamstead, Hertfordshire.

COMMONS, OPEN SPACES AND FOOTPATHS PRESERVATION SOCIETY

A Society, known as The Commons Preservation Society, was founded on 19 July 1865 at a meeting held in the Inner Temple in London; the aim of the Society being the preservation of commons in and around London. Almost immediately the Society was involved in several law suits, notably those involving Hampstead Heath, Wimbledon Common and Epping Forest. In 1899 the Society amalgamated with the National Footpaths Society to form the Commons and Footpaths Preservation Society; the present title being adopted in 1910.

The objects are to preserve commons, public open spaces, greens, footpaths and bridleways and to protect the beauty and promote the fullest enjoyment by the public of the countryside. The Society notes all applications for the inclosure of common land and path extinguishment or diversion orders and enters objections where appropriate. It acts as a pressure group on the Government. Finally, it advises local authorities, other amenity bodies and individuals on the protection of open spaces and rights of way. It has published several books on the law of commons, footpaths and bridleways.

Membership is open to individuals and public bodies. Members receive the Society's journal and copies of any new publications.

Commons, Open Spaces and Footpaths Preservation Society, Suite 4, 166 Shaftesbury Avenue, London, WC2H 8JH. 01 836 7220.

COUNCIL FOR THE PROTECTION OF RURAL ENGLAND

The CPRE was founded on 7 December 1926. Its aims are:
1. To protect the beauty of the English countryside from disfigurement and injury.

2. To act as a centre for obtaining and giving advice and information on matters affecting the protection of rural scenery.
3. To rouse public opinion to an understanding of the importance of this work and the need to promote it.

It is a registered charity which is dependent entirely upon subscriptions, voluntary contributions and bequests. It has a national office in London with seven full-time senior staff, 41 county branches, about 200 local branches and 31,000 members. Generally speaking, the county and local branches look after matters at local level whilst the headquarters is concerned with affairs at the national level. Similar organizations exist for Scotland and Wales.

Council for the Protection of Rural England, 4 Hobart Place, London, SW1W 0HY. 01 235 9481.
Association for the Preservation of Rural Scotland, 20 Falkland Avenue, Newton Mearns, Renfrewshire, G77 5DR. 041 639 2069.
Council for the Protection of Rural Wales, 14 Broad Street, Welshpool, Powys, SY21 7SD. Welshpool 2525.

COUNTRYSIDE COMMISSION

The Countryside Commission is an independent statutory body established under the Countryside Act (1968). 'It seeks to reduce the conflict between town and country interests through the development of an understanding of the countryside and care for it, and through help with the provision of facilities and services for visitors to the countryside.'

The Commission has approximately 15 members who are appointed jointly by the Secretary of State for the Environment and the Secretary of State for Wales. The staff of the Commission are civil servants. A separate committee, set up by the Commission, deals specifically with work in Wales. The Countryside Commission receives a grant from the Government to finance its own projects.

The main activities of the Commission are listed below. Further information can be found in Chapters 7 and 8.

1. *The National Parks.* This is the main field of activity of the Commission. It is responsible for designating areas of wild country as National Parks. The parks, once established, are then administered locally by National Park boards or committees which are financed separately. The Commission however continues to advise and assist on their planning and management.
2. *Areas of Outstanding Natural Beauty.* The Commission designates certain areas as AONB's and is consulted about developments within them.
3. Assists local government and private owners to provide recreation facilities, e.g. country parks and picnic sites, by advice and grant aid.
4. Promotes the development of information services, e.g. the provision of study centres, information centres and guided walks.
5. Provides and maintains National Long Distance Routes.
6. Advances knowledge of countryside recreation and conservation by initiating research and experimental work and communicating the results widely.
7. Advises on issues of importance to the countryside, e.g. National Park organization, development control, conservation and recreation management.
8. Liaises with other government agencies and voluntary organizations working in the same field.

Brochures on National Parks, National Long Distance Routes and other subjects are available on request.

Countryside Commission, John Dower House, Crescent Place, Cheltenham, Gloucestershire, GL50 3RA. Cheltenham 21381.

COUNTRYSIDE COMMISSION FOR SCOTLAND

The Commission was established under the Countryside (Scotland) Act 1967. There are no National Parks, Areas of

Outstanding Natural Beauty or National Long Distance Routes in Scotland at present. Otherwise the duties of the Commission are broadly similar to those of the Countryside Commission.

Countryside Commission for Scotland, Battleby, Redgorton, Perth, PH1 3EW. Perth 27921.

THE COUNTRY-WIDE HOLIDAYS ASSOCIATION

The CHA was officially formed in 1897 as the Co-operative Holidays Association which set out 'to provide recreative and educational holidays by purchasing or renting and furnishing houses and rooms in selected centres, by catering in such houses for parties of members and guests and by securing helpers who will promote the intellectual and social interests of the party with which they are associated'.

It was the inspiration of T. Arthur Leonard who in 1891 began to organize holidays from the Congregational Church in Colne, Lancashire, of which he was the minister. The first property, the Abbey House at Whitby, was leased in 1896.

The Association now owns 21 guest houses situated throughout the British Isles and also holds tenancies of several other centres during the peak holiday period. These provide full accommodation for walkers and a wide variety of optional excursions which vary from easy rambling to strenuous fell-walking. Guests provide their own entertainment in the evenings under the general direction of a host and/or hostess.

Adventure Holidays for young people are also offered a well as special midweek holidays giving tuition in a variety of subjects such as bridge and photography. A number of holidays abroad are also now arranged including very ambitious ones to the Himalayas.

Guests automatically become members of the Association for one year after taking a CHA holiday and may re-new membership for a further year for a small fee. There are currently 20,000 members with 1,000 life members. About 100 local rambling groups have been formed throughout the country. Members receive copies of the holiday brochures and two issues of the CHA magazine each year.

The Country-wide Holidays Association, Birch Heys, Cromwell Range, Manchester, M14 6HU. 061-224 2887.

DEPARTMENT OF THE ENVIRONMENT

The DOE, Welsh and Scottish Offices are responsible for the conservation, maintenance and display of buildings and sites of historical interest within the United Kingdom.

At present over 700 monuments and buildings are in care of the State and are open to visitors. In addition, the owners of houses of historical interest may be given grants on condition that they open their properties to the public over reasonable periods; over 1,800 buildings have been assisted under this scheme since 1953. The Departments also maintain lists of buildings and sites of particular architectural or historical interest which then acquire extra protection from demolition or unsightly alterations; designate conservation areas (3,000 have been designated since 1967), provide grants for excavation, conducts research and provide an advisory service on conservancy.

A large number of guides to ancient monuments and historic buildings have been published. A season ticket can be purchased which admits the holder to all ancient monuments in the care of the Department.

HMSO Publications (inquiries and catalogues): Her Majesty's Stationery Office, Atlantic House, Holborn Viaduct, London, EC1P 1BN. 01 583 9876. [Sectional List 27 for Ancient Monuments and Historic Buildings].

Other guides from DOE (London), Welsh Office (Cardiff) and Scottish Office (Edinburgh).

THE EXMOOR SOCIETY

The Society was formed in 1958 as a branch of the Council for the Protection of Rural England, mainly as a result of a campaign against afforestation led by John Coleman-Cooke.

It is concerned with the conservation of Exmoor, watching and, whenever necessary, fighting against any proposal which is likely to damage the character of that area. It has also been involved in several appeals which have raised funds for the purchase of important properties; for example the endowment of Woody Bay which is a property of the National Trust.

It publishes a Newsletter and an annual magazine called *The Exmoor Review*, organizes social events and is building up a collection of photographs and reference books at its headquarters.

The Exmoor Society, Parish Rooms, Dulverton, Somerset. Dulverton 23335.

FIELD STUDIES COUNCIL

The Field Studies Council is a registered charity which exists to promote a better understanding of our environment and the way we use it. It was founded in 1943 by Francis Butler.

The Council runs ten Field Centres in England and Wales, which provide courses on a wide range of subjects concerned with the natural environment. Nine centres offer residential courses usually of one week duration, whilst one is a day-centre. The courses generally run from Wednesday to Wednesday but some shorter courses are available. Some non-residential courses are offered for those who wish to stay in local hotels, and a few centres offer family courses with baby sitting in the evening. In 1976 more than two hundred courses were planned for adults at the residential centres alone. Subjects covered include landscape painting, nature photography, bird watching, church architecture, spring flowers and garden botany. Each course is supervised by an expert in the subject studied. The residential field centres are mostly converted country houses.

Membership of the Council is open to anyone interested in using a field centre or in the work of the Council. Members receive a course programme and an annual report.

Information Office, FSC, Preston Montford, Montford Bridge, Shrewsbury, SY4 1HW.

FORESTRY COMMISSION

The Forestry Commission was established in 1919, with the object of growing reserves of timber sufficient to serve as a national reserve for a limited period of three years in the event of war, assisting private afforestation, carrying out research and encouraging forest industries. Several Government policy statements have modified these objectives.

Essentially the Commission acts in two ways: (*a*) As Forest Authority it is concerned with the general duty of promoting the interests of forestry by research, dissemination of forestry knowledge, administration of schemes to assist private forestry and the protection of woodlands. In this duty attention is paid to the desirability of conserving the natural beauty of the countryside. (*b*) As National Forestry Enterprise it is responsible for producing wood as cheaply as possible. Attention must be paid however to preserving and improving the landscape, and developing nature conservation and recreation.

The Commission holds about 3,000,000 acres of land of which around 2,000,000 is under tree crops. About 800,000 acres are unsuitable for afforestation, leaving a balance of 220,000 for future planting of which approximately 45,000 acres are used each year. New land, unsuitable for agriculture, is purchased on the open market. The total number of forests is about 230.

A wide variety of recreations are permitted in the forests. At most of the forests open to the public a car park is provided. Camp-sites and cabins are available at some for longer stays. Numerous picnic sites have been established. In 1975 there were 288 waymarked forest walks and 133 forest nature trails; these vary in length but most of them are about two miles long. There were also 22 Information Centres and 25 Arboreta.

Useful publications are:

Forestry Commission Camping and Caravan Sites.
Recreation in your Forests.
Wayfaring in your Forests.
See your Forests (Four pamphlets for Southern and Northern England, Scotland and Wales).

Information Branch, Forestry Commission, 231 Corstorphine Road, Edinburgh, EH12 7AT. 031 334 0303.

FRIENDS OF THE LAKE DISTRICT

The Friends of the Lake District is 'a society to protect and cherish the landscape and natural beauty of the Lake District, to unite those who share these aims, and to take common action with other societies when need arises'.

The Society was formed in 1934 and has played a large part in protecting the countryside of the Lake District. It has played a major role in the evacuation of the military training areas in Martindale and Torver, in ensuring that electricity cables were placed underground in Borrowdale, Langdale and in other dales, and in campaigns to prevent controversial schemes by Manchester Corporation for Ullswater and Windermere. A campaign, launched jointly with the Council for the Protection of Rural England, resulted in an agreement with the Forestry Commission that there would be no further planting in the central 300 square miles (777 sq km) of the Lake District. More recently the Society has been deeply engaged in the problems produced by the increase of motor car traffic in the area. Throughout, there has been an interest in the preservation of rights of way with the provision of new footbridges and paths.

The Society is managed by an executive committee of not more than fifteen members in addition to several honorary officials. Members receive an illustrated Newsletter twice each year.

The Secretary, Friends of the Lake District, Gowan Knott, Kendal Road, Staveley, Kendal, Cumbria, LA8 9LP. Staveley 201.

THE GOWER SOCIETY (CYFEILLION GŴYR)

The Society was founded in 1947 and aims to encourage an appreciation and love of Gower, to oppose any threat to its amenities, to safeguard rights of way and open spaces and to further the study of its features, antiquities and history. It is affiliated to the Royal Institute of South Wales, Swansea.

The interests of the Society are not confined to the Gower Peninsula but cover the whole of the ancient Lordship of Gower which extended over a wider area of South Wales.

There is a present membership of about 1,500 who receive regular newsletters. The Society holds over 50 meetings each year for walks, footpath clearance work and folk dances. The Society has also published a guide to Gower and a number of booklets on the region.

Miss K. M. Matthison, Administration Secretary, The Gower Society, 55 Beechwood Road, Uplands, Swansea. Swansea 298107.

THE HERTFORDSHIRE SOCIETY

The Society was formed in 1936 and also incorporates the Hertfordshire branch of the Council for the Protection of Rural England. The object of the Society is to promote the preservation and improvement of the amenities and character of the County and to promote the protection and preservation of lands, buildings and scenery of beauty or historic or local interest within the County.

It is administered by an Executive Committee and has a permanent staff of two. Membership is open to individuals, councils, societies, industrial concerns, etc.

Each member receives a copy of the Annual Report and Newsletters.

The Hertfordshire Society, Campden Cottage, Much Hadham, Hertfordshire, SG10 6BS. Much Hadham 2267.

HISTORIC HOUSES ASSOCIATION

The Association was formed in 1973. It acts as a trade association for the owners of houses which are of historic interest and which are open to the public. It represents their interests with the Government, gives advice to owners on preservation and management and undertakes publicity on their general behalf. It works in liaison with other bodies such as the British Tourist Authority.

Full membership is restricted to owners of historic premises, Corporate Membership is available to firms who are dependent on historic houses for their business, and lastly individuals, who are in sympathy with the aims of the Association, may become Friends of the HHA. A Friend is entitled to free admission to most of the properties of the Association, may attend certain conferences and seminars and receives a journal three times per year. There are currently about 2,000 members representing over 700 properties.

Historic Houses Association, 10 Charles II Street, London, SW1. 01 839 5345.

THE HOLIDAY FELLOWSHIP

The Holiday Fellowship was formed in 1913 at the insti-
gation of T. A. Leonard who wished to extend the work of
the Co-operative Holidays Association of which he was
General Secretary. This was intended as a companion
organization to the CHA, and goodwill between the organizations continues to this day. (See The Country-wide
Holidays Association).

The HF has now about 30 adult centres and seven youth
guest houses in the British Isles. The arrangements at HF
centres are very similar to those of the CHA.

Guest houses are open to all, but membership of the HF
is effected by taking up at least ten £1 shares. The magazine
Over the Hills is published usually each spring. There are
over one hundred HF rambling and social clubs in various
parts of the country.

The Holiday Fellowship Ltd, 142–144 Great North Way,
London, NW4 1EG. 01 203 3381.

LONG DISTANCE WALKERS ASSOCIATION

The LDWA was founded at the end of 1971 by Alan
Blatchford, who proposed its formation, and Chris Steer.
The early years of the Association were marked by rapid
growth and by 1979 there were about 1,500 members.

The Association is mainly concerned with walks of more
than 20 miles in length. These may be organized group walks,
challenge walks (e.g. Tanners Marathon, Fellsman Hike) or
walks along the long distance footpaths. The LDWA is not
concerned with competitive events and therefore race walking, cross country running, fell running and orienteering are
excluded.

Each member receives a Newsletter three or four times a

year. This contains reports on past events, a calendar of future activities and articles on topics of interest to people who enjoy walking.

Several local groups have now been formed which are autonomous bodies, although conforming fully to the principles and rules of the LDWA. These organize a programme of regular walks and social events.

One of the notable events directly sponsored by the LDWA was the Downsman Hundred in 1973. This was probably the first event of this type over such a distance organized anywhere in the world and was a considerable success. Since that time a similar challenge walk of 100 miles has been organized annually by the LDWA: 1974 the Peakland Hundred in the Peak District National Park, 1975 the 2nd Downsman Hundred, 1976 the Cleveland Hundred in the North York Moors National Park, the 3rd Downsman Hundred in 1977 and the 2nd Cleveland Hundred in 1978.

In 1976 LDWA members completed the route of the London Countryway, a long distance footpath around London (Chapter 8).

Membership Secretary, Long Distance Walkers Association, 1 Lowry Drive, Marple Bridge, Stockport, Cheshire, SK6 5BR. 061 449 8336.

MOUNTAIN BOTHIES ASSOCIATION

The MBA is a charity formed in 1965 'to maintain simple unlocked shelters in remote country for the use of walkers, climbers and other outdoor enthusiasts who love the wild and lonely places'.

Members have been responsible for the renovation of bothies, mainly in the Scottish Highlands, but also in other areas, e.g. Greg's hut on the Corpse road over Cross Fell (named after John Gregory). The main renovations are carried out around Easter and in the summer with other tasks undertaken at week-ends throughout the year.

Membership is open to individuals and clubs. Members receive a Newsletter four times each year.

Read 'Dibidil'. I. Butterfield. From B. & B. Heath, 18 Brownhill, Thurso, Caithness. This is the story of the rebuilding of a bothy on the Isle of Rhum by MBA members and other workers.

Richard Butrym Membership Secretary, Mountain Bothies Association, 15 Merton Road, Histon, Cambridge.

MOUNTAIN LEADERSHIP TRAINING BOARDS

The Mountain Leadership Training Board (England and Wales) consists of representatives from various organizations concerned with outdoor pursuits. The Scottish (SMLTB) and the Northern Ireland Mountain Leadership Training Boards (NIMLTB) have very similar compositions. At the time of writing, after considerable dispute, an arbitration panel is meeting to discuss the future administration of the MLTB and is expected to report mid 1979.

The Boards have introduced training schemes to improve the knowledge and competence of leaders taking parties, particularly of young people, into mountainous country.

The following schemes are available:

(a) *Mountain Leadership Certificate* (*Summer*)

To obtain this Certificate a candidate must have attended a training course of at least one week; have gained experience in expeditions in mountain country over at least one year; and completed a residential course of one week at which an assessment of his suitability was made. A valid Adult Certificate in First Aid must also be held.

(b) Mountain Leadership Certificate (Winter)

The standard is much more demanding than that required for the above certificate and is awarded to those who have successfully completed training in the skills necessary to lead parties on Scottish mountains in winter time.

(c) The Mountaineering Instructor's Certificate and The Mountaineering Instructor's Advanced Certificate

These are awarded to mountaineering instructors who have demonstrated their ability in rock and mountain climbing as well as hill walking.

Mountain Leadership Training Board (England and Wales), Crawford House, Precinct Centre, Booth Street East, Manchester, M13 9RZ. 061 273 5839.

Scottish Mountain Leadership Training Board, 1–3 St Colme Street, Edinburgh, EH3 6AA. 031 225 5544.

Northern Ireland Mountain Leadership Training Board, 49 Malone Road, Belfast, BT9 6RZ.

MOUNTAIN RESCUE COMMITTEE

In 1933 a Joint Stretcher Committee was formed by The Rucksack Club and The Fell and Rock Climbing Club to design a stretcher suitable for use in the British mountains. Three years later a further committee, called The First Aid Committee of British Mountaineering Clubs, was set up on a more permanent basis with representatives from many prominent organizations. The name was changed to The Mountain Rescue Committee in 1946 and it became a Charitable Trust in 1950. A separate organization, The Mountain Rescue Committee of Scotland, was formed in 1964 but both groups work closely together on an entirely voluntary basis.

The aim of the Committee is the provision and maintenance of mountain rescue equipment, teams and posts in the United Kingdom. It is also concerned with investigation into new methods and equipment for mountain rescue with the intention of improving the efficiency of the service.

The Department of Health and Social Security is responsible for supplying basic first-aid equipment to Mountain Rescue Posts run by organizations affiliated to The Mountain Rescue Committee. Individuals and clubs may make donations to help the work of the Committee.

The Committee publishes bi-annually a handbook 'Mountain and Cave Rescue' which lists official rescue teams and posts.

Mr R. Davies, Secretary MRC, 18 Turnside Fold, Simmondley, Glossop, Derbyshire.

THE NATIONAL TRUST

The idea of the National Trust was first suggested during a lecture delivered by Robert Hunter, honorary solicitor to the Commons Preservation Society, in 1884. He advocated the establishment of an organization which could buy and maintain suitable land and buildings for the benefit of the nation. This immediately received support but an association was not formed until 1895. This was known as The National Trust for Places of Historic Interest and Natural Beauty.

The Trust acquired its first property almost immediately in 1895; by 1914 62 properties had been acquired, 28 by gift and the rest by purchase.

The National Trust is a statutory body controlled ultimately by a Council of 52 members. This works through several committees, both national and regional, supported by a number of full-time staff under the direction of a Director-General. There is a separate committee for Northern Ireland.

The income derives from five sources: (*a*) membership subscriptions, (*b*) income from invested funds, (*c*) admission fees, (*d*) donations and legacies, (*e*) property endowments (these are funds tied to the maintenance of specific properties). The total income in 1976 was about £5,000,000.

The main responsibilities of the Trust are:

1. Land. The Trust owns or protects 486,000 acres. The public have access to over half of this total, in most cases free of charge.
2. Country facilities. Over 200 car parks and 80 camp/caravan sites have been provided.
3. Historic Buildings. The majority of the buildings of the Trust were built in the late seventeenth or eighteenth centuries. These range enormously from small cottages to large country houses. In some cases these are untenanted, but under the Country House Scheme others are still family houses, parts of which are open to the public at certain times.
4. Gardens. In 1948 the Trust launched its Garden Fund which enables it to hold and preserve gardens of outstanding importance. These are now among the most frequented of Trust properties.

There are several types of membership open on payment of an annual subscription. Members have the right to visit any Trust properties free of charge.

For a full account read: 'The National Trust, Past and Present'. Robin Fedden, Cape.

The National Trust, 42 Queen Anne's Gate, London, SW1 H9AS. 01 222 9254.

THE NATIONAL TRUST FOR SCOTLAND

The initiative for the foundation of the Trust came from the Association for the Preservation of Rural Scotland and a special committee was set up in 1929. The Trust was founded on 1 May 1931 as 'The National Trust for Scotland for Places of Historic Interest or Natural Beauty'.

The Trust acquired its first property almost immediately; this was Crookston Castle, Glasgow, now in the care of the

Department of the Environment. It extended its scope in 1932 to include the historic site of Bruce's command post at Bannockburn, began its restoration work in the Fife burgh of Culross and went on to purchase the scenic heart of Glencoe in 1935. It is also a statutory body.

Currently the Trust has some 80 properties and a total holding of over 80,000 acres. Membership, currently over 82,000, is open to the public and to organizations. Members may visit the properties free of charge. There is also a Ranger Service of guided walks from many centres, in particular from the Culzean Country Park, Maybole, Ayrshire. The Trust has an extensive list of publications describing its properties.

The Director, The National Trust for Scotland, 5 Charlotte Square, Edinburgh, EH2 4DU. 031 226 5922.

NATURE CONSERVANCY COUNCIL

The Council was set up by Act of Parliament in 1973 to be responsible for nature conservation throughout Great Britain. Financed by the Department of Environment, but is free to express independent views.

At the end of June 1977, the Council had responsibility for 155 National Nature Reserves which cover nearly 300,000 acres. These are owned or leased directly by the Council, or are the result of an agreement between the Council and the owners where the latter retain their ownership but agree to some conditions of land-use. The reserves are generally open to the public and leaflets are available describing the reserves and nature trails which have been provided within them. Access to a few reserves is allowed only by permit which may be obtained from the appropriate regional office.

In addition, over 3,600 Sites of Special Scientific Interest (SSSI) have been notified to local planning authorities. In such cases the Council must be consulted by the authority before permission for development is granted.

The Council also advises the Government, local authorities and private individuals on nature conservation and undertakes or commissions appropriate research programmes.

A list of publications is available on application to the library of the Great Britain Headquarters.

Nature Conservancy Council: Great Britain Headquarters, 19 Belgrave Square, London, SW1X 8PY. 01 235 3241.

THE NORTHUMBERLAND AND NEWCASTLE SOCIETY

Formed in 1924 as the Newcastle upon Tyne Society at the suggestion of Lt Col. J. Douglas Mitchell. After the formation of a county section the name was changed to its present form in 1930. The Society is affiliated to the Council for the Protection of Rural England and acts as the Council's Northumberland Branch.

The Society has a current membership of about 450 with 60 company or group members. It keeps a constant watch upon developments within the area, consults with local authorities and is represented at public inquiries. It organizes symposia each year and has a social programme.

Mrs J. M. Grieve, The Northumberland and Newcastle Society, 24 The Grove, Gosforth, Newcastle upon Tyne, NE3 1NE. Newcastle 855381.

OFFA'S DYKE ASSOCIATION

This organization was established in 1969 as a formal successor, with membership open to the public, of the Offa's Dyke Action Committee originally based upon Staunton Youth Hostel. Its main object was the opening of the long distance footpath along the line of the Dyke. After the official opening of the Path in 1971 the organization continued in being, widening its objects to 'promote the conservation, improvement and better knowledge of the Welsh border region along the Offa's Dyke Path'.

The Association with support from public authorities runs a heritage and information centre at Knighton. It acts by helping and encouraging those official organizations which are responsible for the maintenance of the Path and protection of the Dyke and other features of historic or natural interest situated in the Welsh-English border country. It is also active in encouraging farms along the Path to provide accommodation and has published a number of guide books and maps. There is one full-time official supplementing the work of the committee and other volunteers.

Full members receive various publications of the Association including a journal three times per year, and are also covered by third party insurance arrangements. Present membership is about 1,000.

Offa's Dyke Association, Old Primary School, West Street, Knighton, Powys, LD7 1EW. Knighton 528753.

PEAK AND NORTHERN FOOTPATHS SOCIETY

The Society was formed on 16 August 1894 as the 'Peak District and Northern Counties Footpaths Preservation Society'. This was in response to an anonymous letter published in the *Manchester Guardian* which drew attention to the large areas of moorland, notably Kinder, from which the public was excluded. Within one year the Society had 600 members and within three years its first great success – the establishment of a right of way over the Snake footpath (Hayfield-Woodlands). The Society changed its name to the present form in 1968.

The PNNS has no full-time staff and relies upon voluntary help. The Closure and Diversions Secretary notes any proposed footpath diversion or extinguishment orders and automatically lodges an objection, although this may be withdrawn later. The Society appoints Footpath Inspectors who regularly walk the footpaths within an area and report upon their condition. Any obstruction is reported to the appropriate highways authority. A Signpost Supervisor is responsible for the repair and erection of signposts. The Society is mainly active in the counties of Greater Manchester, Cheshire, Derbyshire, Lancashire and Staffordshire.

Membership is open to individuals and related organizations; at present there are about 500 and 90 members respectively in these categories. Members receive an annual report on the work of the Society.

Mr D. Taylor, 15 Parkfield Drive, Tyldesley, Manchester, M29 8NR. 061 790 4383.

THE RAMBLERS' ASSOCIATION

The main aims of the Ramblers' Association are to secure, improve and protect the access of the walker to the countryside, and to conserve the beauty of the countryside.

The RA was formed in 1935 by a coalition of several ramblers' federations, which had been established in various parts of the country from the turn of the century. These had been formed by groups of rambling clubs interested in the protection of footpaths and the right of access to open country. The RA was run entirely by voluntary help in the early years, the first full-time official being appointed in 1951. Probably the most influential member of the RA to date is Tom Stephenson who was secretary from 1948 to 1969.

The Association is still developing, but basically it has a three-tier structure. The first tier is The National Organization, which has a full-time staff and office in London run by a general secretary. The Areas, which are based upon the old federations, make up the second tier; there are at present 31 which are tending to be identified with individual counties. Lastly, there are over 100 Groups which are based upon towns or districts. 1978 membership was 29,017 with 432 affiliated clubs and societies. Generally speaking, the

National Organization deals with Government legislation and general policy, the Areas are responsible for contacts with County Councils and the Groups for contact with District Councils.

The RA at National level, along with other conservation organizations, acts as a pressure group for the protection of the countryside. Activities in recent years have included campaigns against new reservoirs on Dartmoor, the A66 in the Lake District and mining on the North York Moors. The RA also led the successful fight against the curtailment of Ordnance Survey 1 : 25 000 map series.

Voluntary Inspectors are appointed by Area and Group who are responsible for maintaining a watch over public footpaths within their district. The local organization then fights any attempt to close or divert a path if this is thought to be against the interest of ramblers. A great deal of very valuable work is carried out by RA working parties on the clearance of overgrown footpaths, provision of bridges over streams and in the building of new stiles. Local groups are very active with programmes of walking and social activities.

Members are allocated to Areas and are entitled to attend at Area AGM, take part in Area activities and receive literature. Members are not automatically allocated to a local Group, but may join in most cases without a further subscription. Members receive copies of the magazine 'Rucksack' three times per year and the annual 'Bed, Breakfast and Bus Guide'.

A wide variety of pamphlets and guides are published by the RA.

The Ramblers' Association, 1/4 Crawford Mews, York Street, London, W1H 1PT. 01 262 1477.

RIVER THAMES SOCIETY

The Society was founded by the late Roger Gresham Cooke. It aims to encourage an active interest in the history, present affairs and future of the River Thames and its whole environment; to preserve and extend the present amenities as well as the natural beauty of the Thames; and to promote the need for nature conservation and to assist in the development of art, science, sport and recreation associated with the River Thames.

It is a voluntary body with over 2,000 members and seven branches which cover the Thames from its source near Cirencester to the estuary.

A Thames Information Centre has been established at Feltham, Middlesex. This is an independent organization formed to provide information on the activities and facilities of the river. It publishes 'Thames Topics', the 'Handbook of Thames Information' and surveys of the river.

River Thames Society, Gresham House, Twickenham Road, Feltham, Middlesex, TW13 6HA. 01 894 5511 (Ext. 100).

SCOTTISH RIGHTS OF WAY SOCIETY

The objects of this Society are the preservation, maintenance and defence of rights of way throughout Scotland.

Founded in 1845 as an 'Association for the Protection of Public Rights of Roadway in and around Edinburgh' by Adam Black, then Lord Provost of Edinburgh, it soon began to take an interest in rights of way over a wider area. Reconstituted as 'The Scottish Rights of Way and Recreation Society Ltd' in 1883–4 with an interest in public rights of way throughout Scotland, it has remained an active body since. The Society was again reconstituted in 1946 under its present title.

The Society is a purely voluntary body with a current membership of about 1,500 (1977). Individuals may become members and walking clubs and similar organizations may take Corporate Membership. Members are given free copies of the Society's publications on joining and also receive a copy of the annual report.

Honorary Secretary, Scottish Rights of Way Society, 28 Rutland Square, Edinburgh, EH1 2BW.

SNOWDONIA NATIONAL PARK SOCIETY
(CYMDEITHAS PARC CENEDLAETHOL ERYRI)

The Society was founded at a public meeting held on 10 June 1968. It is a purely voluntary body with the main object of preserving the character and beauty of the National Park and protecting it from exploitation by commercial interests.

Members maintain a constant vigilance for any scheme which may adversely affect the Park and where possible take appropriate action. The Society also undertakes the marking of farm paths, putting up suitable notices and fixing stiles and thus works in a practical way to promote better understanding between those who come to enjoy the mountains and the hill farmers. It has inaugurated an 'Adopt a Mountain' scheme whereby members of affiliated clubs keep a mountain of their choice free from litter.

Snowdonia National Park Society, Betws-y-Coed, North Wales.

THE SOCIETY OF SUSSEX DOWNSMEN

The Society was founded in 1923 by a group of local walkers who were alarmed at the urban development of the South Downs. The aims are to foster interest in the Sussex section of the South Downs, to preserve the character of the Downs, and to protect beauty spots, ancient monuments and rights of way.

Management of the Society is by a council of the officers and 12 elected members. A Preservation Committee, meeting ten times each year, decides policy and action on planning and conservation matters. District Officers are appointed who keep watch on rights of way and other matters within their area. The Society employs two part-time staff.

Membership is open to the public, societies and other unincorporated bodies. At present 2,000 individuals are members. Members receive an Annual Report, three news sheets each year and can take part in a programme of walks.

The Society of Sussex Downsmen, 93 Church Road, Hove,
Sussex, BN3 2BA. Brighton 71906.

THE SOUTH WEST WAY ASSOCIATION

The Association was formed in May, 1973 as an independent
body, although it works in co-operation with the Ramblers'
Association.

It was formed to promote the interests of users of the
South West Peninsula Coast Path. Its immediate object is
to obtain the completion of the path. The Association believes that the Way should be a continuous footpath around
the peninsula, as distinct from the present policy of the
Countryside Commission. Furthermore, it believes that the
path should remain along the coast and not be diverted
inland as has occurred in some areas.

A Footpath Guide to the Way is issued annually as well
as descriptions of sections of the path. Membership is open
to individuals, to other associations and to local authorities.

Mrs D. Y. Lancey, Membership Secretary, The South West
Way Association, Kynance, 15 Old Newton Road, Kingskerswell, Newton Abbot, Devon. Kingskerswell 2678.

YOUTH HOSTELS ASSOCIATIONS

YOUTH HOSTELS ASSOCIATION
(ENGLAND AND WALES)

The object of the Association is stated to be: 'To help all,
especially young people of limited means, to a greater knowledge, love and care of the countryside, particularly by providing hostels or other simple accommodation for them in
their travels, and thus to promote their health, rest and
education'.

The development of this movement is generally attributed
to a German schoolmaster, Richard Schirrmann. He was

concerned with the poor conditions found in the cities at the
start of this century and with the lack of adequate provision
for the young. He arranged for school children to be taken
on tours into the countryside, stopping for the night at
village schools. This encouraged him to press for the establishment of special hostels and the first was opened at a
castle, Burg Altena, in 1909. By 1914 there were 200 hostels
in Germany and 2,177 by 1928.

British travellers to the Continent became acquainted with
this movement which had spread to other European coun-
tries during the 1920s. As a result, the National Council of
Social Service arranged two conferences in 1930 at which a
National Association to promote youth hostels in Great
Britain was formed.

The first hostel was Pennant Hall opened on Christmas
Eve, 1930, and by Easter, 1931, twenty hostels had been
opened.

Separate Associations were later formed for Scotland and
Northern Ireland and the name of the parent body was
therefore changed to Youth Hostels Association (England
and Wales). Within a few years the youth hostel movement
was firmly established in England and Wales. In 1932 the
Association joined with other countries to form the International Youth Hostel Federation.

(a) Youth hostels

The main activity of the YHA is the provision of hostels
offering simple and cheap accommodation. These hostels
vary enormously in character including shepherds' huts, old
farmhouses, castles, country and town houses and even
converted shops and mills. Some, however, are purpose-
built and have modern, well-equipped buildings. Hostels are
divided into four grades depending upon the facilities
offered: Simple (68 hostels), standard (149 hostels), superior
(35 hostels) and special (three hostels). The overnight fee
varies according to the grade of the hostel.

Sleeping is in dormitories, usually with two-tier bunks.
Blankets (or duvets) and pillows are provided but a special

sheet sleeping-bag must be bought or hired. Washing
facilities are provided but each hosteller provides his own
toilet articles. Hot suppers and breakfasts can be purchased
at most hostels and self-cooking facilities are always available. A packed lunch can also be provided. Most hostels
have a small store where foodstuffs can be purchased.

Booking beforehand is advisable but walkers may book in
on the day if places are available.

(b) Adventure holidays

The YHA offers a series of holidays, based upon youth hostels, which provide guided or supervised activities. A wide
variety of activities are covered, e.g. walking, rock climbing,
sailing, pony trekking and archaeology. Separate holidays
are provided for certain age groups.

(c) Equipment sales

YHA Services Ltd have three stores in London, Birmingham
and Manchester which provide a wide variety of clothing
and equipment for most outdoor activities. A free catalogue
is available.

(d) YHA Groups

Many local Groups have been set up which provide a range
of outdoor and social activities. These are open to YHA
members in those areas upon payment of a small membership fee.

Membership of the YHA is gained by payment of a fee. It
is possible however to sample hostelling by purchase of a
Guest Pass which entitles the holder to a stay of one night.

Youth Hostels Association (England and Wales), Trevelyan
House, 8 St Stephen's Hill, St Albans, Hertfordshire, AL1
2DY. St Albans 55215.

YOUTH HOSTEL ASSOCIATION OF NORTHERN IRELAND

This is run on similar lines to the YHA and has a total of twelve hostels. All hostels provide self-cooking facilities, but meals are not provided.

Advance bookings must be made directly to the head office of YHANI. Equipment may be purchased at head office.

YHANI, 93 Dublin Road, Belfast, BT2 7HF. Belfast 24733.

SCOTTISH YOUTH HOSTELS ASSOCIATION

The SYHA has 80 hostels, arranged in three grades according to the facilities offered. The organization and hostels are very similar to those of the England and Wales Association.

Scottish Youth Hostels Association, 7 Glebe Crescent, Stirling, FK8 2JA. Stirling 2821.

CHAPTER 12

Backpacking

For many years camping was mainly associated with the Scout, Girl Guides and similar Associations. More recently however there has been a big rise in its popularity amongst the general public; in particular, family camping both here and abroad has grown to be very popular. The main reason for this is probably the rising cost of hotel and boarding house holidays. But a second reason is the enjoyment that many, particularly young people, get out of this kind of holiday. This is equally true of walkers and there are now more walker-campers than ever before.

(a) *The permanent or standing camp*

This provides a permanent base for the walking holiday. The tent and equipment can be taken to the site by car or public transport and collected in the same way at the end. The only limitation is the cost of purchasing or hiring the equipment, weight is of little importance and the walker can make himself very comfortable. Most family camping today is of this type.

(b) *The mobile camp*

The walker carries all his equipment and moves every day or so. The walker enjoys variety in his sites and he can camp in wild country, well away from roads, where cars cannot be used or where public transport is non-existent. The great enemy, however, is weight and equipment has to be chosen carefully.

It is with this second type and its use by walkers that this chapter is mainly concerned. Actually the term 'Mobile Camping' is not very good in that context as it could equally well apply to canoeists or cyclists. The term 'Light-weight

Camping' is also not fully satisfactory as it is quite common for light-weight tents and equipment to be used in permanent camps for cheapness or because the site is too exposed for larger and heavier tents. 'Backpacking' is undoubtedly the best term to use.

Advantages and disadvantages of backpacking

Your first backpacking holiday should not be undertaken lightly. There is a very good chance you will find it all too wonderful for words and be inspired to do lots more. I hope that you do. But, frankly, it will not suit everybody and without proper care it may not be particularly enjoyable. It is appropriate therefore to consider the advantages and disadvantages of backpacking compared to other forms of accommodation right at the start.

The advantages are:

1. *Cheapness*. On the basis of June 1979 prices it should be possible to buy camping equipment of good quality for summer use for about £150; that is tent, sleeping bag, stove, cooking utensils and miscellaneous items. With reasonable care these should last for at least ten years. Allowing a reasonable sum for camping site fees this is about the same, over that period, as a stay of two weeks in a youth hostel each year or, at the most, one week in a modest boarding house. So if you are likely to have or want to have more holiday than that then camping will definitely be the cheapest way to take it. In fact, a maximum life of ten years for camping equipment may be very modest indeed; for example I am still using a paraffin pressure stove which is 30 years old and in excellent condition.

2. *Flexibility*. In youth hostels there are fixed times for rising, meals and lights-out. Hotel rules tend to be somewhat more flexible. With camping there are few, if any, rules – you do as you wish provided, of course, that you do not disturb local residents or other campers who are nearby. You will not have to book ahead as sites are rarely full in this country and you will be able to extend your stay if you wish. You will not be committed to finishing each day at a pre-arranged

place; if you feel like it you can go on for a few extra miles or finish early. The choices are yours.

3. *Scope*. You can camp on wild moorland or in mountainous country where no other accommodation is available.

4. *Pleasure*. There is a great appeal in being self-sufficient and in relying completely upon yourself for once instead of having people to do things for you. It is also extremely pleasant to sit, sipping a hot brew of tea, at a tent-door in the late evening and listen to the countryside as dusk gathers; or to step out in the mornings with the sun sparkling on the dew. If you don't find such things pleasant, then you probably aren't really made to be a walker anyhow.

The disadvantages are:

1. *Weight*. The tent, sleeping-bag, cooking equipment, etc., have to be carried and you are the one that will have to carry them. Generally, this means adding a *minimum* of 10–12 lb (4·5–5·4 kg) to your load.

2. *Convenience*. The space in a tent is fairly restricted and tasks will therefore be harder to carry out, particularly in wet weather.

3. *Work*. You will have to work a lot harder. *You* have to provide the fresh water, cook the meals and wash up. *You* have to erect and then strike the tent. At the end of a day of hard walking *you* will be the person who has to carry out these tasks which may otherwise be done for you.

4. *Keeping dry*. Backpacking is fine in good weather, it is not so attractive in wet weather. Wet clothes cannot easily be dried, whereas this generally presents no difficulty in a hotel or hostel where a drying room is usually available.

EQUIPMENT

1. Tents

Basically backpacking tents fall into two categories:

    (*a*) Ridge
    (*b*) Bell or pyramid

These names are derived from the basic shapes of the tents.

(*a*) *The ridge tent* (Figure 25)

The cross-section of the ridge tent is in the form of an inverted 'V' with two sloping sides which meet at the top in a horizontal ridge. The tent has two poles, constructed in sections from light metal or wood, which support the roof. Each pole ends in a spike, called a tent-pole spindle, which fits through a round eyelet-hole in the roof fabric. The roof is not supported but relies upon the tension of the fabric between the poles. This tension is produced by guylines which are attached to points on the lower edge of the roof-fabric and to pegs driven into the ground. Normally there are three or four guylines along each side of the tent and two at each end. Further pegs, called brailing pegs, are driven through small metal rings attached to the bottom edge of the tent wall to secure this to the ground. The tent fabric is opened at one end to form a door which can be closed by a zip or by tapes. A sheet of fabric, called a flysheet, can be placed over the tent to form a second roof. This fits over the pole spindles in a similar manner and is held under tension by separate guylines. A loose collar is sometimes placed on to the tent spindle to separate the tent and flysheet. The ground inside the tent is covered with a groundsheet to provide a clean and dry floor. The groundsheet can be separate from the tent or can be attached to prevent draughts and insects entering at the base. In the latter case the ground-sheet should extend a few inches up the walls to prevent water entering the tent during very heavy rain.

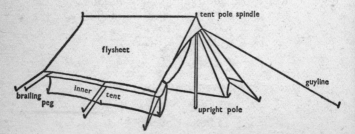

Figure 25. Parts of a typical ridge tent

(b) The bell tent

The bell tent has a single pole placed centrally so that the fabric slopes away in all directions. Other features are substantially as for the ridge tent. Generally it has three main advantages over the ridge tent: (i) It is easier to pitch, (ii) it provides more headroom, and (iii) a large doorway is available which gives easier working in that area. The centre pole tends however to be more of an hindrance inside the tent than the two poles of the ridge tent.

Variations on basic types

1. *Ridge pole.* Some ridge tents have an horizontal pole which supports the ridge of the tent. This improves the shape of the tent and adds stability.

2. *A-poles.* A single upright pole is replaced by two poles running roughly parallel to the tent walls to join at the top of the tent. The poles are usually placed outside the tent and the tent is then suspended underneath the apex of the poles. Thus a ridge tent will have A-poles at each end whilst a bell tent will have A-poles at the centre. This arrangement provides extra room for movement within the tent. It also provides extra stability in windy conditions. A-poles also allow the flysheet to be pitched first, the tent being hung up afterwards. This is an advantage in heavy rain when the tent can be kept dry. (Figure 26).

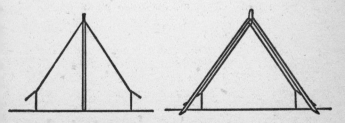

Figure 26. Upright and A-poles

3. *Bell ends*. The flysheet can be brought completely down to the ground at the sides, rear and front of the tent thus giving extra protection in bad weather. At the front of the tent the flysheet can be extended on one side only to form an open porch which provides a useful area for cooking and storage of equipment. A back exit to the tent can also give access to further storage space in the rear end.

4. *Snow valance*. This is a feature of mountain tents and consists of a broad fabric skirt around the base of the tent upon which can be placed rocks or snow. This increases the stability of the tent in high winds.

5. *Tunnel entrance*. The normal triangular door of the ridge tent is replaced by a round opening. This is primarily for use in snow conditions or in very bad weather. The sleeve on the door can be joined to that of another tent for communication.

6. *Sloping ridge*. Based upon the ridge tent with the ridge sloping. This reduces the overall weight and increases the stability in bad weather. This type of sometimes called a Wedge Tent.

Materials

Originally tents were made from a fairly thick cotton or linen fabric, usually called canvas. Large tents are still made from this material. It is strong, windproof, remains free from condensation problems and has given good service for many years but suffers from several disadvantages.

Lightweight cotton fabrics are still used for some modern backpacking tents but the most common material nowadays is nylon. Woven nylon fabrics of similar strength to cotton are very much lighter and hence are preferred where weight is important. They are not as waterproof as cotton however and hence have to be coated with polyurethane to make them completely waterproof. A tent made exclusively from coated nylon would not be very satisfactory however as condensation of water vapour from the body would occur on the inner surface and make life uncomfortable. It is common practice therefore to make the flysheet from coated nylon and the inner tent from cotton. Where nylon is used for both then special precautions are taken to remove condensation, for example by the insertion of cotton panels into the eaves to allow moisture-filled air to escape. Silicone proofed nylon is also used for the inner tent which reduces condensation. PVC or nylon coated with polyurethane or PVC are usually used for groundsheets.

The lightest tents available weigh about 3–4 lb (1·4–1·8 kg).

General care and maintenance. Repairs

The life of a tent can be extended considerably if care is taken both in use and in storage.

In use

(*a*) Pitch the tent on even ground rather than upon an irregular surface where excessive strains may be put upon local areas of the tent fabric.

(*b*) Ensure that the ground is free from stones, such as flints, or twigs that may penetrate the fabric of the groundsheet.

(*c*) Place a sheet of thick polythene over the tent area before the groundsheet is laid as this will reduce deterioration and damage to the groundsheet, but ensure that it does not project beyond the flysheet.

(*d*) Ensure that the guylines are not under excessive tension. With cotton tents guylines should be slackened on wetting and tightened on drying.

(*e*) Take care when moving about inside the tent or when moving objects such as rucksacks as damage may be caused to the wall fabric.

(*f*) Brush out the tent interior each morning and wipe off any traces of mud with a damp cloth.

(*g*) If food has been splashed or dropped in the tent then remove traces as soon as possible with a damp cloth.

(*h*) If possible open the tent in the morning to dry the interior. Try particularly to ensure that the tent is dry before packing; if this is not possible then erect the tent again as soon as possible.

(*i*) Small tears in the fabric should not be neglected. Small repair kits are available, but even a small strip of first-aid plaster will help in an emergency.

Storage

(*a*) Erect the tent and thoroughly dry all parts before packing away. Cotton in susceptible to mildew which causes loss in strength.

(*b*) Check that no items are missing. Are there enough pegs, for example, with a few to spare?

(*c*) Check the tent carefully for signs of damage. Replace all worn or damaged guylines, slides, rubber adjusters and poles. Repair all damage to the fabric such as small tears or loose stitching. Note particularly where the guylines join.

(*d*) When not in use wrap the tent loosely and store in a dry place. Wrap the poles and pegs separately from the fabric and treat all steel parts with an inhibitor to prevent rust.

Re-proofing

The tent fabric will require re-proofing after a few seasons. These proofings may be applied either by brush or by aerosol. The aerosol re-proofers are more convenient but about three times more expensive than brushing solutions. The tent should be erected and surface mud removed with clean water and any grease with special dry cleaning agents before the proofing solution is applied.

2. Sleeping-bags

This is an essential item for backpacking. It consists of a double-walled fabric bag with a filling of insulating material between the walls. The object is to reduce heat loss from the body to the ground and surrounding air during the night so that body temperature is maintained.

At the moment there is a very wide range of sleeping-bags available. Initially it is important to decide on the conditions in which the bag is likely to be most used. Occasional use in somewhat colder conditions will not matter provided that the bag has sufficient room for additional clothing to be worn. The bag must, of course, be of sufficient length and width. It should be long enough to allow you to close the bag without your feet pressing hard against the foot, and wide enough to allow some extra clothes to be worn. But avoid buying a bag which is too large. Reputable suppliers will give advice on the type of bag required and will allow you to get into bags to check size before purchase.

Wall material

This is usually either nylon or cotton, the former being most common. A combination of cotton for the inner wall and nylon for the outer is also used where the greater absorbency of cotton helps to reduce perspiration problems. The outer wall is often made from Ripstop Nylon; a special type of woven cloth which has a few stronger threads inserted at small intervals in both directions to prevent tears developing.

Filling

Various fillings may be used for bags. The main ones are:

(a) Down. This consists of the undercoating of water fowl, either duck or geese, i.e. light, fluffy filaments without any quill shaft.

(b) Down/feather mixtures. A mixture of down and feathers containing not less than 51 per cent by weight of down.

(c) Feather/down mixtures. A mixture of down and feathers containing not less than 15 per cent by weight of down.

(d) Feathers.

(e) Polyester fibres. Sold under trade names such as Terylene or Dacron.

The first four are, of course, natural materials whilst the last is synthetic. Of the natural materials down undoubtedly gives the best insulation for a given weight, but is also the most expensive. Down is therefore used alone for the more expensive bags designed for the coldest conditions. Re-used natural filling materials are inferior to new materials. Polyester fibres are inferior to down and sleeping bags filled with this material tend to be bulkier. Some people, however, who are allergic to the natural materials may prefer the synthetic filling. Polyester fillings are also better in damp conditions.

Construction

The wall of the bag consists of two fabric layers with a filling between. The walls are joined together to form pockets in order to keep the filling uniformly distributed. The simplest method of joining is to sew straight through the two walls so that there is no filling along the lines of stitching (called Simple Quilting). This is a poor method as heat is lost along these lines and it is only used for the construction of cheap bags. Several alternative methods are available but these necessarily increase the cost and weight (Figure 27):

(a) Laminated. Two thin bags with sewn-through construction are joined together so that the stitching lines do not coincide. (Also called Double Quilting).

(b) Box wall. Separating strips are provided to form a 'box' construction. (Also called Wall Quilting or Straight Wall).

(c) Slant wall. Similar to (b) but with a slanting construction.

(d) Overlapping tube. (Also called Continuous V-Baffle).

Closures

Most bags have a zip made of metal or nylon and about 30 inches (76 cm) in length to allow easier entry into the bag. This allows heat to escape and bags designed for cold use either dispense with the zip altogether or have a flap, sometimes down filled, which can fit over the zip. The zip should have a metal ring or tab on both sides.

A drawcord should also be provided at the neck of the bag

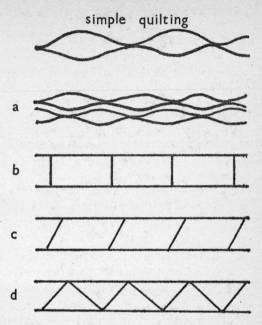

Figure 27. Types of wall construction used in sleeping bags

to allow it to be closed around the shoulders. Some bags designed for cold conditions have an attached hood and drawcord so that only the face is visible; this reduces heat loss from the head.

Liners

It is possible to buy cotton or nylon liners for the sleeping bag. These help to keep the bag clean and hence reduce the need for cleaning.

When not in use the bag should preferably be hung in a dry place and not left compressed in its container. It should be cleaned occasionally, say every year or two, but ask for instructions from the supplier.

3. Ground or sleeping pads

The filling in a sleeping bag which is under the body will be compressed and insulation and comfort will be reduced. It is desirable therefore to provide extra insulation underneath the bag. This can be provided by spare clothing. It is better however to buy ground pads which are light and cheap and give good insulation. These come in two forms:

(a) Cellular pads (closed cell foam). A full-length pad, i.e. 74 × 18 × $\frac{3}{8}$ inch (188 × 46 × 0·9 cm) thick weighs about 1 lb 3 oz (538 gm), but one for the trunk area only, i.e. 38 inches (97 cm) long, weighs as little as 9 oz (255 gm).

(b) Air beds. These have to be inflated by mouth or pump A typical trunk-length air bed weighs about 2 lb 7 oz (1·1 kg).

4. Miscellaneous

Cooking equipment is described in Chapter 13. There are a few smaller items however that should be carried.

1. Water Carrier. It may not always be practicable to camp near a stream and a carrier is very helpful in these cases. Polyethylene or PVC carriers fitted with handle and tap and with capacities of 2–4 gallons (9–18 litres) are available. These weigh about 9 oz (255 gm) empty.
2. Milk Bottle. A polyethylene bottle with wide neck and capacity one pint is useful for milk and is far lighter than the normal glass bottle. Can also be used for other drinks.
3. Air-tight Containers. It is useful to have two or three of these for the protection of perishable foodstuffs. One should have holes in the top for the storage of meat. Two or three pieces of muslin should be carried to drape over meat and milk containers.
4. Egg Containers. Polyethylene boxes with compartments for six eggs and with a carrying handle are useful.
5. Tent Repair Outfit. The tent fabric may become damaged and a small repair outfit can be used to stop more serious damage developing. 'A stitch in time saves nine' is excellent advice.

6. Line. A length of light nylon line (about 20 ft [6 m]) will serve as a clothes line, but in emergencies can be cut as a replacement for a broken bootlace or guyline.

7. Washing Bowl. A collapsible plastic-lined canvas bowl will weigh about 3–5 oz (85–142 gm) and serve for washing, washing-up and cleaning clothes.

8. Torch. Try to get all work finished in the daylight, but this may not be possible particularly in the winter months when night can last for over twelve hours. A torch is useful in this case and also for toilet purposes. A small hurricane lamp is a good buy, operating from gas or paraffin. When using lamps in a tent it is important to provide good ventilation.

9. Cleaning Materials. It will be necessary to carry a small pan scourer, one of the plastic types with foam and scourer being suitable. Liquid detergent is easily available, but a very useful one is Dylon which comes in a $4\frac{1}{2}$ oz (127 gm) tube and can be used with cold water.

10. Insect Repellent. Midges, flies and mosquitoes can be troublesome in some localities. Insect repellents come in three forms: (1) a grease stick to rub over exposed parts of the body, (2) an aerosol spray, (3) an incense coil which will give off a pleasant odour when lit.

11. Trowel. For toilet purposes.

Equipment List

A typical list of equipment for a summer backpacking holiday for two persons in this country would be:

Common Equipment

	lb	oz	gm
Lightweight tent with flysheet, sewn-in groundsheet and upright poles	7	8	3,402
Polyethylene sheet (approx. 10 ft × 6 ft [3 × 2 m])	1	1	482
1 pint pressure stove with paraffin	3	8	1,588
Paraffin container with paraffin (approx. 1 pint)	1	4	567

	lb	oz	gm
Can opener (combined with bottle opener, corkscrew and knife)		5	142
Salt-pepper container		½	14
Matches in waterproof case		1	28
Washing bowl		3	85
Canteen	1	0	454
Cleaning materials (pan scourer, detergent, soap, brush, polish)		13	369
Water carrier (collapsible)		9	255
Milk container (approx. 1 pint)		2	57
Food containers (three)		8	226
Egg container (for six eggs)		2½	71
Tent repair outfit	3	3	85
First aid kit		9	255
Insect repellent		½	14
Light nylon line (approx. 20 ft)		½	14
Trowel		8	226
Torch (with spare battery and bulb)		6	170
Mirror		1½	42
Compass (Silva type)		2	57
Map (1 : 50 000), notebook, ballpoint pen		6	170
Map-case		2	57
Whistle		½	14

Individual Equipment

	lb	oz	gm
Frame and sack (or anatomic)	3	1	1,389
Sleeping-bag (for spring to autumn use)	2	12	1,247
Sleeping-pad (full-length, foam)	1	3	539
Air pillow (plastic)		4	113
Cagoule	1	10	736
Overtrousers (waterproof)		10	283
Belt wallet with money		2¼	64
Handkerchiefs (three)		2	57
Hat (lightweight)		4	113
Shoes or plimsolls	2	0	907
Socks (two pairs walking, two pairs lightweight)		14	397
Shirt		11	312
Sweater	1	6	626
Trousers (lightweight)	1	2	510
Underpants (two pairs)		6	170
Toilet items (toothbrush, toothpaste, comb)		6	170
Towel		10	283

	lb	oz	gm
Cutlery set (knife, fork, spoon)		3	85
Mug (polypropylene, ½ pint)		2	57
Plates (one large, one smaller and deeper, polypropylene)		4¾	135
Weight of common equipment divided by two =	9	12	4,422
Weight of individual equipment =	18	1	8,193
Total weight to be carried =	27	13	12,615

With sufficient food for about four days the overall weight should be about 35 lb (15·9 kg). For reasonably comfortable walking this should be regarded as the maximum. Considerable reduction in weight could be achieved on the above list, e.g. by the use of an ultra-light tent or by the elimination of some items such as torch, tent repair outfit, etc.

CAMPING TECHNIQUE

Always try to arrive at the camp site early, so that you have ample time to set up the camp and have a meal before dusk. Rushing through the jobs often leads to carelessness and bad tempers. On arrival have a light snack and, particularly if the day is hot, a dip or wash before starting work.

1 Selection of camp-site

Careful selection of the site can make a considerable difference to your comfort. The following points should be borne in mind:

1. The ground should be level and well drained. Avoid long grass which will remain wet for a long time in the morning or after a shower. Areas of lush green grass are particularly bad as this usually indicates damp conditions. In general avoid camping in depressions as these tend to be damp due to mist in evening and early morning. To improve the site small stones should be removed.

2. Pitch the tent so that there is shelter from the prevailing winds combined with maximum exposure to the sun.

3. Camp within easy reach of a stream so that ample supplies of water are available for cooking and washing. In hill country it is unwise however to camp very near to streams which can rise rapidly and considerably with heavy rain. Camp at least six feet above the water level.

4. Some cover should be available for latrines. This could be a wall, outcrop of rock, bushes or a peat grough. But downstream and downwind from the camp area.

5. Avoid camping under trees. These shut out the sun, drip for a long time after rain and can be hazardous due to falling branches, lightning and fires.

6. Avoid areas infested with flies and midges. Generally low-lying areas with abundant nettles and thistles, particularly if cattle have been recently grazed, give trouble.

7. Cows, sheep and horses can cause considerable damage to the tent and equipment and are best avoided.

8. Ensure that you have permission to camp. Apart from being inconsiderate and giving campers a bad name, it can be very inconvenient if you are asked to move late in the evening after pitching your tent.

There are a large number of camp-sites which have been established by organizations such as the Forestry Commission, National Trust and County Councils or by local farmers and landowners. Unfortunately, these are often closed from autumn until spring and may be crowded in the summer months, particularly in the popular areas. You will also find that sites are rather unevenly distributed about the country. However, such sites will be preferred by some backpackers as they can provide some or all of the following comforts: flush toilets, wash room with hot water and showers, laundry with drying facilities, a camp shop for fuel and food and possibly a rest room. See index for camp-site directories.

2 Pitching the tent

The procedure for a two pole ridge tent is as follows:

1. Mark out the position of the tent corners and door with small objects.
2. Remove the tent and accessories from the bag noting the method of packing.
3. Unroll the tent, move into the required position whilst folded in half and then finally spread. Untie the guys and assemble the poles.
4. Insert the pegs at the corners of the groundsheet ensuring the groundsheet is fully stretched and smooth.
5. Insert the pegs for the front and rear guylines, hook on the guylines leaving them slack.
6. Insert the front pole spindle into the ridge and erect the pole.
7. Repeat for the rear pole.
8. Close the door.
9. Insert wall guy pegs and attach guylines.
10. Adjust all guylines until the tent fabric is smooth and the ridge is straight.
11. Unroll flysheet and drape over tent inserting pole spindles.
12. Insert all flysheet pegs and attach guylines. Adjust until the flysheet is smooth and does not touch the tent fabric.

Ensure that the pegs are inserted at 90° to the guys (45° to the ground), the side guylines are in line with the seams, the tent poles are vertical, the fabric smooth and the tent symmetrical. If the top soil is too thin to take pegs fully then it is better to insert them at a smaller angle to the ground. If it is impossible to drive pegs altogether then large stones will have to be used to secure the guylines.

Basically the technique is similar for other types of lightweight tents.

3 Camp management

(a) Water supply

Most mountain streams flowing swiftly over rocky beds are probably safe for drinking purposes. In general, however, it is better to regard all water as suspect and to take steps to purify it. This may be accomplished by (*a*) boiling for 10–20 minutes, a procedure which is heavy on time and fuel, or (*b*) by adding one Helazone tablet to every pint of water and allowing this to stand for about 30 minutes. The water should be taken from a swiftly flowing stream or spring and above any points where pollution may occur, such as from cattle or from camp washing.

(b) Latrine

This should be sited downwind from the camp. It may be no more than a hole dug with a trowel where privacy can be assured. Toilet paper can be used or even grass or bracken. The hole should be filled in afterwards and turf replaced.

(c) Personal cleanliness

This is as important on a trek as it is at home. A washing bowl is handy, but a square of polythene sheet in a small depression is adequate. Shaving can be left altogether if necessary.

(d) Camp cleanliness

It is important to keep clothes, tent and sleeping-bag as dry as possible during a camp. Provided that the weather permits, open the tent doors early in the morning so that the sun penetrates into the tent and dries the interior. The tent should be left open as long as possible but remember to close it before dew falls in the evening. The sleeping-bag liner should be removed and both bag and liner turned inside out and hung up to dry. If clothes have been washed or have become wet during the day then lose no opportunity to dry them, even if it means hanging them on the back of the rucksack.

After a meal scrape all food scraps from the plates and then wipe the plates and utensils with grass to remove as much residue as possible. They can then be washed in hot water using a liquid detergent. Wash up as soon as possible after the meal as this will make washing-up easier.

All suitable rubbish should be burnt, but be very careful that fires are kept under control. Bury remaining rubbish in a deep hole, replacing soil and turf afterwards. Or, better keep it until you can put it into a litter bin at the next village.

(e) Protection of food

It is essential to provide protection for foodstuffs, otherwise they will deteriorate and/or become contaminated by flies. This is particularly important in the case of milk, uncooked meats, butter, lard, cheese, cream and eggs. Place the foodstuff into a waterproof container which is immersed in a nearby stream. A stone should be placed on to the top of the container to ensure it remains in place. For meat it is better to use a container with holes in the lid which is then covered with a piece of light cloth and half submerged in cold water. Bottles of milk should be stood in two to three inches (5–8 cm) of water and covered with cloth which drapes into the water; the water will gradually creep up the cloth and cool the milk by evaporation.

Other foodstuffs such as biscuits or cereals will deteriorate if they become damp. They can easily be protected by placing them into airtight containers.

4 Striking camp

Generally the jobs are done in the reverse order to setting up the camp.

(i)   Get ready for the walk before commencing to strike camp.
(ii) Burn all rubbish and bury remains. Replace turf.
(iii) Clean and assemble cooking stove and equipment. Store in rucksack.
(iv) Empty and collapse water container. Store in rucksack.
(v)   Strike tent. (*a*) Make sure that it is clean and dry and that all equipment is removed. (*b*) Release flysheet guy

lines and remove flysheet. Roll up and tie the flysheet
guylines. Fold flysheet. (*c*) Loosen tent guylines and
allow tent to slowly collapse. (*d*) Remove poles and dis-
mantle. (*e*) Straighten fabric into correct position and
fold. Wipe bottom of groundsheet with damp cloth and
then dry. (*f*) Pack folded tent and flysheet into bag.
Poles and pegs are best stored separately.

   As you slacken the guylines remove the pegs in turn
and place into one small pile. Clean and dry pegs and
poles before storing.

(vi) Pack all items into rucksack.
(vii) Make a final thorough search around the camp area to
      ensure that no equipment or litter has been left behind.

FURTHER READING

1. 'Beginner's Guide to Lightweight Camping'. P. F.
   Williams, Pelham.
2. 'The Backpacker's Handbook'. Derrick Booth, Letts.
3. 'Wilderness Camping in Britain'. Eric Hemery, Hale. A
   guide to family outdoor living and not particularly concerned with light-weight camping, but very useful.
4. 'Camping'. Educational Pamphlet No. 58. Department
   of Education and Science. HMSO.
   Concerned particularly with the role of camping in education.
5. 'Backpacking'. Peter Lumley, English University Press.
6. 'Britain. Camping and Caravan Sites'. British Tourist
   Authority.

SUPPLIERS OF CAMPING EQUIPMENT

The firms listed below are some of the leading British manufacturers and suppliers of tents, sleeping-bags and other
camping equipment. In most cases they will supply directly,
but in addition their products can usually be obtained at
numerous shops throughout the country.

1. Banton & Co. Ltd, Meadow Lane, Nottingham, NG2 3HP. Nottingham 868011. (Point Five Sleeping-Bags)
2. Blacks of Greenock, PO Box 6, Port Glasgow, Renfrewshire, PA14 5XN. Glasgow 42333.
3. David Moore & Co. Ltd, Daimor Factory, 75 Holland Street, Butler Street, Manchester, M10 7DD. 061 205 8866. (Daimor Sleeping Bags)
4. Edward R. Buck & Sons, Ltd, Bukta House, Brinksway, Stockport, Cheshire, SK4 1ED. 061 480 9721. (Bukta Products)
5. Karrimor International Ltd, Avenue Parade, Accrington, Lancashire. Accrington 385911.
6. Mountain Equipment Ltd, George Street, Glossop, Derbyshire, SK13 8AY. Glossop 3770. (Sleeping Bags)
7. Robert Saunders (Chigwell) Ltd, Five Oaks Lane, Chigwell, Essex. 01 500 2447. (Lightweight Tents)
8. Scout Shops Ltd, Churchill Industrial Estate, Lancing, Sussex, BN15 8UG. Lancing 5352.
9. Ultimate Equipment Ltd, Willowburn Trading Estate, Alnwick, Northumberland, NE66 2PF. Alnwick 3621.
10. Vango (Scotland) Ltd, 47 Colvend Street, Glasgow, G40 4DH. 041 556 7621.
11. YHA Services Ltd, 14 Southampton Street, London, WC2E 7HY. 01 836 8541.

Do-it-yourself enthusiasts may wish to make their own tents. Materials can be purchased from:

1. Blacks of Greenock (address given above).
2. Scout Shops Ltd (address given above).
3. YHA Services Ltd (address given above).
4. Pennine Boats, Hardknott, Holmbridge, Huddersfield, Yorkshire.

CHAPTER 13

Cooking and Food

EQUIPMENT

Portable cookers and stoves

It is convenient to divide these into two basic types which may be sub-divided further according to the fuel used:

(*a*) Picnic cookers (i) Methylated spirits (ii) Solid fuel
(*b*) Pressure stoves (i) Gas (ii) Paraffin (iii) Petrol

(*a*) Picnic cookers

These are suitable for a brew-up of tea or for heating small amounts of food, but are not really satisfactory for the preparation of the substantial meals that would be required, for example, on a backpacking expedition. They are very light, however, most models weighing between 3 and 14 oz (85–397 gm).

They consist at their simplest of no more than a small fuel container. In some models this is inside an outer case which serves both as a windbreak and a cooking stand. The fuel used is either methylated spirits or solid tablets sold under various trade names such as Meta or Esbit.

(*b*) Pressure stoves

(i) *Gas*. The gas used is either butane or propane, the former being most common. These can be liquefied at ambient temperature by pressure alone and can be stored as liquids in strong containers. When the containers are pierced the liquid begins to vaporize producing a jet of gas which can be ignited.

With butane the efficiency drops with air temperature, so

severely that it is not possible to use it below about 0°C (although conversion kits are available with some models for use at lower temperatures). Propane will vaporize at much lower air temperatures and can be used in severer winter conditions. Propane is stored however under higher pressures than butane and the containers must therefore be stronger and heavier.

Single and double-burner stoves are available, but the backpacker is mainly restricted to single-burner types on account of weight.

The gas is supplied in disposable cartridges which are either piercable or re-sealing. With piercable types the cooker head is fitted on to the cartridge when a pin at the base of the head pierces the cartridge. These cartridges must not be removed from the cooker until they are empty. It is advisable to remove an exhausted cartridge in the open air and away from naked flames as a small residue of gas will still remain. Re-sealing cartridges may be removed with safety even when only partly used. Cartridges are readily available both in this country and abroad, although different makes of cartridge and stove cannot necessarily be used together.

(ii) *Paraffin*. These stoves have been available for a very long time and are still very popular. They take more time to assemble, light and maintain than gas stoves, but are faster and cheaper for cooking. They are also less affected by bad conditions. Operating instructions are:

(*a*) Fill the paraffin container about three-quarters full. The paraffin should be of good quality, strained and stored in a clean, leak-proof bottle (polythene is suitable).

(*b*) Ensure that the burner jet is clear by using one of the cleaning needles (prickers) provided.

(*c*) Fill the priming cup or trough with methylated spirits (solid or paste fuel can also be used) and light. The flame heats the tube through which the paraffin flows to the jet.

(*d*) When most of the methylated spirit has burnt away, close the air-inlet valve and commence pumping. The paraffin is vaporized in the tube and is ignited at the jet by the flames from the methylated spirit.

(*e*) The flame can be reduced by opening the air-inlet valve for a few seconds and then closing it again. To extinguish the flame leave the valve open.

When assembling the stove use a spanner of the correct size to tighten the vaporizing tube. Regularly inspect the stove seals and jet and replace them if necessary. The retailer will have a special tool for easy removal of the jet.

(iii) *Petrol*. These are similar to paraffin stoves but priming with methylated spirit is not required. The petrol normally sold in garages is called leaded petrol and will be suitable for some types of petrol stoves; other types use unleaded petrol which must be ordered specially from a garage. Petrol is best stored in a metal can.

Comparison of different types of pressure stoves.

1. Weight. Gas stoves tend to be lighter than either paraffin or petrol stoves. For example, a typical gas stove with disposable cartridges to give about five hours burning would weigh 2–2½ lb (0·9–1·1 kg); a typical paraffin or petrol stove with equivalent fuel in a suitable container would be about 3¼–4 lb (1·5–1·8 kg).

2. Initial cost. Generally petrol and paraffin stoves cost about the same whilst gas stoves are much cheaper. A single-burner gas stove will cost about ⅓–½ the price of a liquid-fuel model

3. Running costs. Based upon 1977 fuel prices and published data for some stoves, it seems that a petrol stove is about four times more expensive to run than a paraffin stove and a gas stove, using disposable cartridges, about fifteen times more expensive.

4. Ease of handling. Paraffin stoves are undoubtedly the most difficult to assemble and light. Gas and petrol stoves are fairly easy.

5. Smell and contamination. None of these stoves gives an unpleasant smell during use and they do not contaminate food in any way although all fuels have a pronounced smell. Petrol and paraffin must be carried in strong containers

with tight-fitting screw tops to prevent spillage in the rucksack. They should be also kept in an outside pocket of the rucksack to reduce risk of contamination.

6. Efficiency. In good conditions all types of stove should boil a pint of water in about $3\frac{1}{2}$–$5\frac{1}{2}$ minutes. The efficiency of butane gas stoves will however be seriously reduced in cold weather, whilst petrol and paraffin stoves will be little affected.

For serious backpacking under varied conditions I would regard the paraffin pressure stove as the best buy.

Cooking utensils

Most walkers use a canteen for cooking. A canteen consists of a set of pans which fit together secured by a leather strap or metal clasp. They are made from aluminium and are light and compact. There are a number of different types available but a typical model will have two saucepans and a frying pan with a weight of about 1–$1\frac{1}{2}$ lb (454–679 gm). It should also contain a detachable handle (pot grip) for gripping the hot pans.

Plates, mug and cutlery

Plates and mugs are made from aluminium or polypropylene. The latter is probably best as it is slightly lighter, cheaper and helps to keep food hot for longer periods. A 9-inch (23-cm) diameter plate, a cereal or soup bowl and a $\frac{3}{4}$-pint ($\frac{1}{2}$-litre) mug will weigh about $7\frac{1}{2}$ oz (212 gm). Cutlery is made from stainless steel and is held together by a clip or is in a plastic case.

CAMP FIRES

Open air camp fires can be a delight. They reduce the cost of cooking, can be used for drying clothes and are wonderful to sit around in the evening. There are four essentials however:

1. Do not rely upon a fire for cooking, particularly if you have not become experienced with its use beforehand.
2. Never light a fire unless you have the site owner's permission.
3. Ensure that you will be able to collect sufficient fuel without doing any damage to trees, fences, etc.
4. Be sure that the fire is completely safe at all times and thoroughly extinguished before you leave the site.

Construction

Site the fire so that you can see it from the tent door, but about 20 ft (6 m) away so that there is no danger from flying sparks or discomfort from smoke.

1. Clear away all leaves, pine needles and flints from an area about 5 ft by 3 ft (1·5 by 0·9 m).
2. Remove a layer of turf about 3 ft × 1½ ft (0·9 × 5 m) wide from this area; place it to one side so that it can be replaced later.
3. Place large stones along the sides of the cleared area to give two walls about 12 inches (30 cm) high. Two thick logs will also serve.
4. Place a small quantity of dry kindling in the centre of the space with a small pyramid of thin twigs over it. Light the kindling and, when the twigs are alight, gradually build up the fire with thicker sticks.
5. To maintain a medium heat use small logs of sound dead-wood. Large logs can be used to produce more intense heat.

Kindling: Use dry gorse, heather or small chips cut from dead wood. Keep them in a polythene bag.

Fuel: Suitable woods are ash, beech, any conifers, hornbeam or oak. Always use sound wood from the ground or a tree, never use rotten wood or cut live tree branches. Cover with a polythene sheet secured to the ground.

FOOD

Introduction

Food is basically the fuel which we need to keep our bodies alive and active; i.e. it is a source of energy. Even a person who is lying down in a relaxed manner will be using some energy to keep his essential body processes working. If he begins to move around to do any work his energy requirements will immediately increase, and the harder he works the higher will be his requirements.

The energy value of food is measured in kilocalories, or in kilojoules (kJ), 1 kilocalorie being equal to 4·184 kilojoules. The rate of energy consumption by the body is measured in the same units. A young man who is lying down in a relaxed manner will need on average about 293 kJ per hour, i.e. 7,032 kJ per day, although this value will vary with the size, age, sex and physiology of the individual.

Some typical values for energy consumption are given in 'Success in Nutrition', Magnus Pyke, John Murray (Publishers) Ltd:

	kJ per hour
Writing	84
Drawing	167–209
Walking	523–1,003
Marching	1,170–1,672
Fast walking	2,362
Running	3,344–4,184
Walking upstairs	4,184

Actual values will vary greatly from one individual to another.

The most obvious point of this is, of course, that your energy requirements are going to increase considerably if you are doing fast walking, particularly in hilly country. This energy requirement can be met by eating extra food.

Food is made up from a number of constituents which have different functions:

(*a*) Carbohydrate. This is the main constituent and provides most of the energy. Foods which are particularly rich in carbohydrates are sugar, jam, bread and dried fruits.

(*b*) Fat. This also provides energy and a given weight will provide more than any other constituent. Foods which are particularly rich in fat are cooking oil, butter, pork, lamb, beef, cheese and nuts.

(*c*) Protein. The main function of protein is 'body-building', although excess protein will contribute to the energy requirements of the body. Meats, fish, dried egg and milk, cheese and peanuts are examples of food with high protein content.

(*d*) Trace elements and vitamins. Although present in small amounts they are essential to the healthy functioning of the body.

Dehydrated foods

Fresh foods contain a proportion of water: for example, the water content of vegetables and fruit is as high as 80 to 90 per cent by weight. It is possible to remove this water by a number of methods, of which the most common is air-drying. Most vegetables, e.g. peas and carrots, are dried in small dice or cubes and remain uncooked after dehydration. Potatoes and apples, however, can be treated by a somewhat different process of air-drying and the product is both dehydrated and cooked. Generally the nutritional value of the food is unaffected by the dehydration process.

Re-hydration of the product is simple. Vegetables can be re-hydrated by soaking in cold water, after which they have to be cooked. Pre-cooked foods can be re-constituted by stirring rapidly with boiling water for a few minutes. The yield on re-hydration can be expressed as the ratio between the weight of dried food and the weight of the final product. For example, 1 lb (0·45 kg) of dried peas will give 3½ lb (1·58 kg) of eatable peas and 1 lb (0·45 kg) of dried cabbage will give 6½ lb (2·95 kg) of eatable cabbage after re-hydration.

These foods are very attractive to the backpacker as (1) food preparation is considerably reduced as no peeling, washing or slicing is necessary, and (2) weight and volume are considerably less than for fresh foods (about $\frac{1}{16}-\frac{1}{4}$). A disadvantage is the limited range of products available. Bulk quantities can be obtained from retailers or directly from manufacturers. These will keep unopened in a dry place for several months. Special packs are available which provide one complete meal, and some which provide a number of different meals, breakfasts and dinners, suitable for a walking week-end.

Alexa Products, 23 Oxendon Road, Arthingworth, Market Harborough, Leicestershire, LE16 8LA. (Raven Meals)

Springlow Sales Ltd, Marsland Industrial Estate, Werneth Oldham, Lancashire, OL8 1TA.

Swel Foods Ltd (Lightweight Foods), Crowle, Near Scunthorpe, South Humberside, DN17 4JR.

Food for different occasions

1 Ordinary rambling

The majority of ramblers are quite content if they walk about ten to twelve miles over six or seven hours. In terms of energy requirements this would be very similar to light manual work such as housework or painting. So, depending upon your normal work, you would not expect to have to eat much more than you do normally.

Frankly, I think that the best advice is to take what you like and forget all about balanced diets or energy requirements. Take rather more than you think you are likely to need and you will be fine. Most people take sandwiches, but try to put in nice, thick, tasty fillings. Salads are grand at any time and you can work out all sorts of variations. A small tin of rice pudding, a slab or two of cake or biscuits to finish. You should also take a few things to eat as you go along: small sweet apples, nuts and raisins and boiled sweets are all excellent.

It is always wise to carry a drink, fruit squash or tea. This is more important now than it used to be as tea shops and

pubs which will cater for ramblers are becoming more
scarce, preferring to provide for the car brigade.

Wrap the food up carefully so that it will not get squashed.
Sandwiches are nowhere near so attractive if they have been
mangled at the bottom of a rucksack. Oblong polythene
boxes with snap-on lids are ideal.

2 Challenge walking

Really tough challenge walks will demand a higher energy
consumption than very hard manual work. It is also quite
common to develop an aversion to food during an event,
particularly if the weather is very hot. The usual rule therefore is to experiment with foods rich in carbohydrates and
discover which of these you still find attractive even under
trying conditions. But experiment before, and not during,
the event.

Some possibilities which have been found successful are:

1. Complan, either hot or cold, and flavoured with, for
   example, blackcurrant juice.
2. Cereal mixtures (Muesli).
3. Rice pudding, hot or cold.
4. Fruit salad, tinned or fresh.
5. Crushed fruit, such as pears or peaches, with honey.
6. Chocolate bars, boiled sweets, Kendal mint cake, glucose
   tablets.
7. Fresh fruit, provided that it is sweet.

It is important to replace liquids and salts lost through
sweating. Fruit squashes diluted with water are popular, so
also is hot sweet tea. Salt can be added to the fruit squash
or taken in tablet form. Accolade and Dynamo are two
drinks which are worth trying.

3 Backpacking

There are a number of factors which must be considered
here. (1) Weight. Obviously important if you are going into
a wilderness area well away from shops. (2) Backpacking is

hard work, your energy requirements are going to be high.
(3) Variety. We all have our favourite foods, but yours might
not be the same as those of your companions. (4) Balance.
The longer your holiday period the more important it is to
achieve a balanced diet. (5) Effort. You will have to prepare
the meal after a day of hard walking and after setting up
your camp. It takes time and energy. Therefore it is best to
use foods which are easy to prepare.

It is best to aim at a cooked breakfast and a cooked
evening meal and to fill in with a cold rambler's lunch
around mid-day. It is easier to avoid cooking during the
walk, but if the stove is in a side pocket it can easily be taken
out for hot tea or soup.

(1) Plan your meals beforehand. Avoid experiments on the
trek itself, these are best carried out before you start. Only
take those foods which you know you like and which are
relatively easy to prepare and cook. Keep weight in mind,
dehydrated foods in particular are light and take up little
space. But there are other ideas such as lemonade powder
and Nestle's milk in handy 'toothpaste tubes'.

(2) If you have to take food for several days then it is a
good plan to wrap each day's food separately in a polythene
bag. This will save you time later and help you to keep to
your plan.

(3) Wrap your food in convenient and light containers.
Glass bottles and tins will increase your load unnecessarily,
polythene bags and containers are much better.

(4) Keep a record of the type and amount of foods that
you take and how you find them. Your catering should be a
gradually improving process.

It is well worthwhile to spend some time on the planning
of your food supply. Don't 'make-do'. You may get away
with it for a few days, but you will start to deteriorate
physically. You will probably have got fed-up with it by then
anyhow.

For more information see the reading list in Chapter 12.

CHAPTER 14

The Rambler and the Law (including Footpath Clearance and Waymarking)

Most walkers are aware that there exists a framework of law which protects their use of the countryside, but they are usually very hazy about the actual nature of their rights. This chapter is intended therefore to describe in outline the rights and responsibilities of walkers, landowners and local authorities and the action that can be taken in cases of obstruction or trespass.

It cannot be too strongly emphasized that this is an outline only. The law is far too complex for a full account to be given. In case of difficulty it is better to retreat unless or until you are sure of your position. Legal action should only be considered after advice has been obtained from a qualified person.

The keynote in all cases should be tolerance. A recognition that others also have to work or take their leisure in the countryside and that their rights and lives should be respected.

A short section on the clearance of footpaths and bridleways is also included.

1. FOOTPATHS AND BRIDLEWAYS (ENGLAND AND WALES)

Public Rights of Way

County councils are required by the National Parks and Access to the Countryside Act of 1949 to prepare maps which show all paths over which the public has a right of way. When these maps were being prepared individuals or organizations had the right to object if they considered that a way had been incorrectly included or excluded from the map. The final form of the map is called a definitive map.

The inclusion of a footpath on a definitive map can be taken as proof that there was a public right of way when the map was prepared. These rights of way, may be for footpaths (for walkers only) or bridleways (for walkers, horse-riders and cyclists). Each path or way is identified by a number. The map will be accompanied by a statement which may give further information on the paths and ways within the area.

Definitive maps have now been prepared for most of England and Wales. Copies are held at the offices of the county council and district councils and sometimes with the parish council. These copies may be inspected by the public during the normal office business hours.

A 'Road used as a Public Path' or RUPP was classified by the 1949 Act as a road that is used by the public mainly for the same purposes as a footpath or bridleway. Thus, a lane with a surface which has not been made-up but is wide enough to take a vehicle (a 'green lane') would come within this category. By the Countryside Act of 1968 however county councils are required to re-classify all such roads shown on the definitive maps as either footpaths or bridleways or byways open to all traffic. When the new definitive maps have been prepared RUPPs will then be shown and treated as under these categories.

Paths may be added to, removed from or modified on definitive maps under certain circumstances:

(a) An addition may be made if it can be shown that a well-defined footpath has been used by the general public as a right and without interruption for a considerable time. Generally it is assumed that if the public has used a footpath for twenty years or more then the owner accepted its use as a public right of way. An owner may prevent a private path from becoming accepted under this rule by several methods, i.e. by closing the path temporarily at regular intervals, by charging a toll occasionally, by a suitable notice on the path or by notifying the local highway authority.

(b) A new path with public right of way can be created by a county council, district council or National Park Board.

These authorities normally seek to do this by agreement with interested parties but, where this is not possible, they may raise a compulsory creation order for which they require the approval of either the Secretary of State for the Environment or the Secretary of State for Wales. In rare cases the Secretary of State may raise the order. This order is subject to the same procedure for objections as given below under (*c*).

(*c*) A path can be deleted on the basis of an extinguishment or closure order made by a local authority or the Secretaries of State for the Environment and Wales. In all cases the draft order must be published in the *London Gazette*, in at least one local newspaper and on the path itself and other appropriate public authorities must be consulted. Objections may be raised against the order and if necessary these objections will be heard at a public inquiry.

(*d*) A path may be diverted in order to improve it for the general public, for more efficient use of the land or for the purposes of development. The procedure for a diversion order is similar to (*c*) above. Strictly, a diverted path must meet the original path, but in some cases an alternative path may be created which does not meet the original path, e.g. runs approximately parallel to it.

A walker may use a public footpath or bridleway as part of a ramble. He may take anything with him which would be reasonable for that journey and can behave in a manner reasonably consistent with that end. Thus, generally, a rambler can rest on the path or eat a picnic lunch. He can also be accompanied by a dog, provided of course that it is kept under close control and does not bother livestock along the way.

Maintenance of Public Paths

It is the duty of the local highway authority to maintain public paths. With the exception of London the county council is the local highway authority. In London the borough councils act in this capacity. The county council may however arrange for a district council to carry out its functions. A district council may also assume certain powers to maintain public paths independently of a formal arrangement with the county council. It is necessary therefore to make inquiries locally to ascertain the current position. These duties cover all public paths in existence in December 1949 and those new paths which have been formed since that date (with some exceptions due to the dedication of paths from private to public use). Long distance routes created by the Countryside Commission are now the responsibility of the local authorities, but the Commission is continuing to provide grants for their maintenance.

The maintenance duties are:

(*a*) The path must be maintained to such a standard that it is reasonably safe and usable at all times of the year for the type of use for which it was intended.

(*b*) Repair of stiles and gates. A stile or gate must be maintained by the owner of the land so that it is safe to use and does not interfere with its use by walkers. The highway authority contributes a minimum of one quarter of the cost of any repair work carried out by the owner. In the event of an owner failing in his duties the local authority has the power after adequate notice to carry out the work and recover all or part of the costs.

It should be noted that there is no statutory size for a stile or gate or for the width of a footpath or bridleway, with the exception that a gate on a bridleway must be at least five feet wide.

(*c*) Repair of footbridges. Most bridges over railways or canals however are the responsibility of British Rail or the canal authority.

Improvement of Public Paths

In addition to maintenance the highway authorities have the power to improve the standard of footpaths or bridleways.

(*a*) Waymarks. The highway authority has the power to erect waymarks, i.e. signs, at the ends or along the length of a footpath or bridleway. It can do this without the consent of the owner of the land over which the path passes, but it must consult him in a reasonable manner. The highway authority has a duty however to erect a sign at the points where the path leaves a metalled road. This duty can be waived provided that it is agreed with the local parish council that such a sign would be unnecessary.

(*b*) Safeguards. The highway authority can erect barriers or fences or similar structures which will safeguard persons using the path.

(*c*) Footbridges over streams and boggy areas. These can be provided at the discretion of the authority.

(*d*) Draining a path, e.g. by digging a ditch alongside. Again at the discretion of the authority.

Obstructions to Use of Public Paths

There are a number of ways in which the freedom of the rambler to use a public footpath may be reduced. If a person acts in such a way that he hinders, discourages or prevents a walker from using a footpath, then he may be guilty of a common law nuisance. Some of the specific ways in which this can be done are:

(*a*) Ploughing. Farmers do not have the right to damage or destroy a path by ploughing except in the following cases:

(i) Where there is a common law right to plough. This should be given on the statement accompanying the definitive map.

(ii) The right to plough in the interests of good farming. In this case the farmer should give seven days notice to the highway authority and should also make good the surface within six weeks of the ploughing. This means that the surface has to be re-made 'so as to make it reasonably convenient for the exercise of the public right of way'.

(*b*) Blockage of a footpath. The Highways Act of 1959 states that 'If any person, without lawful authority or excuse, in any way wilfully obstructs the free passage along a highway he shall be guilty of an offence.' It would not be necessary to show that the footpath was completely blocked, as anything which made the journey more difficult would fall into this category. Examples are the locking of field gates, blockage of a stile or the placing of barbed wire across a path.

(*c*) Barbed wire which is placed so closely to the side of a path that injury is likely to be caused to the clothing or person of the walker.

(*d*) Excavations or erections by a path which may cause injury. Obviously open quarries with no protective fence would come into this category as these constitute a danger to the walker.

(*e*) Misleading notices. It is illegal to place a notice on or near to a public path which is likely to deter the public from using that path. Thus a notice which states 'Private Footpath' is illegal in this case.

(*f*) Overhanging or overgrown trees or bushes.

(*g*) The deliberate placing of any offensive matter on to a path, or allowing it to flow on to a path. Manure, rubbish or lime could come into this category.

(*h*) The removal of any authorized waymarks.

(*i*) The driving of any motor vehicle on to a footpath or bridleway. This may however be done with the consent of the owner of the land provided that it does not hinder the public in the use of the path or constitute a danger.

(*j*) Subsidence of the ground of the path by quarrying so as to prevent a path being used. Erosion by the sea or by a river would result in the path being lost.

(*k*) Bulls. Generally most areas have a byelaw which prohibits any bull over twelve months old being turned loose into a field through which there runs a public footpath. It is permitted to have a bull in such a field provided that it is secured and strictly controlled. However, some districts have a modified byelaw which permits bulls provided that they are accompanied by cows. As a result of the redrawing of some county boundaries in 1974 a difference in the byelaw may occur not merely between present counties but between different districts of the same county. Unauthorized pasturing of bulls should be reported to the local police.

(*l*) Potentially dangerous animals other than bulls. These may be run loose within a field containing a footpath, but the owner could be liable for damages if an animal injures a walker.

Action in the case of obstruction

An individual has the right to remove an obstruction across a public path. He should first ensure that the path really has a public right of way, and then he should only remove sufficient of the obstruction to enable him to proceed in a reasonable manner. A walker who removes a structure on private land through which there is no right of way, or who removes an unnecesarily large amount where there is a right of way may find himself charged with damaging property without lawful authority.

Where a path has been obstructed by an owner then the owner cannot obtain damages for trespass if walkers go around the obstruction and on to another part of his land.

In the case of obstruction the individual should report the matter to the local highway authority and it is a sound plan to send a copy of all correspondence to the Ramblers' Association or to any local amenity society.

In the last resort the individual or local group can take legal action themselves by writing to the Clerk to the Local Justices.

For further information:

'A Practical Guide to the Law of Footpaths and Bridleways'. Ian Campbell, Commons, Open Spaces and Footpaths Preservation Society. This gives a very detailed account of the subject with many case histories.

Trespass

Trespass consists of entering land which is legally occupied by another person or over which there is no public right of way without the permission of the occupier, or of remaining on that land after permission has been withdrawn.

It does not matter therefore if the entry was intentional or accidental, a trespass will have been committed if there is no public right of way. The entry may also be very slight, for example merely sitting on a fence will be sufficient to constitute a trespass.

If you are trespassing and the occupier asks you to go then you must obey in a reasonably quick and sensible manner. If you do not obey then he may use reasonable force against you. If you resist then he is entitled to use greater force against you, and most certainly in self-defence.

The occupier may also bring an action for trespass in cases where the entry was intentional even if the trespasser thought that there was a right of way, and a further action if any damage has been caused. (The costs of the action may also be awarded against the trespasser.) In the case of accidental trespass, which is very common with ramblers, the position is more uncertain and there is doubt if this is actionable. It is a common practice for ramblers to go around the perimeter of a field when confronted with a path which has been ploughed up or is under a crop. This also constitutes trespass.

It is important to remember also that a public right of way must be used only for passage and cannot be used for other purposes; these also would constitute trespass. However, walkers do not commit a crime by trespassing and notices that indicate that trespassers will be prosecuted do not therefore have any legal standing. Generally a walker has no redress if he injures himself whilst trespassing.

2. FOOTPATHS AND BRIDLEWAYS (SCOTLAND)

The law on rights of way is different from that in England and Wales. A public right of way exists if firstly, the route joins two public places (e.g. roads or churches) and secondly, it has been used 'without let or hindrance' by members of the public as a right for a continuous period of twenty years. Thus, rights of way can be lost or gained depending upon continuing usage. (For example, there is a risk of a path being lost if it has been obstructed for a long period without objections being raised). The situation is therefore fluid and different to that in England and Wales where rights of way have been established by law and can only be changed by the raising of orders. For this reason local planning authorities are not required by law to prepare definitive maps which give rights of way (although some may do this voluntarily) and the O.S. 1 : 50 000 maps for Scotland do not show these.

For development purposes, of course, planning authorities have been given the power to create, divert and extinguish rights of way. Except in the first case where a path has been created by agreement with the landowner, objections may be raised and ultimately the orders have to be confirmed by the Secretary of State for Scotland. The planning authority has the duty to protect and keep open any public rights of way within its area and the power to maintain rights of way. (Except created paths which must be maintained). The landowner has no responsibility to maintain a path but should not obstruct a right of way by placing any obstacle across it which will hinder a walker using the way. (The ploughing of a public path is permitted provided that the local planning authority is notified within a certain time and the surface is reinstated).

Three methods have been suggested to determine if a path has a right of way: (1) Inquire at the planning office of the local authority where maps may be being maintained voluntarily. (2) Inspect the Ordnance Survey 1 : 50 000 maps. A path shown which links two public places will probably have a right of way. (3) Maps showing rights of way have been prepared for some areas by the Scottish Rights of Way Society, i.e. the Cairngorm passes, the Knoydart and Morar passes and West Central Scotland.

In practice, however, although no right of way may exist, walkers are usually allowed to walk freely in mountain and moorland areas, with the exception of some areas during the deer stalking (9 August–20 October) and grouse shooting (12 August–9 December) seasons. Within these periods if possible it is best to inquire locally before starting a walk over country where no rights of way exist.

Read 'A Walker's Guide to the Law of Right of Way in Scotland'. The Scottish Rights of Way Society, 28 Rutland Square, Edinburgh, EH1 2BW.

3. COMMONS

A common is an area of land which is owned by an individual or organization, but over which other persons have certain rights such as the pasture of animals, collection of fuel or the digging of turf or gravel.

These rights descend directly from the feudal system practised in the Middle Ages in which the countryside was divided into manors, each of which was largely a self-contained unit. The lord of the manor actually owned the land but the local inhabitants had certain rights over parts such as the pasturing of their animals or the cutting of wood for fuel. This land was the 'common' land of the manor.

During the latter part of the eighteenth and the first half of the nineteenth centuries many of these rights were taken away by Acts of Parliament called Inclosure Acts. In return the lord and the commoners each received an allocation of freehold land. By 1860–70 however the advantages of inclosure had become less mainly because of the import of cheap food and such acts became much less frequent.

The Commons Registration Act of 1965 required county and county borough councils to maintain a register of common land and rights. Claims for registration had to be made within the period 2 January 1967 to 2 January 1970 and a further period was allowed for objections. This register is now regarded as a legal document in the same manner as the definitive maps are so regarded for public rights of way.

It should be realized that the term 'common' may apply to substantial areas of land which most people probably would not regard in that way, for example Tebay Fell in Cumbria and Ilkley Moor in Yorkshire. It has been estimated that about 1,500,000 acres (6,070 sq. km) are classed as commons in England and Wales.

Commons are owned by an individual or organization and the general public has no common law rights of access on to and across the land. However, a number of Acts made in the last century and in this century have given the public this right in some cases. For example, the National Trust must allow free access to all its commons. Approximately one fifth to one quarter of all common land is open to the public under these Acts.

It should also be noted that owners must not enclose a common by means of a fence or wall without the consent of the Secretary of State for the Environment or Wales and therefore in practice it is easy to gain access to an area of common. Thus, even where no legal right exists, in practice people do use some common land.

For a very thorough treatment:

'A Guide to the Law of Commons'. Ian Campbell, Commons, Open Spaces and Footpaths Preservation Society.

4. THE SEASHORE (FORESHORE)

The foreshore is that land which lies between the high and the low-water marks. This belongs to the Crown, except for a few stretches where the Crown has sold its rights to private individuals. The public has no right to walk over private foreshore unless there is a public right of way or they have obtained the owner's permission. The situation with foreshore owned by the Crown is very similar. The public obviously does walk along long stretches of beach but this is allowed only at the discretion of the Crown or other owner and permission could be withdrawn.

5. MISCELLANEOUS

Dogs

Many walkers like to have the company of a pet dog during a ramble, but it is important that the dog is kept under proper control.

If the dog behaves towards farm animals in a manner which is reasonably likely to cause injury or suffering then the owner, or his agent, may act to protect his livestock. This means that he may kill or injure the dog if there is no other reasonable course of action to take.

If the dog is caught then the owner may apply to a court for the dog to be destroyed, and also for compensation for any damage caused by the dog.

Shooting

Persons shooting in the countryside must not shoot in a manner which may cause injury to a walker using a public right of way, nor can they insist on such walkers waiting before a shoot or drive is completed.

Golf

Some public paths do cross the fairways of golf courses. The position here is as for shooting above, but in both cases the walker should not behave in a manner which aggravates the risk of injury.

A further useful book is:

'The Countryside and the Law'. Charles Fox, David and Charles.

FOOTPATH AND BRIDLEWAY CLEARANCE

By the Highways Act of 1959 each highway authority is responsible for the maintenance of public paths within its own area. Outside London the County Councils act as the highway authorities, whilst the borough councils have this responsibility within the London area. A small proportion of footpaths, which have been created by dedication since 1959 but not accepted by the local authority, do not come into this category and remain the responsibility of the land-owner.

Nevertheless many local rambling and amenity societies,

who are interested in the maintenance of public paths, have, in addition to acting as local pressure groups, themselves undertaken the task of footpath clearance and maintenance. The largest organization in this field is the Ramblers' Association working through its local Groups, but many other societies have played a valuable part. It is due to their efforts that many paths, which were formerly almost impenetrable due to fallen trees, overgrown hedges, brambles or poor drainage, are now freely walked.

The best course of action for any individual who is interested in this type of work is to join the local Group of the Ramblers' Association or a similar organization (Chapter 11). Their members will have the experience, knowledge and equipment necessary and will be glad of extra help. However, there is no reason why an individual or small group of friends should not undertake this work. The following notes are intended as a guide:

(1) Carry out a survey of the local paths. If there are a number of paths in need of clearance then prepare a priority list. Some paths would probably not be freely used even if clear, whilst others could open up an entire area by linking up with other footpaths.

(2) Obtain permission before you start. Approach the owner of the land and consult the local highway authority. Check the exact line of the path that has to be cleared and reach agreement on the amount of clearance to be undertaken. It is essential to secure the willing co-operation of the highway authority and the owner early on.

(3) Appoint a leader for the working party. The leader should notify all workers of the date and time for the clearance, make arrangements for insurance, ensure that suitable tools are carried and that transport is available. On the day he is responsible throughout for the proper conduct of the members.

(4) Tools. Most gardeners will have a variety of tools which can be used, for example secateurs, sickles, shears, forks and saws.

Thin branches can be cut with secateurs whilst pruning or

bow saws can cope with thicker branches. Small tree stumps can be removed with a fork and saw, but a better tool is the mattock which resembles a pick axe with broad blades on each side. Sickles and shears are useful for clearing brambles and young twiggy undergrowth. Forks can be used to dig up stumps and for removing rubbish to the bonfire. A pair of strong gloves is also essential to protect the hands. Inquire from landowner or local parish council if materials are needed.

(5) Safety. People can easily be hurt during a clearance. It is the leader's responsibility to ensure that workers are spaced sufficiently apart to avoid hitting each other with tools. He must ensure that branches are cut in a correct and safe manner, that fires are under control and are extinguished before the party leaves. Suitable insurance can be arranged easily and cheaply. (Some councils may insist upon this and even arrange it if they give permission for parties to act on their behalf.) The insurance should also cover claims for damage in case parties clear or damage trees or other features which are outside the line of the path.

(6) Ensure that the extent of clearance is agreed with the highway authority and landowner beforehand. Reasonable minimum limits are 4 ft (1·2 m) wide and 7 ft (2·1 m) high for a footpath and 6 ft (1·8 m) wide and 9 ft (2·7 m) high for a bridleway.

(7) The debris of cut branches and undergrowth should be burnt. Site the bonfires at strategic points so that carrying is reduced to a minimum. Ensure that bonfires are safe and that fire cannot spread to nearby undergrowth.

(8) The best time for clearance is between October and March inclusive when the trees are bare and when there will be less disturbance to wild life, e.g. nesting birds.

(9) Try to clear a path so that the clearance remains effective for a considerable period. This allows you to direct your resources towards other tasks. Regular use of a footpath may in any case make it largely self-maintaining.

(10) Try to obtain as much publicity as possible for your clearance. This may bring in other volunteers for future work.

In addition to clearance work, a party can also undertake

other tasks such as the repair and erection of stiles, signposts and footbridges. These are excellent summer jobs, but again prior permission should be obtained.

WAYMARKING

Waymarking is the name given to the placing of signs and marks along a footpath to indicate its direction, particularly at bends or at junctions with other paths. This has been a feature of some parts of Europe, e.g. the Black Forest, for many years but, in the main, is a comparatively recent development in this country. Prior to 1968 most paths were not marked, notable exceptions being in the Forest of Dean where footpaths were marked with printed yellow arrows by the Ramblers' Association and Forestry Commission in the early 1960s and in the home area of the Chiltern Society from 1966. A few County Councils had also followed a policy of erecting signposts.

A real impetus came with the Countryside Act of 1968 which requires highway authorities to erect signs at each point where a path leaves a metalled road, and gives them the power to do so along the length of a path. In the latter case the owner of the land must be consulted in a reasonable manner, but his permission is not required. (But it is required if signs are to be fixed to his trees, buildings, fences, etc.) Most of the signposts now to be found in the countryside have been erected since the 1968 Act.

Unfortunately, no time limit was imposed on the work of erecting signposts and highway authorities have varied considerably therefore in their response. In the main where they have responded they have concentrated upon their statutory duty of providing signposts at the end of paths and given low priority to the marking along the path. Exceptions are the long distance routes where organizations, such as the Countryside Commission or County Councils, have been involved and some areas where local volunteer groups have worked by arrangement with the local highway authority. Even so, a variety of different methods of waymarking have evolved. To avoid confusion the Countryside Commission published a report 'Waymarking for Footpath and Bridleway' in 1974 which describes a method of waymarking which is now being adopted by many organizations. The main features of this system are:

(1) The waymarks are painted and are either (*a*) stubby arrows pointing in the direction of the path, i.e. vertically for straight ahead, horizontally for left or right turns or tilted at the appropriate angle for bends; or (*b*) an arrow layout at path junctions rather similar to that in use on roads. Blue indicates a bridleway and yellow indicates a footpath.

(2) The waymarks are placed on existing surfaces whereever possible, preferably man-made rather than natural.

(3) The waymarks should be placed before a bend or junction and facing the oncoming walker. They should be clear from either direction.

The Countryside Commission recommend that waymarks should only be used where a person unfamiliar with the path would have difficulty following the route. On moorlands and mountains this method is not recommended and cairns and posts are considered better. Volunteer groups intending to waymark should read the full report available from the Commission which gives lots of practical information on equipment, materials and methods.

It should be mentioned finally that many walkers are opposed to waymarking in general and a greater number to waymarking in wild country. A policy based upon moderation is probably the best answer.

Read 'Blazing a Trail', Ramblers' Association.

Index

TRAVEL

THE FEARFUL VOID Geoffrey Moorhouse £1.25
There is a fearful void out there in the empty quarter of the
Sahara Desert, but more terrifying still is the void within our
minds – the fear of loneliness and failure. One man's search to
conquer his own self-distrust. Illustrated in full colour.

JOURNEY THROUGH BRITAIN John Hillaby £1.25
It was a magical idea to walk through the over-industrialized
land of Britain from Land's End to John O'Groats, avoiding
all centres of population. Britain's master walker made his
reputation with this book. Illustrated.

JOURNEY THROUGH EUROPE John Hillaby £1.50
John Hillaby gives a splendid potpourri of factual account,
lively anecdote, mythology and private comment in this
account of his walk from the Hook of Holland via the Alps
to Nice. Illustrated.

JOURNEY TO THE JADE SEA John Hillaby 95p
Tired of city-living and ashamed of his toleration of boredom,
John Hillaby made a three-month safari from the Northern
Frontier District of Kenya to the legendary Jade Sea.
Illustrated.

JOURNEY THROUGH LOVE John Hillaby £1.25
Hillaby's most recent and possibly most powerful and
evocative book concerns a series of several walks, in
Yorkshire, Wales, London, the South Downs and North
America, and the thread running through the narrative is the
story of a great tragedy and loss.

A JOURNEY TO THE HEART OF ENGLAND
Caroline Hillier £1.50
A superbly informative and entertaining look at the towns,
landscapes, industries and history of the Western Midlands, an
area rich in tradition and very much the heart of England.

HEALTH AND FITNESS BOOKS
AVAILABLE IN MAYFLOWER BOOKS

Laurence Morehouse & Leonard Gross
Total Fitness   95p ☐

Constance Mellor
Natural Remedies for Common Ailments   £1.25 ☐
Constance Mellor's Guide to Natural Health   80p ☐

Desmonde Dunne
Yoga Made Easy   75p ☐

Sonya Richmond
Yoga and Your Health (illustrated)   95p ☐

Clare Maxwell-Hudson
The Natural Beauty Book   £1.00 ☐

Bruce Tegner
Karate (illustrated)   95p ☐

All these books are available at your local bookshop or newsagent, or can be ordered direct from the publisher. Just tick the titles you want and fill in the form below.

Name ....

Address..

....

Write to Mayflower Cash Sales, PO Box 11, Falmouth, Cornwall TR10 9EN.

Please enclose remittance to the value of the cover price plus:
UK: 25p for the first book plus 10p per copy for each additional book ordered to a maxmum charge of £1.05.

BFPO and EIRE: 25p for the first book plus 10p per copy for the next 8 books, thereafter 5p per book.

OVERSEAS: 40p for the first book and 12p for each additional book.

Granada Publishing reserve the right to show new retail prices on covers, which may differ from those previously advertised in the text or elsewhere.